Women, Men and Language

A Sociolinguistic Account of Gender Differences in Language

Third edition

Jennifer Coates

PEARSON

Longman

Harlow, England • London • New York • Boston • San Francisco • Toronto
Sydney • Tokyo • Singapore • Hong Kong • Seoul • Taipei • New Delhi
Cape Town • Madrid • Mexico City • Amsterdam • Munich • Paris • Milan

PEARSON EDUCATION LIMITED

Edinburgh Gate
Harlow CM20 2JE
United Kingdom
Tel: +44 (0)1279 623623
Fax: +44 (0)1279 431059
Website: www.pearsoned.co.uk

Third edition published in Great Britain in 2004

© Pearson Education Limited 1986, 1993, 2004

The right of Jennifer Coates to be identified as author
of this work has been asserted by her in accordance
with the Copyright, Designs and Patents Act 1988.

ISBN 978-0-582-77186-4

British Library Cataloguing-in-Publication Data
A CIP catalogue record for this book can be obtained from the British Library

Library of Congress Cataloging-in-Publication Data
Coates, Jennifer.
    Women, men and language : a sociolinguistic account of gender differences in
language / Jennifer Coates. — 3rd ed.
        p. cm.
    Includes bibliographical references and index.
    ISBN 0–582–77186–2 (pbk.)
        1. Language and languages—Sex differences. I. Title.
P120.S48C62 2004
306.44—dc22

2004040031

10 9 8 7 6
08

Set in 9/12pt Stone serif by 35
Printed and bound in Malaysia, (CTP-VVP)

The Publisher's policy is to use paper manufactured from sustainable forests.

Women, Men and Language

Studies in language and linguistics

General editors: GEOFFREY LEECH & MICK SHORT
Lancaster University

Already published:

Contents

Preface to the Third Edition

Rewriting *Women, Men and Language* hasn't been easy: when you write a new edition of a book, you can't just say anything you like, but are constrained by the original text. I have tried to preserve the coherence of the second edition at the same time as bringing it up to date. But 'bringing it up to date' was tricky. In the early 1990s, the concepts 'language' and 'gender' seemed clear-cut and unproblematic. Researchers set out to document differences in women's and men's language use and to expose inequalities. This early sociolinguistic work on language and gender built up a solid set of research findings which formed the basis of my book. However, there has been a 'postmodern shift' (Swann 2003: 625) in the way 'language' and 'gender' are perceived, a shift from relative clarity and fixity to relative complexity and fluidity. Gender is no longer seen as given but rather as something that we 'do'; the emphasis is on diversity and on plural masculinities and femininities rather than on a simple binary divide between 'men' and 'women'; and language is examined for ambiguity and mutiple meanings.

This shift has confronted me with many problems, and is one of the reasons a third edition hasn't appeared sooner. I have had to make difficult decisions and have inevitably had to compromise in places. What I have done is to bring chapters up to date in terms of the latest research and to introduce new concepts from the very beginning of the book, so that students can read about early language and gender work at the same time as developing an understanding of new approaches to gender. But I have preserved a great deal of the content of the earlier version, since the early research has helped to define the field of language and gender. This means that there is a constant tension between an older, simpler view of language and gender, and a newer, more complicated and more sophisticated view.

I have added two chapters to Part Two: one on conversational dominance and the other on same-sex talk. These reflect the significant shift in sociolinguistics which took place in the 1980s from work focusing on variation in grammar and pronunciation to work focusing more on gender and conversational practice. The notion that gender is a cultural construction has led researchers to take a much wider view of talk as a gendered performance. I have added a new section on 'Gender in the Workplace' to Chapter 11. I have also added a final chapter (Chapter 12) which talks readers through the latest developments in language and gender research.

The main aim of the book has not changed: it is to introduce the reader to the study of language and gender. The book will focus on gender *differences* in language use, though it is important to remember that women's and men's ways of talking have many similarities, given that gender is intersected by class, age, ethnicity, sexual orientation among other things. I have tried to introduce readers to a wide range of sociolinguistic research in the field, and have aimed to combine general surveys of particular topics with more detailed analysis of specific research projects. I hope this book will help to make readers more aware of the ways in which language is implicated in the construction of gender. And because women and men are still not equal, despite significant changes in western societies, I hope this book will help to show the continuing part played by language in sustaining these inequalities.

J.C.
London, 2003

Acknowledgements

First edition

This book arose from a course I taught for many years at Edge Hill College. I am grateful to Stanley Ellis and Mark Newbrook for providing me with information about their work, and to Chris Baldick, Rhiannon Evans, Sarah Kay and Edward Wilson for their suggestions of folklinguistic material. I have been enormously helped by those who read and commented on earlier drafts of parts of the book: Deborah Cameron, Jenny Cheshire, Margaret Deuchar, Dick Leith, Beryl Madoc-Jones, Lesley Milroy. I would also like to thank my editors, Geoff Leech and Mick Short, for their comments and advice on the manuscript. But my main thanks are reserved for Joy Bowes whose scrupulously careful and detailed comments and criticisms on every chapter of the book have been invaluable. The book is dedicated to the students who took my course – it was their interest in the topic and their frustration with the paucity of texts which stimulated me to write it.

Second edition

In revising *Women, Men and Language*, I've had the unstinting help of my colleagues, Vikki Bell, Linda Thomas and especially Shan Wareing, who have suggested material for inclusion, commented on draft chapters, and always been ready to discuss language and gender issues with me. I would like to thank them for their support and encouragement. I would also like to place on record my gratitude to all those who have participated in my ongoing research on talk in single-sex friendship groups. Although I have used only brief extracts from these data in the book, my understanding of gender differences in language has benefited enormously from working on the project, which would have been impossible without their cooperation. Finally, I'd like to thank my son, William, for his fortitude over the last year, when my obsession with revising the book has sometimes taken priority over his needs, and for his invaluable help as a computer expert!

Third edition

I was only able to complete this third edition with the generous support of my institution, Roehampton University of Surrey, which enabled me to devote myself to writing in the autumn semester 2003. My thanks go to Linda Thomas (as Head of School) and Judith Broadbent (as Linguistics Programme Convener) for facilitating this. Thanks also to Casey Mein and Melanie Carter at Pearson for steering me through the revision process. I am grateful to my ever-supportive colleagues – Judith, Eva, Evi, Frances, and Tope – for their encouragement, and to Amanda and Jane for their invaluable technical assistance. I am particularly grateful to those who read earlier drafts of the revisions, especially Margaret and Pia. I am also indebted to those who gave me access to their sociolinguistic data: Anthea Irwin, Pia Pichler, Louise Mullaney, Kate Segall. Many other sociolinguist colleagues, as well as students on my Language and Gender course, have helped in the shaping of this third edition, through discussions of language and gender in general, and of this book in particular. I would like to single out here Jenny Cheshire, who made me realise a third edition was not an insurmountable task, and who gave me the idea of writing a new final chapter to deal with developments in the field. As ever, thanks go to Margaret for her unstinting support.

Publisher's acknowledgements

We are grateful to the following to reproduce copyright material:

Longman Group UK Ltd for our Table 3.3, from Table 3.2 'Questionnaire for *Atlas linguistic et ethnographique du Lyonnais'* trans. W. Nelson Francis in *Dialectology: An Introduction* (1983); Cambridge University Press and the author Professor Peter Trudgill for our Table 4.1 from *The Social Differentiation of English in Norwich* (1974); CUP and the author Susan Philips for our Tables 9.3 and 9.4 from 'Preschool boys' and girls' language used in pretend play' in Philips, Susan, Steele, Susan and Tanz, Christine *Language, Gender and Sex in Comparative Perspective* (1987); Edward Arnold Ltd for our Table 4.2 and Figures 4.7 and 4.8 in contribution by R.K.S. Macaulay 'Variation and Consistency in Glaswegian English', all in Trudgill, Peter (ed.) *Sociolinguistic Patterns in British English* (1978), also for our Tables 5.1, 5.2 and 5.3 in contribution by Jenny Cheshire 'Linguistic variation and social function' and our Figure 9.1 in contribution by John Local 'Modelling intonational variability in children's speech', all in Romaine, Suzanne (ed.) *Sociolinguistic Variation in Speech Communities* (1982), also Figure 4.15 from Edward, John R. *Language and Disadvantage* (1979) and Figure 10.4 from contribution by Jim and Lesley Milroy 'Belfast: change and variation in an urban vernacular' in Trudgill, Peter (ed.) *Sociolingustic Patterns in British English* (1978); Heinle & Heinle for Tables 7.1 and 7.2 and Figure 7.1 in contribution by Don Zimmerman and Candace West 'Sex roles, interruptions and silences in conversation' in Thorne, Barrie and Henley, Nancy (eds) *Language and Sex: Difference and Dominance* (1975), also our Figure 10.9 in contribution by Patricia Nichols 'Linguistic options and choices for black women in the rural South' in Thorne, Barrie, Kramarae, Cheris and Henley, Nancy (eds) *Language, Gender and Society* (1983); Sage Publications for our Table 7.5 from article by Victoria L. DeFrancisco 'The sounds of silence: how men silence women in marital relations' in *Discourse & Society* 2 (4) 1991; Australian Professional Publication for our Table 6.1 in article by Janet Holmes 'Hedging, fencing and other conversational gambits: an analysis of gender differences in New Zealand speech' and our Figure 4.11 in an article by Edna Eisikovits 'Sex differences in inter-group and intra-group interaction among adolescents', both in Pauwels, Anne (ed.) *Women and Language in Australian and New Zealand Society* (1987); The Linguistic Society of New Zealand (Inc.) and the author Janet Holmes for our Table 6.2 from 'Hedging your bets and sitting on the fence: some evidence for hedges as support structure' in *Te Reo 27* (1984): 54; Longman Group UK Ltd for our Table 6.3 in contribution by Deborah Cameron, Fiona McAlinden and Kathy O'Leary 'Lakoff in context: the social and linguistic functions of tag questions' and our Table 11.1 in contribution by Joan Swann 'Talk control: an illustration from the classroom of problems in analysing male dominance in education', both tables in Coates, Jennifer and Cameron, Deborah (eds) *Women in their Speech Communities* (1989); Praeger Publishers, an imprint of Greenwood Publishing Group, Inc., Westport, CT, for our Tables 6.6 and 6.7 in a contribution from Penny Brown 'How and why are women more polite: some evidence from a Mayan community' in McConnell-Ginet, S. et al. (eds) *Women and Language in Literature and Society*; Routledge Publishers for our Table 9.2 in Gordon Wells' contribution 'Variation in child language' in Lee, V. (ed.) *Language Development* (1979); Editions Payot & Rivages for Figure 3.1 from *Les Mots et les Femmes*, page 27 (1978); Basil Blackwell Publishers and Lesley Milroy for our Figures 5.3, 5.4 and 10.5 in *Language and Social Networks* (1980); Basil Blackwell Publishers and Suzanne Romaine for our Figure 9.2 in *The Language of Children and Adolescents* (1984); Cambridge University Press and Jenny Cheshire for our Figures 5.5 and 5.6 from *Variation in an English Dialect* (1982); CUP Press and the authors Eckert, P. and McConnell-Ginet, S. for our Figures 4.12, 4.13, 10.6 and 10.7, adapted from 'New generalizations and explanations in language and gender research' in *Language in Society*, 28 (2), (1999); Blackwell Publishers and the author Brown, P. for our Table 6.8, adapted from 'How and why are women more polite: some evidence from a Mayan community' in *Language and Gender: A Reader* edited by J. Coates (1998); Pearson Education Ltd for our Figure 7.2, adapted from *Women, Men and Politeness* (Holmes, J. 1995); Blackwell Publishers and the authors Herring, S., Johnson, D. and DiBenedetto, T. for our Table 7.3, adapted from 'Participation in electronic discourse in a "feminist" field' in *Language and Gender: A Reader* edited by J. Coates (1998); Pearson Education Ltd for our Table 7.4 adapted from 'Talking shop: sex and status as determinants of floor apportionment in a work setting' in *Women in their Speech Communities* edited by J. Coates and D. Cameron (Woods, N. 1989); Routledge/Taylor & Francis Books, Inc. and the authors Eckert, P. and McConnell-Ginet, S. for our Figure 10.8, adapted from 'Constructing meaning, constructing selves: snapshots of language, gender and class from Belten High in *Gender Articulated: Language and the Socially Constructed Self* edited by K. Hall and M. Bucholtz (1995); Hodder Arnold for our Figure 10.10, adapted from 'Linguistic change in intonation: the use of high-rising terminals in New Zealand English' in *The Sociolinguistics Reader Vol. 1: Multilingualism and Variation* edited by P. Trudgill and J. Cheshire (Britain, D. 1998); and Blackwell Publishers and the authors Holmes, J. and Stubbe, M. for our Table 11.2, adapted from '"Feminine" workplaces: stereotypes and reality' in *The Handbook of Language and Gender* edited by J. Holmes and M. Meyerhoff (2003).

We have been unable to trace the copyright holders for Figures 4.4 (10.1) and 6.1 and Tables 3.1 and 6.5 and would appreciate any help that would enable us to do so.

To Simon, Emily and William

PART ONE

Introductory

CHAPTER 1

Language and gender

1.1 Introduction

Do women and men talk differently? Gender differences of all kinds fascinate people, and so it is not surprising that there is curiosity about the way women and men talk and whether there are *linguistic* gender differences. We all have our own views on gender differences – in language and in other aspects of human life. Tabloid newspapers and television chat shows, for example, provide answers to the question 'Do women and men talk differently?' which could be described as 'folklinguistic'. They are likely to say that women gossip, or that men swear more than women. These answers are widely believed – but are they true? or are they myths?

And what about the question itself? By asking 'do women and men talk differently', we make a series of assumptions that are currently under challenge. First, the question assumes that we can divide speakers neatly into two groups called 'women' and 'men'. Secondly, the question assumes that we are interested in *differences* between women and men rather than *similarities* between them. At this point, you may think these are ridiculous points to make – of course there are women and men; what's wrong with being interested in differences rather than similarities. But I want to make clear that if I had asked a different question, there would have been different answers.

I shall attempt to answer the question 'Do women and men talk differently?' by drawing on evidence from anthropology, dialectology, discourse analysis, ethnography, sociolinguistics and social psychology. Over the last twenty years, there has been an explosion of research in the field of language and gender. Many books have been published, as well as many articles, both in learned journals and in edited collections. It is one of the aims of this book to provide a coherent account of such work; to bring together the many accounts of gender differences in language that have been written and to make them accessible to the interested reader. The book is intended both for those with an interest in sociolinguistics who want to study one aspect of linguistic variation in depth, and also for those interested in gender differences in general. It will concentrate on sociolinguistic work carried out in Britain and other English-speaking countries.

This book, then, is primarily a sociolinguistic account of the co-variation of language and gender. It is not about the relationship between language and sexism, except in a very general sense; that is, it is not about language which denigrates, or is believed to denigrate, women. It will describe language *use*, in particular the differing usage of women and men as speakers.

As far as terminology is concerned, **gender** rather than **sex** will be the key category under discussion. 'Sex' refers to a biological distinction, while 'gender' is the term used to describe socially constructed categories based on sex. Most societies operate in terms of two genders, **masculine** and **feminine**, and it is tempting to treat the category of gender as a simple binary opposition. Until recently, much of the research carried out on language and gender did so. But more recent theorising challenges this binary thinking. Gender is instead conceptualised as plural, with a range of femininities and masculinities available to speakers at any point in time. (These new conceptualisations will be explored in Chapter 8.)

In this introductory chapter, I shall begin with an overview of the way language and gender studies have developed within sociolinguistics. I shall then give a brief account of the main approaches adopted by linguists to the question of gender differences in language. Finally, I shall provide a brief outline of the structure of the book.

1.2 Sociolinguistics and gender

It is only relatively recently that sociolinguists have turned their attention to gender. Why is this? I should like to suggest three reasons: the first two stem from sociolinguistics' antecedents in dialectology and linguistics; the third is linked to changes in the position of women in contemporary society.

First, in traditional dialectology, the informants selected were typically *non-mobile, older, rural* and *male* (see Chambers and Trudgill 1980: 33). This bias in informant selection was observed by sociolinguists and rejected, but rejection consisted initially of choosing urban rather than rural and younger as well as older informants. While many studies included informants of both sexes, studies confined to male speakers continued to be carried out (e.g. Labov's (1972b) study of black adolescents in Harlem; Reid's (1976) study of Edinburgh schoolboys). It was only in the late 1980s that studies appeared which concentrated on *female* speakers (e.g. Bate and Taylor 1988; Coates and Cameron 1989).

Second, as sociolinguistics began to establish itself as a discipline, reaction against mainstream linguistics led to a shift in emphasis from standard to non-standard varieties. All sorts of minority groups have come under scrutiny, in particular working-class groups, ethnic minority groups, adolescents. Women, however, were not perceived as a minority group. Linguistic variation co-extensive with social class, ethnicity or age was what appeared salient to early sociolinguists.

So why wasn't gender perceived as salient? The answer is that, until relatively recently, men were automatically seen as at the heart of society, with women being peripheral or even invisible. (This pattern of **androcentricity** will be explored further in the next chapter.) This is difficult to comprehend today, when gender differences are big business (see, for example, the success of books like *Men are from Mars, Women are from Venus* or the more recent *The Essential Difference: Men, Women and the Extreme Male Brain*),[1] but if we look back at the period following the Second World War, all important positions in society were held by men. So Britain was headed by a king, George VI (the father of Queen Elizabeth II), the Prime Minister was male as were virtually all MPs, the most important people in the Law and the Church were male, business was run by men. However, the maleness of these important men was not remarked upon: in the 1940s and 1950s, men were persons first and male persons second. The major change that has occurred since that time, due in large part to the political activism of the Women's Movement, is that women have achieved the legal right to be treated as the equals of men (both the Equal Pay Act and the Sex Discrimination Act came into effect in Britain in 1975). This has led to changes both in the workplace and in the home – changes in practice and also changes in attitudes.

The publication of Robin Lakoff's *Language and Woman's Place* in 1975 was a symbolic moment. While Lakoff's book has been criticised for its sweeping claims and lack of empirical evidence, its significance cannot be underestimated, as it galvanised linguists all over the world into research into the uncharted territory of women's talk.

Men, ironically, remained unexamined for much longer, precisely because *man* and *person* were often interchangeable concepts, but in the last decade the whole issue of men and masculinity has come into focus. There has been a shift in men's view of themselves – a shift from seeing themselves as unmarked representatives of the human race to focusing on themselves *as men*. A good example of this shift can be seen in the titles of sociolinguistics books. Labov's study of black male adolescents in Harlem (Labov 1972b, referred to earlier in this section) was one of the most important sociolinguistic works of the 1970s. Its title was *Language in the Inner City*. This title ignores the fact that the language analysed in the book is *male* language. By contrast, a collection of articles on the language use of male speakers published in the 1990s is entitled simply *Language and Masculinity* (Johnson and Meinhoff 1997). This latter book was the first to focus explicitly on men and language.

1.3 Differing approaches to language and gender

Since the publication of Lakoff's classic work, *Language and Woman's Place*, in 1975, linguists have approached language and gender from a variety of perspectives. These can be labelled the **deficit** approach, the **dominance** approach, the **difference** approach, and the **dynamic** or **social constructionist** approach.[2]

They developed in a historical sequence, but the emergence of a new approach did not mean that earlier approaches were superseded. In fact, at any one time these different approaches could be described as existing in a state of tension with each other. It is probably true to say, though, that most researchers now adopt a **dynamic** approach.

The **deficit** approach was characteristic of the earliest work in the field. Most well known is Lakoff's *Language and Woman's Place*, which claims to establish something called 'women's language' (WL), which is characterised by linguistic forms such as hedges, 'empty' adjectives like *charming, divine, nice*, and 'talking in italics' (exaggerated intonation contours). WL is described as weak and unassertive, in other words, as deficient. Implicitly, WL is deficient by comparison with the norm of male language. This approach was challenged because of the implication that there was something intrinsically wrong with women's language, and that women should learn to speak like men if they wanted to be taken seriously.

The second approach – the **dominance** approach – sees women as an oppressed group and interprets linguistic differences in women's and men's speech in terms of men's dominance and women's subordination. Researchers using this model are concerned to show how male dominance is enacted through linguistic practice. 'Doing power' is often a way of 'doing gender' too (see West and Zimmerman 1983). Moreover, all participants in discourse, women as well as men, collude in sustaining and perpetuating male dominance and female oppression.

The third approach – the **difference** approach – emphasises the idea that women and men belong to different subcultures. The 'discovery' of distinct male and female subcultures in the 1980s seems to have been a direct result of women's growing resistance to being treated as a subordinate group. The invisibility of women in the past arose from the conflation of 'culture' with 'male culture'. But women began to assert that they had 'a different voice, a different psychology, and a different experience of love, work and the family from men' (Humm 1989: 51). The advantage of the difference model is that it allows women's talk to be examined outside a framework of oppression or powerlessness. Instead, researchers have been able to show the strengths of linguistic strategies characteristic of women, and to celebrate women's ways of talking. However, the reader should be aware that the difference approach is controversial when applied to *mixed* talk, as was done in *You Just Don't Understand* (1991), Deborah Tannen's best-selling book about male–female 'miscommunication'. Critics of Tannen's book (see, for example, Troemel-Ploetz 1991; Cameron 1992; Freed 1992) argue that the analysis of mixed talk cannot ignore the issue of power.

The fourth and most recent approach is sometimes called the **dynamic** approach because there is an emphasis on dynamic aspects of interaction. Researchers who adopt this approach take a **social constructionist** perspective. Gender identity is seen as a social construct rather than as a 'given' social category. As West and Zimmerman (1987) eloquently put it, speakers should be seen as 'doing gender' rather than statically 'being' a particular gender. This argument led Crawford (1995: 12) to claim that gender should be conceptualised as a verb, not a noun! The observant reader will notice that the phrase 'doing gender' was also used in the paragraph on the dominance approach. This is because the four approaches do not have rigid boundaries: researchers may be influenced by more than one theoretical perspective. What has changed is linguists' sense that gender is not a static, add-on characteristic of speakers, but is something that is *accomplished* in talk every time we speak.

The deficit approach is now seen as out-dated by researchers (but not by the general public, whose acceptance of, for example, assertiveness training for women suggests a world view where women should learn to be more like men). The other three approaches have all yielded valuable insights into the nature of gender differences in language. While it is true to say that social constructionism is now the prevailing paradigm, discussion of sociolinguistic work in subsequent chapters will demonstrate the influence of the dominance and difference approaches during the 1980s and 1990s.

1.4 Organisation of the book

This book will focus on linguistic variation related to the gender of the speaker. It will describe differences found in the speech of women and men, and will relate these linguistic differences to the social roles assigned to women and men in our culture. Chapter 2 will expose our society's preconceptions about gender differences in language, while Chapter 3 will assess the contribution of anthropology and dialectology to the study of gender differences.

I shall then move on to look in detail at sociolinguistic analyses of gender differences in language. The five chapters that make up Part Two of the book follow the chronological order in which sociolinguistic research on gender developed. Chapter 4 will focus on quantitative sociolinguistic studies, Chapter 5 on studies involving the concept of social network. In Chapter 6 I shall look at those studies which examine women's and men's linguistic behaviour in the wider sense of communicative competence: this will include studies examining the use of hedges, questions, compliments, swearing and politeness, among other things. Chapter 7 will concentrate on the way certain conversational strategies can be used to achieve dominance in talk, looking in particular at interruptions, silence and patterns of floor-holding, while Chapter 8 will focus on single-sex talk and will present a more social constructionist picture of the way masculinity and femininity are accomplished in interaction.

These five central chapters will also try to deal with socio-functional explanations, since the data presented inevitably lead to the question 'Why?' Many explanations for gender differentiation in language have been suggested and these will be reviewed and discussed.

Part Three, entitled 'Causes and consequences', will examine three related areas in detail: the development of gender-differentiated language in children (Chapter 9), the nature of linguistic change and the role of gender differences in promoting change (Chapter 10), and finally the social consequences of gender differences in language, looking especially at the use of language in the school setting and in the workplace (Chapter 11). This last chapter will ask whether women are disadvantaged in these two contexts, or whether it is male speakers who are now 'in crisis'.

Part Four, entitled 'Looking to the future', contains just one chapter, which will provide an overview of recent developments in language and gender research. Language and gender is now such a dynamic area of sociolinguistics that new kinds of data and new ways of conceptualising gender are evolving all the time. Chapter 12 will sketch in the most important of these developments, and will hazard some guesses about the shape of language and gender research in the future.

1.5 Author's caveat

We are constrained by the English language to think in terms of binaries – man/woman, male/female, masculine/feminine. When we use the pronoun 'I', we bring to that use of 'I' a sense of being either a woman or a man. You, reading this book, will bring to your reading your experience of what it means to be a female speaker or a male speaker today. You will also have been socialised into a set of preconceptions about the nature of women and men in general and about female and male speakers in particular. You should be alert to these preconceptions and to your own necessarily partial viewpoint when sifting the evidence presented in this book. Also you should remember that it is not only you, the reader, who have preconceptions and prejudices – I, the writer, have them too, and so have the various scholars whose work on language I shall be referring to. Obviously, the pursuit of any discipline involves an attempt by scholars to rise above their preconceptions. However, it is important for scholars to acknowledge that they are not outside culture, but are part of it and therefore not impartial.

As a first step to coming to terms with our preconceptions, and in order to assess which gender differences in language are fiction and which fact, we will look at the cultural mythology associated with gender differences in language. The next chapter will address this subject directly.

Notes

1 John Gray, *Men are from Mars, Women are from Venus* (HarperCollins, New York and London 1993); Simon Baron-Cohen, *The Essential Difference: Men, Women and the Extreme Male Brain* (Penguin, Harmondsworth 2003).
2 'Social constructionist' is probably the more accurate term, but 'dynamic' has the mnemonic advantage of continuing the pattern of words beginning with the letter 'd'.

CHAPTER 2

The historical background (I) – Folklinguistics and the early grammarians

2.1 Introduction

Differences between women and men have always been a topic of interest to the human species and supposed linguistic differences are often enshrined in proverbs:

A woman's tongue wags like a lamb's tail. (England)
Foxes are all tail and women are all tongue. (England – Cheshire)
Où femme y a, silence n'y a (*where there's a woman, there's no silence*). (France)
The North Sea will sooner be found wanting in water than a woman at a loss for a word. (Jutland)[1]

The comments of contemporary observers, recorded in diaries, letters, poems, novels and so on, also provide us with evidence of folklinguistic beliefs about gender differences in language. Beside these more casual observations we can place the work of the early grammarians. It is not always easy to draw a line between the former and the latter, since much work entitled 'grammar' is no more scientific in its approach to gender differences in language than the observations of 'ordinary' people. In other words, academics and scholars are as much the product of the times they live in as are non-academics, and their work on language can be as subject to prejudice and preconception as are the comments of lay people.

As we shall see, scholarly comments on gender differences in language reflect the ideas of their time. In some cases this tendency has led to startling contradictions. Such contradictions can be accounted for by assuming a general rule, which I shall call **The Androcentric Rule**: 'Men will be seen to behave linguistically in a way that fits the writer's view of what is desirable or admirable; women on the other hand will be blamed for any linguistic state or development which is regarded by the writer as negative or reprehensible'.

In this chapter I shall survey writings from the Middle Ages up to the beginning of this century (that is, work written before the discipline of linguistics was established). Rather than survey the entire field, I shall focus on the following areas of interest: vocabulary, swearing and taboo words, grammar, literacy, pronunciation and verbosity.

2.2 Vocabulary

Interest in the lexical and grammatical structure of the language, that is, in its vocabulary and grammar, was stimulated by the rise of Standard English. Once one variety of a language is selected as the standard, then the process of codification inevitably follows. Codification involves the writing of both dictionaries (dealing with the lexical items of a language) and grammars (dealing with the grammatical structure of a language). In England, the eighteenth century saw the publication of numerous dictionaries and grammars, all written in an attempt to reduce the language to rule and to legislate on 'correct' usage.

Commentary on gender differences in vocabulary is quite widespread in eighteenth-century writings, as the following extracts will demonstrate. The passage below, written by Richard Cambridge for *The World* of 12 December 1754, implies that the ephemeral nature of women's vocabulary is associated with the unimportance of what they say:

> I must beg leave ... to doubt the propriety of joining to the fixed and permanent standard of language a vocabulary of words which perish and are forgot within the compass of a year. That we are obliged to the ladies for most of these ornaments to our language, I readily acknowledge.
> (Cambridge 1754, as quoted in Tucker 1961: 93)

Here we see an eighteenth-century gentleman grappling with the problem of linguistic change. The ultimate aim of codification was to 'fix' the language once and for all. However, vocabulary was an area which appeared to elude control. On what grounds Richard Cambridge judged women to be responsible for ephemeral words, we are not told.

Turning to the early twentieth century, we find Otto Jespersen, a Danish professor of English language, writing on the question of changing vocabulary. He asserts that it is *men* rather than women who introduce 'new and fresh expressions' and thus men who are 'the chief renovators of language' (Jespersen

1922: 247). This apparent inconsistency can be accounted for by the Androcentric Rule (see section 2.1). As the rule would predict, in an age which deplored lexical change, women were held to be the culprits for introducing ephemeral words. On the other hand, Jespersen in 1922 accepted that change was inevitable and saw innovation as creative: he therefore credited men with introducing new words to the lexicon.

An anonymous contributor to *The World* (6 May 1756) complains of women's excessive use of certain adverbial forms:

> Such is the pomp of utterance of our present women of fashion; which, though it may tend to spoil many a pretty mouth, can never recommend an indifferent one. And hence it is that there is so great a scarcity of originals, and that the ear is such a daily sufferer from an identity of phrase, whether it be *vastly*, *horridly*, *abominably*, *immensely*, or *excessively*, which, with three or four more calculated for the same swiss-like service, make up the whole scale or gamut of modern female conversation.
> (as quoted in Tucker 1961: 96)

This characteristic women's language is gently mocked by Jane Austen in *Northanger Abbey* (1813), in the speech of Isabella Thorpe:

> 'My attachments are always *excessively* strong.'
> 'I must confess there is something *amazingly* insipid about her.'
> 'I am so vexed with all the men for not admiring her! – I scold them all *amazingly* about it.'
> (*Northanger Abbey*, Ch. 6, my italics)

It is clearly significant that it is Isabella, who is flirtatious, selfish and shallow, who uses these adverbials, and not Catherine, the heroine (who is altogether less sophisticated).

The use of adverbial forms of this kind was a fashion at this time, and was evidently associated in the public mind with women's speech. Lord Chesterfield, writing in *The World* of 5 December 1754, makes very similar observations to those of the anonymous contributor quoted above:

> Not content with enriching our language with words absolutely new [*again the accusation that women destabilise the lexicon*] my fair countrywomen have gone still farther, and improved it by the application and extension of old ones to various and very different significations. They take a word and change it, like a guinea, into shillings for pocket money, to be employed in the several occasional purposes of the day. For instance, the adjective *vast* and it's [*sic*] adverb *vastly*, mean anything and are the fashionable words of the most fashionable people. A fine woman . . . is *vastly* obliged, or *vastly* offended, *vastly* glad or *vastly* sorry. Large objects are *vastly* great, small ones are *vastly* little; and I had lately the pleasure to hear a fine woman pronounce, by a happy metonymy, a very small gold snuff-box that was produced in company to be *vastly* pretty, because it was *vastly* little.
> (as quoted in Tucker 1961: 92)

Lord Chesterfield concludes with a mock-serious appeal to one of the great legislators of the time, Dr Johnson, whose *Dictionary* (1755) was a landmark in the codification process. 'Mr. Johnson', Lord Chesterfield says, 'will do well to consider seriously to what degree he will restrain the various and extensive significants of this great word' [i.e. *vast*].

Johnson's *Dictionary* is well known for its individualistic and biased definitions (*Patron* is defined as 'Commonly a wretch who supports with insolence, and is paid with flattery'). Johnson stigmatises the words *flirtation* and *frightful* as 'female cant'. Such a comment is value-laden. It seems clear that the anonymous contributor to *The World* quoted above is a man: all these passages reveal that their (male) authors believe women to have restricted and vacuous vocabulary, and to exert a malign influence on the language. Note that 'language' is defined by these eighteenth-century writers in terms of male language; the way men talk is seen as the norm, while women's language is deviant.

The androcentric bias is still present in twentieth-century observations on English vocabulary. Jespersen included a chapter entitled 'The Woman' in his book *Language: Its Nature, Development and Origin* (1922). This chapter has the merit of summarising extant research on women's language in many different parts of the world. It has been justifiably criticised, however, for its uncritical acceptance of sexist assumptions about male/female differences in language. Jespersen includes a section on vocabulary in this chapter. He generalises that 'the vocabulary of a woman as a rule is much less extensive than that of a man'. He supports this claim with data from an experiment by an American, Jastrow, in which male college students used a greater variety of words than female college students when asked to write down one hundred (separate) words. This is the only evidence given.

In his section on adverbs, Jespersen says that women differ from men in their extensive use of certain adjectives, such as *pretty* and *nice*. It should be noted that the American linguist, Robin Lakoff, in *Language and Woman's Place*, the work that for many people marks the beginning of twentieth-century linguistic interest in gender differences, specifically singles out '"empty" adjectives like *divine, charming, cute . . .*' as typical of what she calls 'women's language' (Lakoff 1975: 53).

Women differ from men, according to Jespersen, even more in their use of adverbs. Quoting Lord Chesterfield's remarks on the adverb *vastly* (see pp. 11–12), Jespersen argues that this is 'a distinctive trait: the fondness of women for hyperbole will very often lead the fashion with regard to adverbs of intensity, and these are very often used with disregard of their proper meaning' (Jespersen 1922: 250). (This of course begs the question of 'proper' meaning.) He quotes examples from all the major European languages. This proves that adverbs are widely used in these speech communities, but we are given no evidence to show that it is only, or preponderantly, women who use them.

So is also claimed as having 'something of the eternally feminine about it'. Jespersen quotes *Punch* of 4 January 1896: 'This little adverb is a great favourite with ladies, in conjunction with an adjective'. The extract gives as examples of 'ladies usage': 'It is *so* lovely!'; 'He is *so* charming!'; 'Thank you *so* much!'; 'I'm *so* glad you've come!' Jespersen's 'explanation' for this gender-preferential usage is that 'women much more often than men break off without finishing their sentences, because they start talking without having thought out what they are going to say' (Jespersen 1922: 250). He provides no evidence for this claim, but implies that men always 'think out' what they are going to say before they start talking.

Lakoff also has a section on the intensifier *so*. She asserts that '*so* is more frequent in women's than men's language, though certainly men can use it' (Lakoff 1975: 54). As we shall see in subsequent sections, there are many parallels between Lakoff's and Jespersen's work, which is surprising in view of the fact that feminists welcomed Lakoff's book, but have been very critical of Jespersen's.

2.3 Swearing and taboo language

> A whistling sailor, a crowing hen and a swearing woman ought all three to go to hell together.
> (American proverb)

In this section I shall be considering oaths, exclamations, taboo words: anything which could come under the general heading 'vulgar language'. The belief that women's language is more polite, more refined – in a word, more ladylike – is very widespread and has been current for many centuries.

Vulgarity is a cultural construct, and the evidence suggests that it was the new courtly tradition of the Middle Ages which, by creating gentility, also created vulgarity. The issue of vulgar language forms an important theme of French *fabliaux*, comic tales of the Middle Ages, which seem in part to have been written in direct response to the new vogue for 'clean' language. One – *La Dame qui se venja du Chevalier* (Montaiglon et Raynaud 1872–90: vol. VI) – explicitly supports the courtly taboo stigmatising a man's use of obscene language in front of a woman. The man and woman are in bed together when the man commits his *faux pas*: 'the knight, who was on top, looked right at her face and saw her swooning with pleasure. Whereupon he couldn't suppress his foolishness but said something very vulgar. Right then he asked her "My lady, would you crack some nuts?"' (as translated in Muscatine 1981: 11). *Croistre noiz* (crack nuts) is a synonym for *foutre* (fuck). The woman is extremely offended and proceeds to take her revenge.

In contrast to this, there is a group of three *fabliaux* (the two versions of *La damoisele qui ne pooit oïr parler de foutre* and *la pucele qui abevra le polain*) which can be read as an attack on linguistic prudery in women, and which defend the use of vernacular ('vulgar') terms. In all three versions of the story, the heroine is a stuck-up (*dédaigneuse*) young woman who can't bear to hear any words to do with sex – they make her feel ill. The father can't keep male servants as they don't speak language suitable for his daughter's ears. The hero is a clever young man who arrives on the pretext of looking for work and feigns disgust at hearing obscene language, thus gaining the confidence of the father and daughter. The girl is so convinced of his purity that she invites him to sleep in her bed. A mutual seduction takes place, with the lovers using elaborate metaphors of ponies, meadows, fountains, etc. to avoid the use of taboo expressions. The writer comments in one version: 'I want to show by this example that women should not be too proud to say *foutre* (fuck) out loud when all the same they're doing it' (as translated in Muscatine 1981: 14). The humour in these tales arises from the ludicrous contrast between the woman's dislike of the *words* and her pleasure in the *act*. A famous passage in the *Roman de la Rose* (*c.* 1277) attacks the use of euphemisms and circumlocutions, and calls for plain language. The writer comments: 'If women don't name them (i.e. *coilles*, bollocks) in France, it's nothing but getting out of the habit' (as quoted in Muscatine 1981: 17). Presumably there have always been taboos on language, but it looks as if the courtly tradition of the Middle Ages, which put women on a pedestal, strengthened linguistic taboos in general, and also condemned the use of vulgar language by women, and its use by men in front of women.

The strength of the folklinguistic belief in male/female differences in swearing is reflected in Elyot's strictures on the upbringing of noblemen's children in *The Governour* (1531). Elyot advises that the child of a Gentleman should be brought up by women who will not permit 'any wanton or unclene worde to be spoken' in the child's presence. To avoid the child's hearing such words, he urges that no men should be allowed into the nursery.

Shakespeare on the other hand makes fun of this cultural stereotype. In *I Henry IV*, Hotspur mocks his wife for her genteel use of oaths:

> *Hotspur*: Come, Kate, I'll have your song too.
> *Lady Percy*: Not mine, in good sooth.
> *Hotspur*: Not yours, in good sooth! Heart! you swear like a comfit-maker's wife! 'Not
>   you, in good sooth'; and
>   'As true as I live'; and
>   'As God shall mend me'; and 'As sure as day';
>   And givst such sarcenet surety for thy oaths,
>   As if thou never walk'st further than Finsbury.
>   Swear me, Kate, like a lady as thou art,
>   A good mouth-filling oath; and leave 'in sooth'
>   And such protest of pepper-gingerbread
>   To velvet-guards and Sunday citizens.
> (*I Henry IV*, III. i. 241ff.)

Shakespeare here reveals an awareness that swearing is related not only to gender but also to social class. Hotspur urges Kate to swear *not* like a comfit-maker's wife and other 'Sunday citizens' (the bourgeoisie), but like 'a lady', that is a female member of the aristocracy.

As section 2.2 has shown, eighteenth-century gentlemen were having to come to terms with the fact of linguistic change. Arthur Murphy, in a witty article in *Gray's Inn Journal* of 29 June 1754, suggests that there should be a

Register of Births and Deaths for words. He elaborates on this idea with the following conceit:

> A Distinction might be made between a kind of Sex in Words, according as they are appropriated to Men or Women; as for Instance, *D—n my Blood* is of Male extraction, and *Pshaw, Fiddlestick* I take to be female.
> (as quoted in Tucker 1961: 86)

The idea of distinct male and female swear words is still widely held. Lakoff, 200 years later, makes exactly the same observation as Murphy:

> Consider (a) 'Oh dear, you've put the peanut butter in the refrigerator again.'
>   (b) 'Shit, you've put the peanut butter in the refrigerator again.'
>
> It is safe to predict that people would classify the first sentence as part of 'women's language', the second as 'men's language'.
> (Lakoff 1975: 10)

Lakoff summarises her position later by saying 'women don't use offcolor or indelicate expressions; women are the experts at euphemism' (1975: 55).

While noting that she is talking about 'general tendencies' rather than 'hundred-percent correlations', Lakoff seems happy to present such folklinguistic material without the support of any research findings to confirm her statements. It is less surprising that Jespersen, in 1922, held such views:

> There can be no doubt that women exercise a great and universal influence on linguistic development through their instinctive shrinking from coarse and gross expressions and their preference for refined and (in certain spheres) veiled and indirect expressions.

He goes on to the particular case of swearing:

> Among the things women object to in language must be specially mentioned anything that smacks of swearing.

In a footnote to this, he adds:

> There are great differences with regard to swearing between different nations; but I think that in those countries and in those circles in which swearing is common it is found much more extensively among men than among women: this at any rate is true of Denmark.
> (Jespersen 1922: 246)

These writers claim to *describe* women's more polite use of language, but we should ask whether what they are actually doing is attempting to *prescribe* how women *ought* to talk. Avoidance of swearing and of 'coarse' words is held up to female speakers as the ideal to be aimed at (as is silence, as we shall see in section 2.7 on verbosity). It is clear that people have thought for a long time that women and men differ in relation to the use of swear words and other taboo expressions. As section 6.3 will show, the actual situation is much more complex than folkinguistic claims suggest.

2.4 Grammar

The rise of Standard English stimulated an awareness of variation in language and with it the growth of the notion of correctness. Once a standard was accepted and codified, then forms which deviated from this standard were frowned on as 'incorrect'. Eighteenth-century notions of grammar were less sophisticated than today's: grammars were prescriptive rather than descriptive, laying down rules of correct usage. They often included sections on spelling and punctuation, which demonstrates how early grammarians took the *written* language as the basis for their work.

The earliest writers on grammar and rhetoric were concerned about the 'correct' ordering of elements in phrases such as *men and women*:

> Some will set the Carte before the horse, as thus, My mother and my father are both at home, even as thoughe the good man of the house ware no breaches, or that the graye Mare were the better Horse. And what thoughe it often so happeneth (God wotte the more pitte) yet in speaking at the least, let us kepe a natural order, and set the man before the woman for maners Sake.
> (Wilson 1560: 189)

This idea of 'a natural order' and of the superiority of the male is unabashedly prescribed for linguistic usage: 'The Masculine gender is more worthy than the Feminine' (Poole 1646: 21). This idea seems to have been a necessary precursor of the sex-indefinite *he* rule, which proscribes the use of *they* or *he or she* where the sex of the antecedent is unknown. Compare the following three sentences:

1. Someone knocked at the door but they had gone when I got downstairs.
2. Someone knocked at the door but he or she had gone when I got downstairs.
3. Someone knocked at the door but he had gone when I got downstairs.

According to prescriptive grammarians, only the last of these three utterances is 'correct' (the first is 'incorrect' and the second 'clumsy'). John Kirkby's statement, from his *New English Grammar* of 1746, is the one most frequently quoted:

> The Masculine Person answers to the general Name, which comprehends both Male and Female; as *Any Person, who knows what he says.*
> (Kirkby 1746: 117)

This is not the place for a full discussion of the rival merits of generic *he* and singular *they* in contexts requiring a sex-indefinite pronoun (for a detailed account, see Bodine 1998). The important point is that the androcentric (male-as-norm) attitudes so conspicuous in early pronouncements on language were actually used as the basis for certain prescriptive rules of grammar. Many people will see feminist opposition to the use of sex-indefinite *he* as misguided and doomed to failure ('I feel . . . that an attempt to change pronominal usage will be futile': Lakoff 1975: 45). What these people are unaware of is the fact that the present rule was itself imposed on language users by male grammarians of the eighteenth century and after. It is naïve to assume that codification was carried out in a disinterested fashion: those who laid down the rules inevitably defined as 'correct' that usage which they preferred, for whatever reason.

Observations on language by men of letters reveal an assumption that women are frequently guilty of incorrect usage, as far as grammar is concerned. The following passage is typical of its time:

> I came yesterday into the Parlour, where I found Mrs. Cornelia, my lady's third Daughter, all alone, reading a Paper, which, as I afterwards found, contained a Copy of Verses, upon Love and Friendship. . . . By the Hand [i.e. *handwriting*], at first sight, I could not guess whether they came from a Lady, but having put on my spectacles, and perused them carefully, I found by some peculiar Modes in Spelling, and a certain Negligence in Grammar, that it was a Female Sonnet.
>
> (Richard Steele 1713; as quoted in Tucker 1961: 69)

Lord Chesterfield (1741) in a letter to his son remarks: 'most women and all the ordinary people in general speak in open defiance of all grammar'. Henry Tilney tells Catherine Morland that 'the usual style of letter writing among women is faultless, except in three particulars' which are 'a general deficiency of subject, a total inattention to stops, and a very frequent ignorance of grammar' (*Northanger Abbey* 1813). Although he is teasing, we can assume that these were the kinds of taunts about grammatical incorrectness which were commonly made at women's expense at the time.

Jespersen inevitably has much to say on the subject of grammar and male/female differences. As we have seen (in relation to *so*, section 2.2), he believed that women often produce half-finished sentences (as a result of not thinking before speaking!). He claims that this happens particularly with exclamatory sentences, and he illustrates his claim with the following examples (both taken from literature):

> 'Mrs. Eversleigh: I must say!' (but words fail her).
> (Hankin, quoted in Jespersen 1922: 251)

> 'The trouble you must have taken,' Hilda exclaimed.
> (Compton-MacKenzie, quoted in Jespersen 1922: 251)

These utterances are precisely the kind of thing that real people, of both sexes, do say. The concept of the half-finished sentence results from treating written language as primary. The sentence is the main unit of written language, but analysis of spoken discourse (a relatively new pursuit) suggests that the sentence may not be a relevant category for speech. In other words, people don't speak in sentences, either finished or half-finished. However, since in the past men received far more education that women, it is likely that their speech was more affected by written norms; in other words, male/female differences may have reflected relative exposure to written language. But we have no quantitative evidence to support this hypothesis.

Jespersen's second claim revolves around the concepts of **parataxis** and **hypotaxis**. Clauses can be joined together in a variety of ways. **Parataxis** is the term used to describe a sequence of clauses where there are no links at all (the clauses are simply juxtaposed): CLAUSE, CLAUSE (e.g. *I got up, I went to work*). Similar to this, but not always included in the term 'parataxis', is **coordination**, where the clauses are linked by **coordinating** conjunctions (*and, but,* etc.): CLAUSE ***and*** CLAUSE (e.g. *I got up **and** I went to work*). **Hypotaxis** is the term used to describe a sequence of clauses where the links are **subordinating** conjunctions (*after, when, because,* etc.): ***after*** CLAUSE, CLAUSE/CLAUSE ***after*** CLAUSE (e.g. ***After** I got up, I went to work/I went to work **after** I got up*).

The crucial difference between these two modes is that parataxis involves a series of main clauses, each clause being of equal value, while hypotaxis consists of a main clause with one or more subordinate clauses dependent on it. The logical connections between the clauses are made *explicit* in a hypotactic style, but left *implicit* in a paratactic style.

There is a long tradition in our culture of scorning parataxis and praising hypotaxis. Paratactic constructions tend to be called 'primitive', presumably because of their surface-structure lack of logical connectives. Hypotactic constructions, on the other hand, are universally admired, especially from the Renaissance onwards. It should be remembered that the classic Latin sentence involves complex subordination, and classical models were revered.

Jespersen's analysis of male/female differences in syntax makes use of this distinction:

> If we compare long periods [i.e. *sentences*] as constructed by men and by women, we shall in the former find many more instances of intricate or involute structures with clause within clause, a relative clause in the middle of a conditional clause or vice versa, with subordination and sub-subordination, while the typical form of long feminine periods is that of co-ordination, one sentence or clause being added to another on the same plane and the gradation between the respective ideas being marked not grammatically, but emotionally, by stress and intonation, and in writing by underlining. In learned terminology we may say that men are fond of hypotaxis and women of parataxis. (Jespersen 1922: 251)

The distinction between *grammatically* and *emotionally* is obscure, but *emotionally* is presumably pejorative, and suggests that Jespersen finds the hypotactic style superior. He continues with two famous similes:

> a male period is often like a set of Chinese boxes, one within another, while a feminine period is like a set of pearls joined together on a string of *ands* and similar words. (Jespersen 1922: 252)

At his most sexist, Jespersen still produces elegant imagery.

More recently, the paratactic/hypotactic distinction has been used to distinguish between Bernstein's restricted and elaborated codes.[2] Without using these terms, Bernstein appeals to our culturally conditioned notion that hypotaxis is a superior mode of construction: he claims that subordination is typical of elaborated code, while restricted code makes use of 'simple' coordinated clauses. Linguists argue that there is nothing intrinsically superior about a construction involving subordinate clauses, but note that hypotactic constructions are typical of written language, while paratactic constructions are typical of speech. We can draw up a simple table (Table 2.1) to show the correspondences.

Table 2.1: The linguistic domains (real and hypothesised) of parataxis and hypotaxis

	Parataxis	Hypotaxis
Typically found in:	Anglo-Saxon prose	Renaissance and post-Renaissance prose
	Speech	Writing
Supposed to be typical of:	Restricted code	Elaborated code
	Women's language	Men's language

As has been said earlier, there has been a tendency for scholars to measure everything against the bench-mark of formal written prose. Both Jespersen's claims about women's syntax seem to relate to differences between the spoken and written language. Written language (in particular, printed material) was produced mostly by men (see section 2.5); this means that Jespersen could judge men on their written syntax but he was more likely to have judged women's syntax on the basis of their spoken language.

2.5 Literacy

This section is closely linked to the preceding one. There is no doubt that, until the coming of state education for all in the twentieth century, women had less access to literacy than men. Before the nineteenth century, only women of the middle class and above were likely to be literate, and even then, when we say literate, we mean literate in the vernacular. The brothers and husbands of these same women were literate in the classical languages as well. Classical Latin and Greek were no longer spoken as mother-tongues by anyone: they survived as languages only in the male worlds of the school, the university and the church. Latin, in particular, had become 'a sex-linked language, a kind of badge of masculine identity' (Ong 1967: 250). When Milton was asked whether he would teach his daughters other languages, he is alleged to have replied: 'One tongue is sufficient for a woman.'

The following extract shows that, while seventeenth- and eighteenth-century gentlemen agreed that women's language had its defects, especially their written language, they were not all opposed to the idea of changing this state of affairs through education. The extract is taken from the introduction to a work entitled *The Many Advantages of a Good Language to any Nation: with an Examination of the Present State of our own: As also, An Essay towards correcting some Things that are wrong in it*. This work has been ascribed to Thomas Wilson

(1663–1755), Bishop of Sodor and Man. After emphasising the Power of Words, the writer warns that an improper use of words reflects badly on the user.

> We could heartily wish that the fair sex would take notice of this last Reason; for many a pretty Lady by the Silliness of her Words, hath lost the Admiration which her Face had gained. And as the Mind hath more lovely and more lasting Charms than the Body, if they would captivate Men of Sense, they must not neglect those best kind of Beauties. As these Perfections do not depend upon the Strength of the Hand, but the Quickness of the Wit, and Niceness of the Eye and Ear; and as in these Talents Nature hath doubtless been as bountiful to that Sex as to our own, those improprieties in Words, Spelling and Writing, for which they are usually laughed at, are not owing to any Defect in their Minds, but the Carelessness, if not injustice to them in their Education. These following Essays are intended for a Help to them as well as others.
> (Wilson? 1724: 37)

He goes on to point out the importance of educating the mothers of the nation's children. We can all admire the liberality of his sentiments, while noting that he addresses his remarks exclusively to men ('Nature has doubtless been as bountiful to that Sex as to our own'). At the time this was written (1724), women's writing was clearly the subject of mockery; moreover, women obviously received very little and very poor education. Swift makes the same point, with typical exaggeration, in his *A Letter to a Young Lady on her Marriage* (1727):

> It is a little hard that not one Gentleman's daughter in a thousand should be brought to read or understand her own natural tongue, or be judge of the easiest Books that are written in it.

Henry Tilney's teasing of Catherine about women's letter writing (quoted in the previous section), shows that little had changed nearly a century later.

Rousseau (1712–78) condemns women's writing, but on different grounds from those we have heard so far. He says:

> that burning eloquence, those sublime raptures which transmit delight to the very foundation of the soul will always be lacking from women's writings. They are all cold and pretty like their authors. They may show great wit but never any soul.
> (Rousseau, *La Lettre d'Alembert sur les Spectacles*, as translated by Peggy Kamuf 1980: 290)

In the Romantic Age, then, women are seen as inferior because their writings lack passion. We can contrast this with Jespersen's claim that women prefer paratactic modes of expression (see section 2.4), a claim which rests on the assertion that they are 'emotional' where men are 'grammatical'. This contradiction is more easily understood if we take the view that each era redefines what is admirable in language and what is to be avoided (**The Androcentric Rule**). There is consistency in Rousseau's and Jespersen's finding that women are performing less admirably than men.

It is not until the twentieth century that we can take it for granted that women are literate, that women have equal access to education, and that women's voices are heard equally with men's (at least in theory). Women's comments on writing give us an insight into the problems of using a medium which has over the centuries been in the hands of men. Virginia Woolf is particularly concerned with the form of the written sentence:

> But it is still true that before a woman can write exactly as she wishes to write, she has many difficulties to face. To begin with, there is the technical difficulty – so simple, apparently; in reality, so baffling – that the very form of the sentence does not fit her. It is a sentence made by men; it is too loose, too heavy, too pompous for a woman's use. Yet in a novel, which covers so wide a stretch of ground, an ordinary and usual type of sentence has to be found to carry the reader on easily and naturally from one end of the book to the other. And this a woman must make for herself, altering and adapting the current sentence until she writes one that takes the natural shape of her thought without crushing or distorting it.
> (Woolf 1929, as published in Woolf 1979: 48)

Woolf's concern that the written sentence is 'made by men' is part of a wider debate over whether language as a whole is man-made. The inadequacy of 'male' language as a medium for writing about women's experience has been deplored by women writers for centuries.[3] French feminists in particular have pursued this line of argument; Luce Irigaray (1990: 82) claims that even the syntax of the written sentence is irredeemably male, and urges a new 'feminine' syntax. But it is not only the form of the written sentence that has come under attack. The 1980s have seen the publication of several feminist dictionaries and other works on vocabulary,[4] and radical innovations by feminist writers have begun to seep into public consciousness (if only to be ridiculed). Lexical forms like *herstory* (as an alternative to *history*) and *malestream* (to replace *mainstream*) may not, in the long run, be permanent additions to the English lexicon, but they draw attention to the essential **androcentricity** of the written word, and of the culture it represents.

2.6 Pronunciation

The rise of a standard variety of written English was followed by the rise of a standard variety of *spoken* English. After the development of a standard grammar and lexicon, the need was felt for a standard in pronunciation. The accent normally associated with standard English is RP (Received Pronunciation), an accent which differs from all other English accents in that it no longer has links with any particular geographical region. The growth of a spoken standard is accompanied by the growth of ideas about what constitutes 'good' speech. As the educated speech of the Court in London became prestigious, so other accents began to be stigmatised. Comments by contemporary writers reveal again an androcentric view of linguistic usage with women's speech singled out as deviating from the (male) norms.

Elyot, in *The Governour* (1531), gives the following advice on the subject of nurses and other women who look after noblemen's children when they are infants:

[they shall] at the lest way . . . speke none English but that which is cleane, polite, perfectly and articulately pronounced, omittinge no lettre or sillable, as folisshe women oftentimes do of a wantonnesse, whereby divers noblemen and gentilmennes chyldren (as I do at this daye knowe) have attained corrupte and foul pronuntiation.
(Elyot 1531)

Note that the appeal to the idea that no letters or syllables should be omitted is an appeal to the notion of written language as norm. As we have seen (section 2.4), spoken English has been compared with written ever since the growth of a written standard. Where writing and speech differ (and we are only now beginning to understand how great these differences are), there has been a tendency to see the spoken form as incorrect, or as deviating from the ideal. The above passage reminds us again that gentlemen, as the educated literate group in society, had a different view of language from women.

The following extract (taken from Gill's *Logonomia Anglica* (1619–21) links the speech of women with that of low-status men:

in speech the custom of the learned is the first law. Writing therefore is to be adjusted, not to that sound which herdsmen, girls [*mulierculae*] and porters use; but to that which the learned or cultivated scholars [*docti aut culte eruditi viri*] use in speaking and recitation.
(as translated in Dobson 1969: 435, n. 4)

The pronunciation of female speakers (*mulierculae*) is explicitly compared with that of male speakers (*viri*), and readers are urged to imitate educated *men*. The grouping of herdsmen, porters and girls together shows us that non-prestigious speech was clearly associated with lack of education. It is not clear, however, whether women and men of the same social class in the seventeenth century *did* talk differently – it is only in the twentieth century that quantitative socio-linguistic analysis has been applied to speech.

Jespersen includes an excellent survey of male/female differences in pronunciation in his chapter on 'The Woman', in a section oddly entitled 'Phonetics and Grammar' (where is the grammar?). He interprets the comments of early grammarians as showing that women had a more advanced pronunciation than men. For example, he quotes Mulcaster (1582): '*Ai* is the man's diphthong, and soundeth full: *ei*, the woman's, and soundeth finish (i.e. fineish) in the same both sense, and use, *a woman is deintie, and feinteth soon, the man fainteth not bycause he is nothing daintie*'. Jespersen comments: 'Thus what is now distinctive of refined as opposed to vulgar pronunciation was then characteristic of the fair sex' (Jespersen 1922: 243). He demonstrates that this tendency to innovate was not confined to English women, giving examples from France, Denmark and even Siberia. He devotes a paragraph to 'the weakening of the old fully trilled tongue-point r' (1922: 244). He argues that this change, which has occurred in many languages, has been brought about to a large extent by women. His evidence is slight, and his explanation bizarre: 'The old trilled point sound is natural and justified when life is chiefly carried on out-of-doors, but indoor life prefers, on the whole, less noisy speech habits'

(Jespersen 1922: 244). He argues, in effect, that sounds which are appropriate in a rural setting are inappropriate in an urban one. His observation of differences between the speech of 'the great cities' and 'the rustic population' seems plausible, but his correlation of city life with 'refined domestic life' (and therefore under women's influence) seems naïve.

Writing in 1922, Jespersen concludes with the statement: 'In presentday English there are said to be a few differences in pronunciation between the two sexes'. They are listed in Table 2.2 as he gives them (the first two are attributed to Daniel Jones, who was Professor of Phonetics at London University). It is interesting to note that, while Jespersen here demonstrates differences in women's and men's pronunciation, his examples, if accurate, do not reveal a consistent pattern: the more 'advanced' forms – [sɔft], [gəːl], [waɪt], [tʃɪldrən] and [weɪskʊt] – are not correlated with gender.

Table 2.2: Gender differences in pronunciation in England, 1922 (based on Jespersen 1922: 245)

Men	Women	
[sɔːft]	[sɔft]	soft
[gəːl]	[gɛəl]	girl
[waɪt]	[hwaɪt]	white
[tʃɪldrən]	[tʃʊldrən]	children
['weskət]	['weɪs'kout]	waistcoat

Jespersen concludes that these are isolated instances: 'on the whole we must say that from a phonetic point of view there is scarcely any difference between the speech of men and that of women: the two sexes speak for all intents and purposes the same language' (Jespersen 1922: 245). However, his earlier observations on women's more advanced pronunciation have been borne out by much twentieth-century work in sociolinguistics. The relationship between women's speech and linguistic change will be pursued in Chapter 10.

2.7 Verbosity

Many women, many words; many geese, many turds.
(English proverb)

There is an age-old belief that women talk too much. The cultural myth of women's verbosity is nicely caught in this fifteenth-century carol which describes the many virtues of women, but undermines the message with a refrain telling us that the opposite is true:

Of all creatures women be best
Cuius contrarium verum est. [of which the opposite is true]
(Davies 1963: 222)

Women are described as 'not liberal in language but ever in secree'. The reader is encouraged to confide in women:

> For tell a woman all your counsaile
> And she can kepe it wonderly well.

The writer, tongue in cheek, defends women against the charge of being chatterboxes:

> Trow ye that women list to smater [*chatter*]
> Or against their husbondes for to clater?
> Nay! they had lever [*would rather*] fast, bred and water,
> Then for to dele in suche a matter.

The humour of this poem derives from the reader knowing that the writer intends the opposite meaning throughout. Since the key to understanding this joke is the Latin phrase in the refrain, the joke is clearly a male one, since Latin and Greek were taught only to boys (see section 2.5).

English literature is filled with characters who substantiate the stereotype of the talkative women. Rosalind, in *As You Like It* (III.2.264), says: 'Do you not know I am a woman? When I think, I must speak'. Dion, in Beaumont and Fletcher's *Philaster* (II.4.1–3), advises:

> Come, ladies, shall we talk a round? As men
> Do walk a mile, women should talk an hour
> After supper; 'tis their exercise.

Aurora Leigh, the eponymous heroine of Elizabeth Barrett Browning's poem of 1856, says: 'A woman's function plainly is – to talk'.

In a section on 'the volubility of women', Jespersen quotes examples from literature such as those above to prove his point, and refers to research done on reading speed which found that women tended to read a given passage faster than men and to remember more about the passage after reading it. In the face of this evidence, Jespersen asserts: 'But it was found that this rapidity was no proof of intellectual power, and some of the slowest readers were highly distinguished men'! (Jespersen 1922: 252). To support his prejudice, Jespersen refers to Havelock Ellis's work *Man and Woman* (1894), which 'explains' that 'with the quick reader it is as though every statement were admitted immediately and without inspection to fill the vacant chambers of the mind' (Jespersen 1922: 252), and to Swift's assertion that

> the common fluency of speech in many men, and most women, is owing to the scarcity of matter, and scarcity of words; for whoever is a master of language, and hath a mind full of ideas, will be apt in speaking to hesitate upon the choice of both: whereas common speakers have only one set of ideas, and one set of words to clothe them in; and these are always ready at the mouth.
> (Swift, quoted in Jespersen 1922: 252)

It must be obvious to any reader today that none of this represents a valid argument. Jespersen obviously accepts the cultural stereotype of the voluble chattering woman; he presents us with some tangential data on reading speed; he then argues that women's facility with words does not correspond to any intellectual power (but rather the contrary), and quotes the dogmatic statements of two famous men, as if this constituted supporting evidence. Since he provides no data on the speed and quantity of women's speech, the passage tells us nothing except that scholars of language in the early part of the twentieth century were subject to the prejudices of their times.

The other side of the coin to women's verbosity is the image of the silent woman which is often held up as an ideal – 'Silence is the best ornament of a woman' (English proverb). This ideal is found very early in literary texts, for example, in the Arthurian romances, in stories such as Erec and Enyd. This exists in versions by Chrétien de Troyes (*c.* 1170), in *The Mabinogion* (*c.* 1300), and in Tennyson's *Idylls of the King* (1859). The crucial episode involves Erec (Geraint in *The Mabinogion*/Tennyson) and Enyd riding alone on a journey during which Erec tests his wife's loyalty to him. Erec says:

> and this
> I charge thee, on thy duty as a wife,
> Whatever happens, not to speak to me,
> No, not a word!
> (Tennyson, *Geraint and Enid*)

Silence is made synonymous with obedience.

The tale of Patient Griselda also appears in many different forms, for example, as 'The Clerk's Tale' in Chaucer's *Canterbury Tales*. Again, a wife's loyalty and obedience are tested: this time her children are forcibly taken from her. Even though Griselda believes they may be killed, she does not protest: 'Ne in this tyme word ne spak she noon' ('The Clerk's Tale', 1. 900). Silence is again portrayed as intrinsic to obedience. (It should be noted that Griselda passes the test of obedience with flying colours, and is thus a character twentieth-century readers have difficulties with; Enyd, on the other hand, breaks her husband's command in order to warn him of danger – she saves his life by refusing to remain silent.)

During the Renaissance, eloquence was highly acclaimed, but Tasso, in his *Discorso della virtu feminile e donnesca* (1582), makes it clear that, while eloquence is a virtue in a man, *silence* is the corresponding virtue in a woman. As one scholar comments: 'The implication is that it is inappropriate for a woman to be eloquent or liberal, or for a man to be economical and silent' (MacLean 1980: 62).

The model of the silent woman is still presented to girls in the second half of the twentieth century: research in English schools suggests that quiet behaviour is very much encouraged by teachers, particularly in girls. This will be discussed at greater length in section 11.2. Such conditioning begins very early in a child's life. It is reported that nursery school children in Bristol are taught a song which goes: 'All the Daddies on the bus go read, read, read . . . All the Mummies on the bus go chatter, chatter, chatter' (quoted in *The Guardian*). Primary school children on Merseyside are taught this song too.

Dale Spender comments on the issue of women and silence:

> The talkativeness of women has been gauged in comparison not with men but with
> *silence*. . . . When silence is the desired state for women . . . then any talk in which a
> woman engages can be too much.
> (Spender 1980a: 42)

The idea that silence is 'the desired state for women' is supported by the theory
of 'muted groups' proposed by the anthropologists Shirley and Edwin Ardener
(Ardener 1975, 1978). Briefly, they argue that in any society there are dominant
modes of expression, belonging to dominant groups within that society. If
members of a 'muted group' want to be heard, they are required to express
themselves in the dominant mode (this ties in with Virginia Woolf's comments: section 2.5 above). While muted groups are not necessarily silent, their
mutedness means that they have difficulty making themselves heard by the
dominant group. However, in many cultures, muted groups are indeed silenced
by rules laid down by the dominant group. 'Ritual silence may be imposed on
women: in synagogues, for example, and in Greece after weddings' (Ardener
1978: 23). In Britain, the muting of women is more subtle, but there is still
overt opposition to women as radio or TV announcers, for example, and the
controversy over women's ordination arises in part from the dominant group's
resistance to women speaking in authoritative voices.

In relation to the specific topic of women's supposed verbosity, this section
has demonstrated that pre-Chomskyan linguistic inquiry provides us with no
evidence that women talk more than men. Yet there is no doubt that western
European culture is imbued with the belief that women *do* talk a lot, and there
is evidence that silence is an ideal that has been held up to (and imposed on)
women for many centuries.

2.8 Conclusion

In this chapter we have looked at folklinguistic views of male/female differences in language and those of the early grammarians. We have concentrated
on six areas: vocabulary, swearing and taboo language, grammar, literacy, pronunciation and verbosity. Modern sociolinguistic work on gender differences
in grammar and pronunciation will be the subject of Chapters 4 and 5. Chapter
6, which looks at the general topic of communicative competence, will include
a discussion of contemporary linguistic research on gender differences in swearing, and Chapter 7 will summarise recent research on verbosity.

Notes

1 The first proverb is taken from *The Oxford Dictionary of English Proverbs*,
   edited by Smith and Heseltine (1935); the second is from *Cheshire Proverbs*,

collected and annotated by Joseph C. Bridge (1917); the last two are taken from Jespersen (1922: 253, n. 1).

2 According to Bernstein (a sociologist) restricted code is distinguished from elaborated code in the following ways: it is used in relatively informal situations, and speakers assume a great deal of shared knowledge; this is reflected linguistically in the high proportion of pronouns and tag questions, and in the simple syntax. Linguists are not happy with the codes, and Bernstein's claim that the ability to use them correlates with social class is highly controversial.

3 See Donovan (1980) for a fascinating survey.

4 Examples are: Cheris Kramarae and Paula Treichler (1992) *Amazons, Bluestockings and Crones: A Feminist Dictionary* (originally published as *A Feminist Dictionary* in 1985); Mary Daly (1988) *Webster's First New Intergalactic Wickedary of the English Language*; Jane Mills (1989) *Womanwords: A Vocabulary of Culture and Patriarchal Society*.

CHAPTER 3

The historical background (II) – Anthropologists and dialectologists

3.1 Introduction

There are two major disciplines whose work touches on gender differences in language. These two disciplines – Anthropology and Dialectology – have aims and objectives which are quite distinct from those of sociolinguistics, but there are areas of overlap. Anthropologists have observed language as part of their observation of the whole spectrum of social behaviour in a given community. Dialectologists have analysed the speech of rural communities in order to investigate linguistic change and the decline of rural dialects. Both anthropologists and dialectologists have commented upon gender differences in language; it is these comments which form the basis of this chapter.

3.2 Anthropologists

Differences between the language of male and female speakers have been noted in anthropological literature since the seventeenth century. Missionaries and explorers came across societies whose linguistic behaviour caused them to speak of 'men's language' and 'women's language'. These terms overstate the case: what we find in these languages are phonological, morphological, syntactic and lexical contrasts where the speaker's gender determines which form is chosen. I shall briefly survey some of this work to illustrate the kind of male/female variation in language that anthropologists commented on.

3.2.1 Phonological differences

The Chukchi language, spoken in Eastern Siberia, varies phonologically, depending on the gender of the speaker. Women use /ʃ/ where men use /tʃ/ or /r/. For example, the word for *people* is pronounced /ʃamkɪʃʃɪn/ by women and /ramkɪtʃɪn/ by men.

The men and women of the Gros Ventre tribe in Montana also make consistent differences in their pronunciation (Flannery 1946). The velar plosive /k/ is replaced by an affricate in the men's speech, so where the women say /wakinsihiθa/ (newborn child), the men say /wadʒinsihiθa/. The word for bread is pronounced /kja'tsa/ by the women, and /dʒa'tsa/ by the men. In this community, pronunciation is a defining marker of sexual identity: if anyone uses the wrong form, they are considered to be bisexual by older members of the tribe. Flannery hypothesises that fear of being laughed at for such errors has helped to erode the use of the language by the younger generation, who tend to speak English.

3.2.2 Morphological differences

Edward Sapir (1929, quoted in Yaguello 1978) describes a language spoken by the Yana (in California) where the language used between men differs morphologically from that used in other situations (men to women, women to men, women to women). The words used in this men-to-men variety are longer than those used in the communal language. It seems that in a minority of cases the men add a suffix to the primary form, following a rule which can roughly be stated as follows: *When a word in the communal language ends with a long vowel, a diphthong or a consonant, or if the word is a monosyllable, the men's language adds a suffix /-na/, e.g. /ba/ (stag) → /bana/; /au/ (fire) → /auna/*. In the majority of cases the form in the communal language appears to be a logical *abbreviation* of the male form, following a rule which can roughly be stated as follows: *When a word in the men's language ends in a short vowel – /a, i, u/ – this vowel is lost and the preceding consonant becomes voiceless; thus /b, d, g, dʒ/ + short vowel → /pʼ, tʼ, kʼ, tʃʼ/, e.g. /gagi/ (crow) → /gakʼ/; /pʼadza/ (snow) → /pʼatʃʼ/*.

This second rule can be accounted for by the principle of morphophonemic economy (there is a tendency in all languages for words to get simplified – cf. *omnibus → bus, refrigerator → fridge*, etc.). In other words, the men's language seems to preserve historically older forms. Sapir suggests that the reduced female forms symbolise women's lower status: the men's fuller forms are associated with ceremony and formality. This is an interesting case of male speech being associated with conservatism and linguistic purity, characteristics now conventionally associated with women's language (this will be discussed at greater length in Chapters 4 and 10).

Among the Koasati, a Muskogean Indian tribe in Louisiana, certain forms of the verb vary according to the speaker's gender (Haas 1944). For example, where the women's form ends in a nasalised vowel, the men's form ends in -*s*.

The following are examples:

Women	Men	
lakawtakkǫ́	*lakawtakkós*	I am not lifting it
lakawwa	*lakawwá.s*	he will lift it
ká.	*ká.s*	he is saying

Where the women's form has the falling pitch-stress on its final syllable and ends in a short vowel followed by /l/, the men's form involves high pitch-stress and replaces /l/ with /s/.

Women	Men	
lakawwîl	*lakawwîs*	I am lifting it
molhîl	*molhís*	we are peeling it
lakawhôl	*lakawhós*	lift it! (to 2nd person plural)

In this community, it is the women's language which is conservative and which represents an earlier stage in the language. In 1944 Haas found that only the older women were maintaining the distinction; the younger women used the men's forms. The women's forms are presumably obsolete now.

3.2.3 Lexical differences

Gender differences in vocabulary were frequently reported by early anthropologists. I shall look at two examples here; two other examples are given in the next section (section 3.3).

In most languages, the pronoun system marks gender distinctions in the third person (e.g. *he/she*), but the distinction is less commonly made in the first and second persons where speaker's gender is involved. Japanese is a language

Table 3.1: Japanese personal pronouns (Ide 1991: 73)

	Men's speech	Women's speech
First person		
formal	watakusi	watakusi
	watasi	atakusi*
plain	boku	watasi
		atasi*
deprecatory	ore	φ
Second person		
formal	anata	anata
plain	kimi	anata
	anta*	anta*
deprecatory	omae	
	kisama	φ

* marks variants of a social dialect

30

which marks gender in all three persons of the pronoun (Bodine 1975; Ide 1991). There is a formal first person form *watakusi* which can be used by either male or female speakers and a formal second person pronoun, *anata*, which can be used to male or female addressees. However, when we look at the full repertoire of personal pronouns available in Japanese, we find that there are significant differences between those used by men and those used by women (see Table 3.1). This table shows us, first, that certain forms are exclusive to men: *boku* as a first person pronoun, and *kimi* as a second person pronoun. The deprecatory pronouns *ore* (first person), *omae* and *kisama* (second person) are also exclusive to men; women have no deprecatory pronouns available to them. Secondly, Table 3.1 reveals differences in levels of formality: *watasi*, for example, is formal for men, but plain for women. This has the effect of making women's speech sound more polite than men's (see section 6.6 on gender differences in politeness).

In his work on the Trobriand islanders, Malinowski (1929, quoted in Yaguello 1978) established that their kinship terminology is organised on the basis of two criteria:

1. Same/different gender as the speaker
2. Older/younger than the speaker

This means that the word for *sister*, for example, will vary according to whether the speaker is male or female, and whether the speaker is older or younger than the sibling. Figure 3.1 shows how the system works for the relationships of brother, sister, brother-in-law and sister-in-law. In the case of the relationship we call *sister*, the Trobrianders have three terms (*luguta, tuwagu, bwadagu*) for our one. Conversely, they make no distinction between a man's sister and a woman's brother (both are *luguta*), nor between a man's brother *and* a woman's sister if the age difference is the same in both cases (*tuwagu* or *bwadagu*).

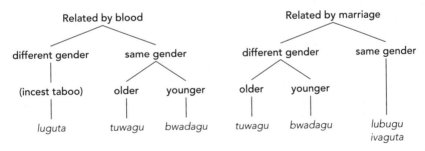

Figure 3.1 Trobriand islanders' terms for sister, brother, sister-in-law, brother-in-law (based on Yaguello 1978: 27)

We can see why earlier scholars were misled into talking of men's and women's languages. In particular, where English and other European languages distinguish kin on the basis of **gender of the spoken about**, the Trobriand language, like Chiquito, Yana, and many others, distinguishes kinship terms on the basis of **gender of the speaker**. This means that Trobriand islanders give different names to relationships we see as 'the same', but only one name to relationships we perceive as 'different'.

3.3 Anthropological explanations

It is clear that none of these examples constitutes a case of separate languages for women and men. Observers mistakenly described the phenomena they came across in terms of separate male/female languages as a result of both linguistic naïvety and a tendency to exaggerate. Their hypotheses about the origins of gender differences in language were inevitably skewed by their belief in polarised gender varieties. The two main explanatory factors put forward by anthropologists were **taboo** and **contact with speakers of other languages**.

Taboo operates in all societies, proscribing certain forms of behaviour, including linguistic behaviour. In British society today, topics of conversation such as excretion or sexual activity are taboo in many contexts. In so-called 'primitive' societies, what is or is not permitted is stringently controlled socially. Taboos are part of the structure which maintains social order.

A good example of taboo and its effects on language is reported by Caroline Humphrey in an article on women and taboo (Humphrey 1978). She investigated what constituted incorrect or improper behaviour for women in Mongolia. Most linguistic taboos in Mongolia are concerned with *names*. Mongols avoid using the names of dead people, predatory animals and certain mountains and rivers thought to be inhabited by spirits. More particularly, women are absolutely forbidden to use the names of their husband's older brothers, father, father's brothers or grandfather. This taboo extends beyond the names of the husband's male relatives: women are not allowed to use *any word or syllable* which is the same as, or sounds like, any of the forbidden names. For example, where the name *Shar* is taboo, the woman must not use either the name or the word *shar* (= yellow), but has to substitute *angir*, a word which refers to a yellow-coloured duck. Or if the tabooed name is *Xarzuu* (derived from *xarax* = to look at), the woman must also avoid the word *xar* (= black) and has to use instead *bargaan*, which means 'darkish or obscure'. It is not surprising that earlier reports talked of 'women's language' among the Mongols. However, such taboos affect only vocabulary; other aspects of language are unaffected. Moreover, each woman affected by such a taboo will have different linguistic problems, depending on the names of her male relatives-by-marriage. So while it can result in distinct female vocabularies, taboo as a social force is hardly sufficient explanation of the other gender differences which occur in language.

Contact with speakers of other languages occurs when there is an invasion, or when men marry women from outside their village or tribe (as is the custom in some societies). The most well-known case of gender differences in language said to result from the marrying of people speaking different languages is that of the Carib Indians. In his account of the people of Lesser Antilles, written in 1665, Rochefort claimed that the men and women spoke different languages:

> The savage natives of Dominica say that the reason for this is that when the Caribs came to occupy the islands, these were inhabited by an Arawak tribe which they exterminated completely, with the exception of the women, whom they married in order to populate the country. Now, these women kept their own language and taught it to their daughters. . . . It is asserted that there is some similarity between the speech of the continental Arawaks and that of the Carib women.
> (as quoted in Jespersen 1922: 237)

It is clear from other evidence that this is another case of separate lexical items for women and men in certain areas; it is not a case of two separate languages. Moreover, the invasion theory is not totally convincing, especially as the linguistic variation found among Carib Indians is similar to that found in other American Indian groups (Trudgill 1974b: 86). Contact with speakers of other languages will not do as an explanation for gender differences in language in general, since such differences occur in all known languages.

3.4 Some problems with anthropological work on gender differences

The major defect of anthropological work is that anthropologists failed to see that gender differences in language were not exclusively a feature of 'primitive' people and of distant exotic cultures. It is reasonable to ask the question: Why did they ignore gender differences in the European languages they were familiar with? The answer seems to be that they defined the problem in terms of **gender-exclusive** differences. That is, they commented on differences between women's and men's usage where certain linguistic forms were reserved exclusively for the use of one gender or the other. All the examples quoted so far in this chapter are of this kind. The variation in male/female language found in European languages, however, involves **gender-preferential** differences, that is, while women's and men's language differs, there are no forms associated exclusively with one gender; rather there is a tendency for women or men to prefer a certain form. For example, as we shall see in the following chapters, women in Britain tend to use forms closer to Standard English, while men tend to use a higher proportion of non-standard forms. The difference between gender-exclusive and gender-preferential usage seems to be a reflection of the difference between pre-literate, non-industrialised societies and literate, highly industrialised societies; the former tend to have clearly segregated gender roles, unlike modern European societies where gender roles are much less rigidly structured.

Despite their failure to generalise their discoveries to more familiar societies, anthropologists at least drew attention to the way in which human societies use gender as a salient social category, and to the linguistic differences which arise directly from this social structure and which re-create and perpetuate this structure. More recently, anthropology has had an important influence on the developing discipline of sociolinguistics. In general terms, the anthropologists' insistence on the significance of cultural context has underpinned the sociolinguist's conviction that the study of the ideal speaker/hearer in a homogeneous speech community is too narrow a field. More particularly, sociolinguistic methodology has borrowed directly from anthropological field techniques; the study of groups as working wholes and the concept of the social network as a tool of analysis have led to exciting new developments in sociolinguistic research. Some examples of such research will be described in detail in Chapters 5 and 6.

3.5 Dialectologists

Dialectologists, unlike anthropologists, have always been sensitive to gender differences in their own (i.e. European) languages. Ironically, this has resulted in our having virtually no data on such differences, for reasons which will become apparent during the following discussion. I shall discuss the work of dialectologists as it relates to gender differences under three headings: women as informants, the questionnaire, and the fieldworker.

3.5.1 Women as informants

The choice of informants is of crucial importance in any linguistic survey. Since the Holy Grail of traditional dialectology was 'pure' dialect, which had to be recorded before it died out, dialectologists chose as informants those who, in their view, spoke 'pure' dialect. The circularity of this procedure was uncritically accepted. Their methodology contrasts markedly with that of modern quantitative sociolinguistics, which has adopted the methods of the social sciences, and takes a representative sample of informants chosen randomly from the electoral roll, or some equivalent list. Because dialectologists' choice of informants was so unrepresentative, we have little idea what sort of linguistic variation existed in the rural communities studied. Certain members of the community were included; others were excluded. We have no comparative data to confirm or refute the dialectologists' claim that some members of the speech community spoke a more 'pure' form of the dialect than others.

Who did dialectologists choose as informants? The answer to this question reveals that their choice depended largely on folklinguistic beliefs. Dialectologists favoured older members of the community as informants (for obvious, if not scientific, reasons), but they disagreed about the merits of female as opposed to male informants. One view was that women were the best informants because of their innate conservatism. This view was expressed by a great variety of dialectologists, from the end of the nineteenth century up to the 1940s, in areas as different as Slovenia, Switzerland, Flanders and Romania. The general view is that stated by Wartburg in his review of Griera's Linguistic Atlas of Catalonia (which is criticised for its lack of women informants):

> Everyone knows that as far as language is concerned women are more conservative than men; they conserve the speech of our forebears more faithfully.[1]
> (Wartburg 1925: 113 as quoted in Pop 1950: 373)

This view is supported by the following 'reasons':

1. Women hardly ever leave their village, unlike men.
2. Women stay at home and talk ('chat') to each other, and don't mix with strangers.
3. Women don't do military service.

The opposite view – that women are *not* conservative – was held by many other dialectologists, including the hugely influential Gilliéron, director of the linguistic survey of France (the first major survey to use a trained fieldworker). These dialectologists preferred *men* as informants, since they considered men's speech to be closer to the 'pure' dialect. The general view is clearly stated by Harold Orton in his *Introduction to the Survey of English Dialects*:

> In this country men speak vernacular more frequently, more consistently, and more genuinely than women.
> (Orton 1962: 15)

The innovative nature of women's speech is stressed:

> Women's speech is not conservative. Women, who are usually said to be more conservative than men, accept new words quite readily.[2]
> (from Pop's account of Gilliéron 1880)

Unlike those who believe in women's conservatism, these dialectologists offer us no explanations. Gauchat, for example, tells us that women are more innovative and then describes their lives as follows:

> They spend much more time in the home, with other people, cooking and washing, and talking more than men, who are busy with their agricultural work; you see the men at their work, silent and often on their own for the whole day.[3]

We are presumably meant to infer from the different lifestyles of the two sexes a reason for their differing linguistic usage. But this description does not explain why women should be more innovative than men. In fact, the female way of life described here is virtually identical to that described by dialectologists in the 'women are conservative' camp. As far as we can see any difference, it is in the way the *men's* lives are described: the dialectologists in the first group stress the men's interaction with strangers, their involvement in travel and military service; while those in the second group either don't describe the men's lives, or portray them as isolated.

The explanation which seems to underlie the second group of studies is women's supposed sensitivity to linguistic norms. It is assumed that standard norms will have more influence on women's speech than on men's; women, it is argued, have little status in society, and so seek to acquire status through their use of language. Stanley Ellis, chief fieldworker for the Survey of English Dialects, comments:

> Women were always seen as a refining and 'improving' influence. It was suggested that this often came about because young country girls used to have a spell as indoor servants in better class homes and came under the influence of better speech.
> (Ellis, personal communication)

The concepts of both conservatism and status-consciousness on the part of women are introduced into dialect studies in a somewhat *ad hoc* manner, depending on how women's speech is perceived. Neither seems a very satisfactory explanation of gender differences in language. (For a fuller critique of conservatism and status-consciousness as explanatory factors, see Cameron and Coates 1989.)

The evidence suggests, then, that attitudes to informants were preconceived and highly subjective. Not surprisingly, we find contradictions: Gilliéron, whose survey covered the whole of France, argued that women were not conservative linguistically, while Meunier, in his much smaller study of the Nivernais region of France, favoured women as informants because of their conservatism. Jaberg and Jud, in their major dialect survey of Italy and southern Switzerland, also assume the linguistic conservatism of women, but one of their fieldworkers (Rohlfs) is quoted as saying 'the pronunciation of vowels by women doesn't differ only from that of men – who possess vowels which are purer and clearer – but from area to area' (Jaberg 1936: 21, n. 3 as quoted in Pop 1950: 579).[4] Rohlfs definitely seems to be claiming that men's pronunciation of vowels was 'purer' than women's. Pop, in his comprehensive account of dialect study (Pop 1950), can hardly fail to notice such discrepancies. He is basically an adherent of the 'women are conservative' camp, but he advocates a detailed comparative study of the pronunciation of men and women, since, he says, 'it certainly seems, although people often assert the contrary, that women's language displays more innovations than men's in certain cases' (Pop 1950: 195).[5]

Only one dialectologist, out of all those I have surveyed, states specifically that he is *not* aware of gender differences in the speech community he is studying. This is Angus McIntosh, director of the Survey of Scottish Dialects. He writes: 'As to sex, there is no evidence which shows conclusively whether men or women make better informants in Scotland' (McIntosh 1952: 90).

So who did the dialectologists choose as informants? On the basis of their published views, we would expect the first group to select women (since they describe women as linguistically conservative) and the second to select men (since they describe men as linguistically conservative). In fact, with the exception of the German–Swiss survey and McIntosh's Scottish survey (in both of which the fieldworkers interviewed one man and one woman in each locality), *all* the dialect surveys for which I have figures favoured men. Table 3.2 gives details.

Table 3.2: Table to show proportion of women informants in dialect surveys
(source: Pop 1950)

Dialect survey	Date of publication	Male informants	Female informants	Total informants	% women
France (Gilliéron)	1902–10	640	60*	700*	8.57
Catalonia (Griera)	1923–39	107	1	108	0.93
S. Austria (Tesniere)	1925	70	18	88	20.45
Italy/Switz. (Jaberg and Jud)	1928–40	380	40*	420*	9.52
Sardinia (Pellis)	1933–35	55	5	60	8.33
Corsica (Bottiglioni)	1933–42	61	6	67	8.96
Italy (Bartoli)	1933	316	48	364	13.19
Belg. Congo (De Boeck)	1942	?	0	?	0.00
North China (Giet)	1946	495	29	524	5.53
England (Orton)	1962–78	867	122	989	12.34

* = approximate figure

As Table 3.2 shows, women were very poorly represented in dialect surveys. Moreover, a detailed examination of dialect survey findings shows that the few female informants are not spread evenly. The Survey of English Dialects, for example, investigated the thirty-nine counties of England, but this does not mean that 12 per cent of informants in each county were women, as we would expect (see Table 3.2); in fact, in seven counties, *no* women were interviewed (Worcestershire, Gloucestershire, Northamptonshire, Huntingdonshire, Cambridgeshire, Wiltshire and Devon).

When we look for explanations for this uneven pattern of sampling, we find that dialectologists express reservations about women as informants. Even dialectologists who see women as better informants on *linguistic* grounds (because of their supposed conservatism) reject them for non-linguistic reasons. For example, women are said to be too busy or too timid, or embarrassed at being asked to speak patois in front of a researcher. A typical 'explanation' for failing to interview more women is that of Sever Pop, who was director of the dialect survey of Romania:

> The investigator comes up against problems in persuading women to give up two or three days to the project, since household chores prevent them from doing so, and they feel embarrassed at sitting down at the table with a 'city gentleman'.[6]
> (Pop 1950: 725)

Pop at least adduces reasons which seem relevant to the fieldworker's task. Other dialectologists, however, explain their omission of women on blatantly sexist grounds. The following is taken from an article by Griera, a Catholic priest who was responsible for the Linguistic Atlas of Catalonia:

> The reasons for my doing so [*excluding women*] are: the impossibility of their maintaining attention during a long questionnaire lasting several days; the fact that their knowledge of objects is, in general, more limited than men's, and, above all, their lack of firm concepts which is reflected in imprecise naming of objects.
> (Griera 1928)[7]

Even though dialectologists are aware that they tend to favour men as informants, it seems probable, to judge from the following comment of an expert fieldworker, that they had no idea *how few* women were actually involved as informants: 'The informants I used during my spell as fieldworker for the Survey of English Dialects in the 1950s were far more men than women. I would estimate about one informant in four or five were [*sic*] female' (Ellis, personal communication). As we can see from Table 3.2, fewer than one informant in eight was female.

There are two aspects of dialect study which may help us to explain the predominance of men as informants. These are the questionnaire, which was traditionally used to structure the interview, to guarantee comparability, and to ensure that the desired responses were obtained from every informant; and the fieldworker, usually a trained scholar who was sent out into a given area by the director of the survey, to conduct interviews with informants.

3.5.2 The questionnaire

The questionnaire, 'the central instrument used in the systematic collection of dialect' (Francis 1983: 52), may seem an innocent tool of research, but besides determining in advance what linguistic items are to be scrutinised, it predetermines in other ways what is to be included and what not.

Most questionnaires, both those in postal surveys and those employing fieldworkers, were divided into sections, and some of these sections would be aimed specifically at women, and some at men. The German–Swiss Linguistic Atlas based its choice of informants on this division: 'The responses for the dialect of each locality were given by a man and a woman of the district: the man replied to the questions concerning men's work; the women to those concerning feminine occupations'[8] (Pop 1950: 770). The German–Swiss survey was unusual in interviewing as many women as men, but we should note the rigid segregation of questions into those for women and those for men. This presumably reflects the dialectologist's concern with **lexicon**. Traditional dialectology aimed to establish 'what a three-legged milking stool is called in several hundred different places' (McIntosh 1952: 70). Many dialectologists assumed that men's and women's vocabularies differed as a reflection of their social roles. As McIntosh comments:

> Experience has shown that a conventional portmanteau questionnaire cannot be filled in completely with the help of only one person; the housewife lets one down on agricultural terms, the farmer on kitchen terms, and often some local expert has to be hunted out specially to deal with such items as flowers or birds.
>
> (McIntosh 1952: 89)

I shall look at two examples of dialect study to show how the structure of the questionnaire affected the choice of informant.

1. Navarro, who was responsible for the Linguistic Atlas of Puerto Rico, is reported as justifying his virtual exclusion of women informants on the grounds that they wouldn't know the replies to his questions:

   > 'Since the questionnaire was designed to find out in particular about agricultural terminology, women could not give good replies. For this reason there are only two women among the informants.'[9]
   >
   > (Pop 1950: 452)

2. Wirth, director of the Linguistic Atlas of Sorabe (a Western Slav dialect), was particularly interested in domestic vocabulary. As Pop says:

   > 'Since his questionnaire was principally concerned with the terminology of the dwelling place and housework, he was obliged to appeal to women to collaborate.'[10]
   >
   > (Pop 1950: 981)

Table 3.3 (see p. 40) gives details of the thirty-one sections included in the questionnaire for the *Atlas linguistique et ethnographique du Lyonnais* (Gardette 1968). This is one of the more recent regional atlases produced by French dialectologists, yet the built-in assumption of male-as-norm is still there: of the thirty-one sections, two (nos 20 and 21) are specifically marked as 'Women's Life'. Women's life has to be marked because it is taken for granted that the majority of sections will relate to men.

We can see from the preceding discussion that one of the reasons women were not used as informants was that (male) dialectologists defined which areas of life and therefore which lexical sets were worthy of study from an essentially androcentric viewpoint.

> It is especially common for the interviewer to shift to a woman – often the wife of a principal male informant – for those parts of the questionnaire which deal with the house, the kitchen, the children, and other areas commonly considered to be women's province.
>
> (Francis 1983: 86)

Since men's work was regarded as of prime interest, women's work, and therefore women's vocabulary, was normally regarded as peripheral. Since dialectologists were also interested in phonology and grammar, this concentration on male language does not seem defensible. There are indications, however, that women may have been involved more than at first appears. The description of the principal informant at point number 2 for the Dialect Atlas of

Table 3.3: Questionnaire for *Atlas linguistique et ethnographique du Lyonnais* (Francis 1983: 60)

Section		Number of questions
1	Meadow, hay, rake, fork	57
2	Grain, sowing, harvest	58
3	Threshing, the flail	57
4	Yoke, goad	39
5	Plows and working the land	55
6	Carts and wagons	66
7	The vineyard	89
8	The wood	54
9	The garden, potatoes, root vegetables	36
10	Cattle, horses, donkeys	63
11	Sheet, goats, swine	62
12	The barnyard	50
13	The barnyard (concluded), bees, dog, cat	43
14	Milk, butter, cheese	64
15	Bread	43
16	Trees (other than fruit-trees)	59
17	Fruit-trees	59
18	Birds, flies, parasites	58
19	Harmful animals, snakes, water creatures, insects	48
20	Women's life: 1. The bed, housekeeping, meals	59
21	Women's life: 2. Washing, sewing	52
22	The house: 1. Generalities, doors and windows, kitchen	61
23	The house: 2. Lamps, fireplace, bedroom, outbuildings	56
24	Weather: winds, rain, snow, sun	70
25	The stars, landscape	45
26	The calendar	44
27	The day, kinship	48
28	From cradle to grave	107
29	The body	85
30	Clothing; manure; occupations	50
31	Hemp	31
	Total lexical items	1,875
	Morphological items	68

SubCarpathian Poland (published in 1934) tells us that he was called Jean Klamerus, that he was 75 years old, that he was rather deaf and slow. He was interviewed in the presence of his daughter-in-law, who is described as an energetic, intelligent woman, a good informant from a grammatical point of view, and very good from a phonetic and lexicological point of view. Pop comments that it was the daughter-in-law who replied to most of the questions (Pop 1950).[11] How often a female relative gave the responses which are credited to a man, we cannot tell.

THE HISTORICAL BACKGROUND (II)

3.5.3 The fieldworker

Another reason why men were chosen as informants rather than women was probably that the vast majority of fieldworkers were themselves men. This is so much the normal pattern that McIntosh defines the fieldworker as 'a man [*sic*] specially trained to listen to peculiarities of speech' (McIntosh 1952: 66). The first women fieldworkers were those involved in the Linguistic Atlas of New England (two women out of ten fieldworkers) and the Survey of English Dialects (two women out of eleven fieldworkers).

If we imagine Edmont Edmont, fieldworker for the French Linguistic Atlas, arriving on his bicycle at one of the 639 localities he surveyed between 1896 and 1900, it seems plausible to argue that he was far more likely to get into conversation with, and subsequently to interview, other men. Edmont did in fact interview only about sixty women out of his 700 informants. Kurath, director of the New England survey, writes the following in his section on choosing informants:

> After some experience in the field, he [*the fieldworker*] may discover that informal contacts in the general store, barber shop or local tavern can provide him with useful leads. (Kurath 1972: 13)

(Note the use of *he/him* in this extract.) This is the advice of an eminent dialectologist to others in the field after a century of dialect study: presumably it reflects traditional practice. If the norm was male fieldworkers making contact with potential informants in the male setting of the barber shop or the tavern, then it is hardly surprising that women were rarely interviewed.

If we look at what happened when the fieldworker was *female*, we can test the hypothesis that the gender of the fieldworker influenced the selection of informants. An examination of those sections of the Survey of English Dialects where a woman was the fieldworker shows a significant increase in the number of women interviewed. As Table 3.2 shows, for the survey as a whole, 12 per cent of informants were women. For Leicestershire and Rutland, the two counties wholly investigated by a woman fieldworker, the figures are 33 per cent and 40 per cent respectively.

The fieldworker's gender should be taken into account for other reasons too. Only recently have linguists become fully aware of the effect an interviewer can have on an informant's language. Labov (1969) has demonstrated convincingly that by replacing a white middle-class interviewer with a younger, black interviewer (and also by reducing the formality of the situation by sitting on the floor, eating crisps, etc.), the black child who was previously thought to have virtually no language can be shown to be a fluent speaker. It seems highly probable that women feel constrained in the presence of a male interviewer (see Pop's comment quoted above, p. 37), and will therefore produce more formal language. This may help to explain the experience of Orton and others that women's speech was closer to standard norms. (However, modern sociolinguistic surveys, carried out by both women and men, are still finding that in Britain women's speech tends to be closer to standard, as we shall see in Chapter 4.)

In more recent dialect surveys, despite the growth of sociolinguistic research and methodology, the presence of women as fieldworkers is still a matter for comment. The following is an extract from Gardette's discussion of methodology in his *Atlas linguistique et ethnographique du Lyonnais*:

> The four female fieldworkers of our team had in general as good results as those of Monsieur Girodet and myself. Those who interviewed in areas where they were known, among informants who claimed common friends, often received a particularly sympathetic welcome.
> (Gardette 1968: 44)

This shows an understanding that the relationship between fieldworker and informant is one which can vary. But it is also patronising, since it is surely gratuitous to comment on the women's results being as good as those of the two male fieldworkers. In a discussion of women as fieldworkers, Francis (1983) argues that women may not be ideal, since male informants may not want to respond frankly in their presence. I shall quote this passage in full as it is very revealing of attitudes in dialectology:

> It has been pointed out that women [*as fieldworkers*] do have one disadvantage: the kind of old-fashioned rustic who constituted the usual informant in traditional surveys is likely to be squeamish about discussing some topics and using some lexical items considered to be improper in the presence of a woman. This is true, but such items constitute a very small part of most questionnaires. On the other side it may be said that a woman fieldworker may have much better success than a man in eliciting some of the special vocabulary of women from female informants.
> (Francis 1983: 84)

Note how the writer doesn't feel any need to make explicit the fact that the 'old-fashioned rustic who constituted the usual informant' is obviously male. Just as women are often included as informants only for the sake of special 'women's vocabulary', so women fieldworkers become accepted since they may be better at eliciting this 'women's' language. Female informants and female fieldworkers are viewed as essentially tangential to the central concerns of traditional dialectology.

3.6 Conclusion

It is now seen as a major weakness of traditional dialectology that it selected informants on such an unscientific basis. Because of assumptions made by fieldworkers and their directors about male/female differences in language, women have been largely ignored in dialect studies. Where they have been included, it has been to supplement the fieldworker's information, rather than as full members of the speech community. Dialectology, in other words, has marginalised women speakers. Traditional dialectologists defined the true vernacular in terms of male informants, and organised their questionnaires around what was seen as the man's world.

A desire to improve on the methodology of dialect surveys, combined with a growing interest in *urban* dialects, gave impetus to the growth of sociolinguistics. Sociolinguists, like dialectologists, are interested in variation in language and in the phonology, grammar and lexicon of non-standard varieties. But where dialectologists focused on the *spatial* dimension, studying regional variation, sociolinguists have shifted attention to the *social* dimension and study variation due to factors such as age, gender, social class, education, ethnic group. Dialectologists tended to ignore the speech of women, for all sorts of conscious and unconscious reasons: some dialectologists claimed that women's speech was more standard than men's and therefore less interesting for their research; others, as we have seen, saw women as more conservative linguistically. We have no hard evidence that women's speech was more or less standard, more or less vernacular than men's. If dialectologists had sampled populations in the way quantitative sociolinguists do, by interviewing a representative cross-sample, then we might have had some very interesting data on linguistic gender differences. As it is, we have, as the end-product of most dialect surveys, a record of the language of non-mobile, older, rural *men*, and we don't know whether women's language differed significantly from theirs or not.

It is only with the advent of quantitative sociolinguistic studies that we have reliable data on gender differences in language. Quantitative sociolinguistic studies which explore gender differences in language will be described in the two following chapters (Chapters 4 and 5).

Notes

1 'Tout le monde sait qu'en matière de langage les femmes sont plus conservatrices que les hommes, qu'elles conservent plus fidèlement le parler des aieux' (Wartburg 1925: 113, as quoted in Pop 1950: 373).

2 'Le parler des femmes n'est pas conservateur. Les femmes, que d'ordinaire on affirme être plus conservatrices que les hommes, acceptent assez facilement les mots nouveaux' (Pop's account of Gilliéron, *Patois de la commune de Vionnaz (Bas Valais)* (1880), Pop 1950: 180).

3 '[les femmes] passent beaucoup plus de temps à la maison, en société, à cuisiner, à laver et qui parlent plus que les hommes, pris par les travaux de la campagne, au milieu desquels on les voit taciturnes, et souvent isolés toute la journée' (Pop's account of Gauchat, *L'Unité phonétique dans le patois d'une commune* (1905), Pop 1950: 194).

4 'La prononciation des voyelles chez la population féminine ne diffère pas seulement de celle des hommes – qui possèdent des voyelles plus pures et plus claires – mais de quartier à quartier et quelquefois même d'individu à individu' (K. Jaberg, *Aspects géographiques du langage*, 1936, as quoted in Pop 1950: 579).

5 'il semble bien, quoique l'on affirme souvent le contraire, que le langage des femmes présente dans certains cas plus d'innovations que celui des hommes' (Pop 1950: 195).

6 'L'enquêteur rencontre des difficultés à persuader les femmes de sacrifier deux ou trois jours pour l'enquête, car les soins du ménage les en empêchent, et elles se trouvent gênées de s'attabler avec "un monsieur de la viells"' (Pop 1950: 725).

7 'Les raons que m'hi obligaren son: l'impossibilitat de guardar atencio durant un llarg interrogatori d'alguns dies; el tenir els coneixements de les coses, generalment, mes limitats que els homes i, sobretot, la falta de fixesa s'idees que es tradeix en una denominacio imprecisa de les coses' (A. Griera, *Entom de l'Atlas linguistique de l'Italie et de la Suisse Meridionale*, 1928, as quoted in Pop 1950: 373). I am grateful to Max Wheeler for translating this extract.

8 'Les réponses pour le parler de chaque localité ont été données par *un homme et par une femme du pays*: le premier répondait aux demandes concernant les travaux faits par les hommes; la seconde à celles touchant les occupations féminines' (Pop 1950: 770).

9 'Le questionnaire ayant été rédigé en vue de connaître surtout la terminologie agricole, les femmes ne pouvaient pas donner de bonnes réponses. Pour cette raison, il n'y a que deux femmes parmi les informateurs' (Pop's account of Navarro's fieldwork for the *Linguistic Atlas of Puerto Rico*, 1948, in Pop 1950: 432).

10 'Son questionnaire regardant en premier lieu la terminologie de l'habitation et du ménage l'obligeait d'ailleurs à faire appel à la collaboration des femmes' (Pop 1950: 981).

11 'c'est plutôt elle [i.e. the daughter-in-law] qui a donné les réponses' (Pop 1950: 977).

PART TWO

The sociolinguistic evidence

CHAPTER 4

Quantitative studies

4.1 Introduction

In this chapter I shall look at gender differences in language revealed by quantitative sociolinguistic studies. The chapter begins with a brief description of classic sociolinguistic work, with its analysis of linguistic variation in relation to social class of speaker and speech style (formal or informal). The central section will examine in some detail five examples of sociolinguistic work which reveal significant gender differences. The chapter ends with a discussion of the reasons underlying this kind of sociolinguistic variation.

4.2 The standard paradigm

Classic sociolinguistic research, such as William Labov's in New York and Peter Trudgill's in Norwich, aimed to examine the correlation between linguistic variation and other variables, in particular social class. These quantitative studies revealed clear social stratification, and gave rise to the related concepts of **prestige** and **stigma**. **Prestige** is said to be attached to those linguistic forms normally used by the social group with the highest social status. The process of standardisation almost always leads to the development of notions of correctness; members of a given speech community will come to acknowledge that one particular variety – the standard dialect – is more 'correct' than other varieties. Correct usage will be seen as being enshrined in this variety, which will accordingly have high prestige. The use of the standard variety in the major institutions of society – the law, education, broadcasting – perpetuates this prestige. Conversely, **stigma** is attached to non-standard forms. This stigma may be overt, as in the case of forms which are the subject of heated condemnation on newspaper correspondence pages, or which are frowned on in school (e.g. 'dropping' initial /h/, *ain't*, *I* instead of *me* as in *for you and I*);[1] or it may be beneath the level of public consciousness, as in the case of many of the forms investigated by sociolinguists. As interest in the use and persistence of non-standard forms has grown, non-standard varieties have come to be known as the **vernacular**.[2]

Another important concept employed in quantitative sociolinguistic studies is that of the **linguistic variable**. A variable, to put it simply, is something which varies in a socially significant way. A linguistic variable, then, is a linguistic unit with various realisations: these are called **variants**. An example of a linguistic variable in contemporary British English is (t) (note that round brackets are used to indicate that we are talking about a variable, not a sound – [t] – or a letter – <t>). When (t) occurs intervocalically (between vowels) in words like *butter* or phrases like *bit of*, it has two variants, the voiceless alveolar plosive [t] and the glottal stop [ʔ]. In other words, depending on circumstances, *bit of* may be realised as [bɪtəv] or [bɪʔəv]. Linguistic variables can be phonological (like (t) in the example) or grammatical or lexical. Not all linguistic units are variables, of course.

Sociolinguists are interested in linguistic variables because they don't vary randomly – they vary systematically in relation to other variables, such as social class, age and gender. In other words, linguistic variables are involved in **co-variation** with other variables. Londoners who say [bæʔə] for *butter* will still be referring to a substance made from cream which we spread on bread, but they will be revealing something of their social/regional origins in choosing that particular variant. Speakers' use of linguistic variables is one of the ways in which they locate themselves in social space. Linguistic variables, in other words, are linguistically equivalent but socially different ways of saying something.

4.2.1 Social stratification

The classic pattern of social stratification revealed by quantitative studies is shown in diagrammatic form in Figure 4.1. The vertical axis represents group score (measured as the average of the scores of all the individuals in that group and converted to a percentage figure); a score of 100 per cent represents consistent use of the prestige form. The horizontal axis represents the degree of formality in the speech situation. Notice the following three points:

1. Each social class group uses a higher proportion of prestige forms (has a higher score) in formal speech, and a lower proportion of prestige forms (a lower score) in informal speech: this produces the sloping lines.

2. In any given speech style (i.e. at any point on the horizontal axis from least formal to most formal) social class stratification is maintained; each group maintains its position relative to other groups: this produces the parallel, non-overlapping lines in the diagram.

3. Use of the imaginary linguistic variable plotted here varies from 100 to 0 per cent: the prestige variant is used consistently by the upper middle class in the most formal contexts, but it is not used at all by the lower working class in the least formal contexts (such consistent use of non-standard forms in non-formal contexts is what many sociolinguists are now trying to observe, in order to arrive at accurate descriptions of the vernacular).[3]

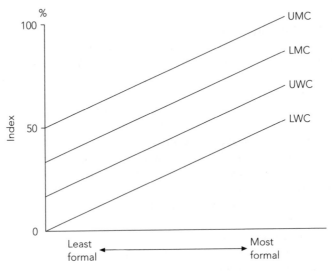

Figure 4.1 A diagrammatic representation of social stratification

As you might expect, representations of social stratification as it is actually found in modern urban communities are not as tidy as Figure 4.1. Figure 4.2 is adapted from Peter Trudgill's Norwich survey (Trudgill 1974a), and shows the relative scores for the variable (ng), as found at the ends of words like *hopping*,

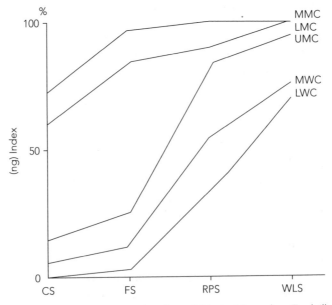

Figure 4.2 Social stratification in Norwich – the variable (ng) (based on Trudgill 1974a: 92)

skipping. Trudgill's informants are divided into five social class groups: the middle middle and the lower middle class, the upper, middle and lower working class. Four different speech styles are represented: Casual Speech (CS), Formal Speech (FS), Reading Passage Style (RPS) and Words List Style (WLS). These names are roughly self-explanatory: informants were interviewed by the investigator (who was not known to them) – this produced Formal Speech. Informants were asked to read a passage aloud and to read a list of words. Data obtained from these tasks were labelled Reading Passage Style and Word List Style respectively. Casual Speech occurred spontaneously when, for example, a third person interrupted the interview or during breaks for coffee; it also occurred in planned contexts, for example, in response to the interview question 'Have you ever been in a situation when you had a good laugh?' The variable (ng) is scored for two variants only. A score of 100 per cent represents consistent RP pronunciation: [ŋ] (*hopping*), while a score of 0 represents consistent non-standard pronunciation: [n] (*hoppin'*).

In Figure 4.2 you can see that, although the five lines do not slope evenly (as in the idealised diagram), they all rise from left to right; in other words, all five social class groups in Norwich use the prestige variant [ŋ] more in more formal speech styles. And while the lines are not equidistant from each other, they do not cross over each other; in other words, social stratification is maintained in all the four speech styles investigated. Note the difference between the three working-class groups and the two middle-class groups in the two less formal speech styles: there is a noticeable gap between the two sets of lines at the left-hand side of the diagram. Scores range from 0 per cent (the lower working class in Casual Speech) to 100 per cent (the two middle-class groups in Word List Style). Figure 4.2 demonstrates the range of social class and stylistic variation which (ng) is involved in in Norwich.

The complex but regular pattern exhibited here by (ng), and represented in idealised form in Figure 4.1, is thought to be typical of a linguistic variable with stable social significance, that is, a linguistic variable not involved in change.

4.2.2 Linguistic variables undergoing change

The other classic pattern revealed by quantitative sociolinguistic research is typical of a linguistic variable undergoing change. An idealised diagram is given in Figure 4.3. Note that both social stratification and the slope up from left to right are maintained. The main difference between Figure 4.3 and the diagram for a stable linguistic variable (Figure 4.1) is the **crossover** pattern which Figure 4.3 shows. The lower middle class (the second highest status group) shows a much greater shift towards the prestige form in formal styles than any other social group – note the steepness of the slope – so great in fact that it has a higher score than the upper middle class in these more formal styles. In less formal styles, however (where Labov argues less attention is paid

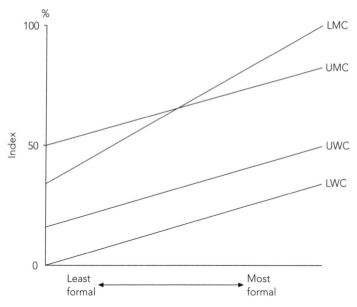

Figure 4.3 A diagrammatic representation of a linguistic variable undergoing change

to speech and pronunciation is therefore less under the speaker's control), the lower middle class, like the two working-class groups, uses proportionately few of the prestige variant. This results in the line which joins lower-middle-class scores **crossing over** the line joining upper-middle-class scores.

The behaviour of the lower middle class here, reflected in their scores, is known as **hypercorrection**. The most famous example of hypercorrection is that of post-vocalic (r) in New York City, as analysed by Labov (1972a). The variable post-vocalic (r) involves pronunciation or non-pronunciation of (r) in words such as *car* or *guard*, where (r) occurs after a vowel. Figure 4.4 reproduces Labov's diagram. Only two variants are involved: presence or absence of post-vocalic (r) (e.g. /kar/ or /kaː/). A score of 100 represents consistent usage of (r) after a vowel; a score of 0 represents consistent absence of (r). Labov's informants were divided into six groups, and their speech measured in five different styles. (The fifth style, MP – Minimal Pairs – involves pairs of words where (r) is the only differentiating element, e.g. *sauce: source*.)

Figure 4.4 reveals clearly that, while in less formal styles only the upper middle class (UMC) uses the prestige variant with any degree of consistency, in the more formal styles lower middle class (LMC) usage surpasses that of the UMC. The reason for hypercorrection seems to be the sensitivity of the LMC as a group to social pressures: their insecurity (because of their position on the borderline between the middle and working classes) is reflected in their concern with correctness and speaking 'properly'. When a linguistic variable

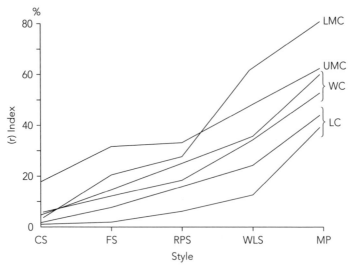

Figure 4.4 Social stratification of a linguistic variable in process of change: post-vocalic (r) in New York City (Labov 1972a: 114)

is in the process of change, Labov argues, the LMC becomes sensitive to the use of the new prestige variant (in this case, use of r-full pronunciation). In more formal styles (i.e. when paying more attention to speech) they make a conscious effort to speak 'correctly', and style-shift sharply from a virtually r-less casual (informal) style to a keeping-up-with-the-Jones', more r-full formal style.

4.3   Gender differences

Most early sociolinguistic work was concerned primarily with social class differences. However, it was soon apparent that other non-linguistic variables, such as ethnic group, age and gender, were involved in structured linguistic variation. In the case of gender, it was established that in many speech communities female speakers will use a higher proportion of prestige forms than male speakers. In other words, the prestige norms seem to exert a stronger influence on women than on men. In the case of stable linguistic variables, we can expect a pattern like the one shown in Figure 4.5. In the case of linguistic variables in the process of change, it appears that LMC *women* are particularly sensitive to the new prestige variant and are therefore prone to hypercorrection. Let's look at five examples of sociolinguistic research where gender differences have emerged as significant, to examine in detail the form such differences take. (The relationship between gender differences in speech and linguistic change will be taken up in Chapter 10.)

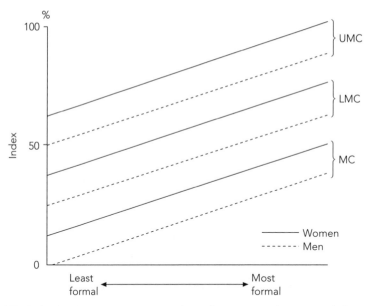

Figure 4.5 A diagrammatic representation of stratification according to social class and gender

4.3.1 Norwich

Trudgill's demonstration of social stratification in the case of the variable (ng) in Norwich has been given in Figure 4.2. A closer analysis of the data, including speaker's gender as well as social class and contextual style, reveals that scores for male and female speakers are quite different. The general pattern revealed here is that shown in Figure 4.5: women speakers in Norwich tend to use the prestige variant [ŋ] more (and the stigmatised variant [n] less) than men, and this holds true for all social classes.[4] Such a diagram is highly complex and difficult to read; Figure 4.6 (see p. 54) gives the results for formal style only, in histogram form. The contrast between the scores of women and men of the same social class is very striking.

Table 4.1 gives the actual scores of women and men in five social class groups and in four styles. As in Figure 4.2, a score of 100 represents consistent [ŋ] pronunciation (the prestige form), and a score of 0 represents consistent use of [n] (the stigmatised variant). The most interesting point to notice is that in fourteen out of twenty cases (i.e. 70 per cent) women's scores are higher than men's scores. Among other things these figures tell us the following:

1. In all styles, women tend to use fewer stigmatised forms than men.
2. In formal contexts (where Trudgill got informants to read lists of words) women seem to be more sensitive to the prestige pattern than men (look at the last column – the lowest score for women is 80).

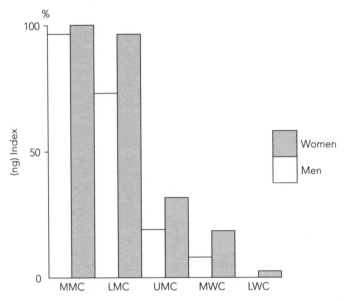

Figure 4.6 Histogram for (ng) in Norwich, showing social class and gender differences (based on Trudgill 1974a: 94)

Table 4.1: The variable (ng) in Norwich – index scores broken down by social class, sex and contextual style* (based on Trudgill 1974a: 94)

		CS	FS	RPS	WLS
MMC	M	69	96	100	100
	F	100	100	100	100
LMC	M	83	73	80	100
	F	33	97	100	100
UWC	M	5	19	82	100
	F	23	32	87	89
MMC	M	3	9	57	76
	F	12	19	54	80
LMC	M	0	0	0	34
	F	0	3	46	83

* I have reversed Trudgill's scores for consistency's sake (i.e. to keep 100 as the score representing the most prestigious pronunciation)

3. Lower-middle-class *women* style-shift very sharply: in the least formal style, they use quite a high proportion of the stigmatised variant, but in the three more formal styles, they correct their speech to correspond to that of the class above them (the middle middle class) – Labov argues (1972a: 243) that extreme style-shifting of this kind, often resulting in hypercorrection, is particularly marked in LMC women.

4. Use of non-standard forms (i.e. of the vernacular) seems to be associated not only with working-class speakers, but also with *male* speakers.

4.3.2 Glasgow

Ronald Macaulay's (1977, 1978) study of Glasgow English revealed a similar pattern (though Macaulay's results are based on one style only, that of the formal interview). The diagram for the variable (i), as in *hit, kill, risk,* is given in histogram form in Figure 4.7. A score of 100 represents consistent pronunciation of (i) as [ɪ] (the prestige form); a score of 0 represents consistent pronunciation of (i) as [ʌ̂] (Glasgow vernacular form).

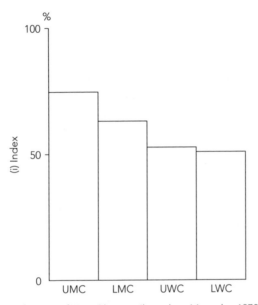

Figure 4.7   Social stratification of (i) in Glasgow (based on Macaulay 1978: 135)

The diagram showing social class stratification presents the usual tidy picture: each social class group uses proportionately more of the prestige form than the next group down in the social class hierarchy. When the figures are broken down into male and female scores, however, as in Figure 4.8, this superficial tidiness disappears. Women in each social class are revealed as using more of the prestige form [ɪ] than men of the same social class. Note that the women in each social class pattern like the men in the group *above* them. Conversely, the men in each social class pattern like the women in the group *below* them (see Table 4.2). Macaulay pointed out that the major break in the women's scores comes between the lower middle class and the upper working class, while for men it comes between the upper middle class and the lower middle class. So LMC women speak more like UMC women, while LMC men

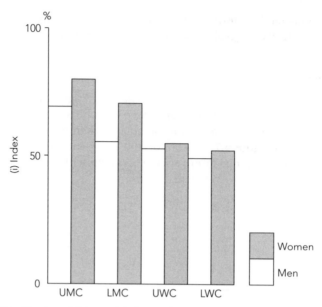

Figure 4.8 Stratification of (i) by social class and gender (based on Macaulay 1978: 135)

speak more like upper working class (UWC) men. This shows yet again the pivotal nature of the lower middle class.

Macaulay's data, like Trudgill's, suggests that social class scores conceal more than they reveal. In the case of the variable (i) in Glasgow, social class scores give us only an average of male and female scores, and fail to differentiate male and female usage.

Table 4.2: Male and female scores for (i) in Glasgow (based on Macaulay 1978: 135)

	Men	Women
UMC	69.00	80.00
LMC	55.25	71.25
UWC	53.25	55.00
LWC	50.00	53.00

4.3.3 West Wirral

Mark Newbrook's (1982) study of West Wirral aims to establish how far the urban vernacular of Liverpool ('Scouse') has spread into the surrounding area and, in particular, how far Scouse features have replaced local Cheshire forms as the usual non-standard forms occurring in this locality. He investigated a number of phonological variables, and found that there were significant gender

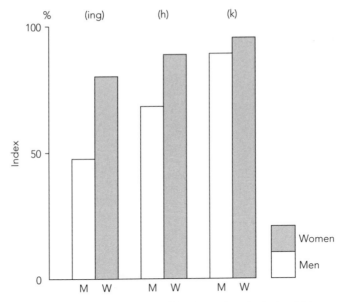

Figure 4.9 Gender differences in West Wirral for three phonological variables: (ing), (h) and (k)

differences for most of them. Figure 4.9 shows male and female group scores for the three variables (ing) as in *jumping*, (h) as in *house*, and (k) as in *kick*. The variants for (ing) are [ɪŋ] and [ɪn]; the variants for (h) are [h] and ø; the variants for (k) are the standard form [k] and the non-standard affricated form [kˣ] (or sometimes [x]). In all cases, a score of 100 indicates consistent use of the prestige variant.

With all three variables, we find the expected pattern: women's pronunciation is closer to the prestige standard than men's. Moreover, these group scores conceal the fact that the range of individual scores involved differs greatly between men and women. The typical score for a working-class man was much lower than that for a middle-class man, whereas women's scores covered a much narrower range. This suggests that social class is a more important factor in determining men's speech than women's, at least in West Wirral.

Figure 4.10 is the histogram for the variable (a) as in *bath, grass*. In this case, informants are analysed in terms of age as well as gender. A score of 100 represents consistent RP pronunciation: [ɑː]; a score of 0 represents consistent non-standard pronunciation: [æ]. Note that women's scores are higher than men's in each age group. Note also the age-grading that occurs with this variable: scores are higher for older speakers than for younger ones. Older *women* are much closer to the standard norms than other speakers, while young men are virtually consistent [æ] users. It looks as if young women are participating in the increasing dominance of [æ]. This non-standard variant seems to be a marker not only of male speech, but also of the speech of the young.

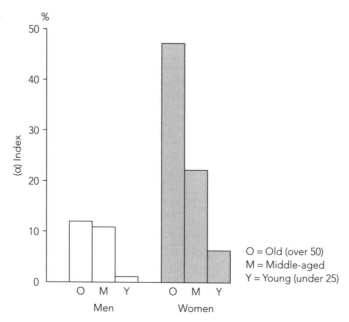

Figure 4.10 The variable (a) in West Wirral showing stratification by age and gender

4.3.4 Sydney, Australia

The studies we have looked at so far were all carried out in Britain, and all investigated phonological variation. But gender-differentiated language seems to be a world-wide phenomenon, and is not confined to pronunciation. Our fourth example comes from Australia and involves grammatical variation. Edina Eisikovits (1987, 1998) investigated the speech of adolescents living in working-class areas of Sydney. Three of the grammatical features she studied were the following:

1. Non-standard past tense forms such as *seen* and *done*
    e.g. *he woke up an' seen something*

2. Multiple negation
    e.g. *they don't say nothing*

3. Invariable *don't*
    e.g. *Mum don't have to do nothing*

Figure 4.11 gives the results for these three forms in the speech of her 16-year-old informants. (Note that, because of her focus on non-standard forms, Eisikovits' results are scored with 100 representing consistent *non-standard* usage.)

Here we see the expected pattern once again, with female speech closer to the standard, and male speakers consistently using a higher proportion of non-standard forms. However, this pattern was *not* apparent in the speech of younger adolescent speakers interviewed by Eisikovits. The development of gender-

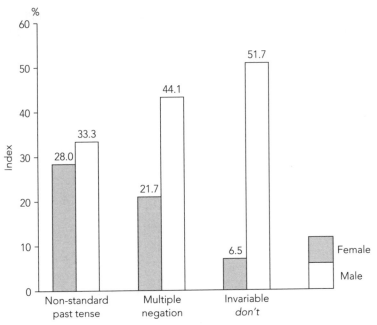

Figure 4.11 Gender differences in Sydney, Australia, for three non-standard grammatical features (based on Eisikovits 1998)

appropriate speech will be discussed in Chapter 9; I shall look at Eisikovits' results in more detail as part of that discussion (section 9.3.1).

4.3.5 Detroit, USA

Our final example comes from research carried out by Penelope Eckert in Detroit in the United States.[5] I have chosen to finish the section with this study because it shows very clearly how variationist studies have progressed. Eckert's data were obtained through participant observation: her subjects were students at Belten High, a high school in the suburbs of Detroit. The students she focuses on belong to two dominant groups in the school: 'jocks' and 'burnouts'. 'Jocks' are students who participate enthusiastically in school culture and aim to go on to college; 'burnouts' are students who reject the idea of the school as central to their lives, and who are more interested in activities outside school. To put it simply, the jocks constitute a middle-class culture, the burnouts a working-class culture.

Eckert studied phonological variation in the speech of these students: her analysis reveals the complex correlation between pronunciation, gender and social category (jock or burnout). Two of the variables she studied were (uh) as in *fun, cuff, but* and (ay) as in *fight, file, line*. These sounds are in flux in the local variety of (white) American English spoken by the students: the vowel in words like *but* is moving back (so *but* can sound more like *bought)*, while the first element (the nucleus) [a] of the diphthong in words like *file* is being raised so that *file* may sound more like *foil*. Most students use the full range of pronunciations but they vary in the frequency with which they use the more conservative and more innovative pronunciations. Figures 4.12 and 4.13 present the results for these two variables.

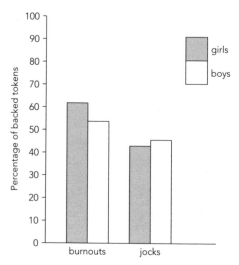

Figure 4.12 Percentage of backed tokens of (uh)

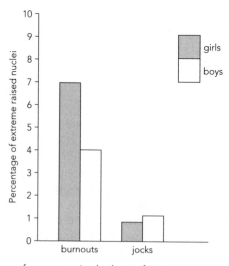

Figure 4.13 Percentage of extreme raised tokens of (ay)

4.12 and 4.13 adapted from Eckert, P. and McConnell-Ginet, S. (1999), pp. 196 and 197. Cambridge University Press.

As Figures 4.12 and 4.13 show, the patterning of these two variables is more complex than anything we have seen before. These variables are not simply gender markers – gender and social category are intertwined. Overall, the burnout girls are the most advanced speakers in terms of new vernacular forms, while the jock girls prefer more conservative variants. This means that the girls' usage is more polarised than the boys': 'the jock and burnout girls' values for both (ay) and (uh) backing constitute the linguistic extremes for the community' (Eckert and McConnell-Ginet 1999: 195). This finding is very different from the simple binary oppositions between male and female speakers that were evident in the other examples we have looked at.

4.3.6 Summary

These six studies show us the complexity of gender differentiation in speech. Where variation exists, it often seems to be the case that gender is involved, with male and female speakers preferring different variants. And where it is possible to label one of the variants as prestigious, then it is often female speakers who are found to use this variant. This was the case with Norwich (ng), Glasgow (i) and West Wirral (ing), (h) and (k). So for some communities studied, use of non-standard, non-prestige forms seems to be associated not only with working-class speakers, but also with male speakers. But this is obviously not the case in Detroit, where the Belten High girls are found at both ends of the scale: the jock girls have a more conservative accent, which fits the pattern of earlier research, but the burnout girls have the strongest local accent.

4.4 Explanations

The five studies discussed in the last section deal not just with differences in linguistic usage between male and female speakers, but also with explanations for these differences. The following subsections will looks very briefly at some of these explanations. Some of these are now out-dated and some are mutually contradictory. My aim here is to give a sense of the range of explanatory models that have been available in sociolinguistic work.

4.4.1 Women's sensitivity to linguistic norms

Women's sensitivity to linguistic norms is often asserted, and this is attributed to their insecure social position. Such insecurity on the part of women offers a clear parallel with the lower middle class, who, as we saw in section 4.2.2, provide the classic example of hypercorrect linguistic behaviour. Are sociolinguists really saying that women's linguistic behaviour is hypercorrect (see, for example, Labov 1972a: 243)? Let's look at some examples.

1. *(ng) in Norwich*
   Besides showing a regular pattern of gender differentiation, Table 4.1 (index scores for (ng) in Norwich) also exemplifies the extreme style-shifting of LMC women. In formal styles, LMC women pattern like the UMC as a whole, but in more informal speech they use a high proportion of stigmatised forms.

2. *The glottal stop in Glasgow*
   The glottal stop is the most overtly stigmatised feature of Glasgow speech. Macaulay found that it was widely used, but with clear social stratification (working-class groups using it considerably more than middle-class groups). The biggest contrast was between LMC men and women: LMC female informants used 40 per cent fewer glottal stops than LMC male informants. One LMC woman used fewer glottal stops than *any* UMC informant, a finding which conforms to the classic definition of hypercorrect behaviour.

3. *(o) on Merseyside*
   This linguistic variable – which occurs in words like *coat, go* – has many variants. One of these, [ɛʊ], is generally considered to be hypercorrect.[6] In his work in West Wirral, Newbrook established that, when they used Scouse variants, a minority of male informants but *all* the females preferred this variant.

The first two examples show that the hypercorrect pattern of the second highest status group, the lower middle class, is crucially connected with the usage of LMC *women*. The third example shows a more general pattern, with women of all classes showing sensitivity to [ɛʊ] But these examples, and the material examined earlier in this chapter, do not justify labelling women's speech as a whole as hypercorrect. As Figure 4.5 shows, gender differences lead to regular stratification, with women using fewer stigmatised forms and more prestige forms than men in each social class. It is no more justifiable to call this pattern of female usage hypercorrect than it would be to call the usage of the middle class hypercorrect in relation to that of the working class.

4.4.2 Self-evaluation tests

In order to test sensitivity to linguistic norms, Trudgill (1972, 1974a) carried out self-evaluation tests on his informants. He presented them with a recording of certain words, with two or more different pronunciations, varying from prestigious pronunciation (RP) to non-standard Norwich pronunciation. Informants were asked to indicate which of the forms most closely resembled the one they habitually used. The variables (er), as in *ear, here, idea*, and (a) as in *gate, face, name*, were both involved in this test. In the case of (er), only 28 per cent of male informants and 18 per cent of female informants responded accurately (i.e. claimed to use the form which corresponded to their actual usage in Casual Speech, as recorded in the interview). A staggering 68 per cent of the women (and 22 per cent of the men) **over-reported**, that is, claimed to use the prestige form when their index scores revealed they actually didn't. On the other hand, half the men (50 per cent) and 14 per cent of the women **under-reported**, that is, they claimed to use non-standard forms when their index scores revealed that they habitually used forms closer to standard pronunciation.

The results for the variable (a) repeat this pattern: 50 per cent of the men and 57 per cent of the women evaluate their pronunciation accurately; 43 per cent of the women (and 22 per cent of the men) *over*-report, while 28 per cent of the men (and none of the women) *under*-report. Table 4.3 summarises these figures.

Table 4.3: Percentage scores for self-evaluation for (er) and (a) in Norwich (based on Trudgill 1972)

	(er)		(a)	
	M	F	M	F
Over-report	22	68	22	43
Under-report	50	14	28	0
Accurate	28	18	50	57

The first thing to notice is that Trudgill's test reveals significant *over*-reporting by *women*. This suggests that women *are* sensitive to prestige norms. Many women in Norwich believe that they are producing forms close to standard pronunciation when they are not. This suggests that they are *aiming at* standard pronunciation, and that they are trying to avoid stigmatised forms.

The second thing to notice is that Trudgill's test reveals significant *under*-reporting by *men*. They claim to use non-standard forms when in fact they do not. Such behaviour can be explained by hypothesising that non-standard speech must have **covert prestige**.

4.4.3 Covert prestige

The concept of covert prestige arose when linguists attempted to explain the persistence of vernacular (non-standard) forms in the speech of working-class speakers. In view of the resistance of working-class speakers to the overt prestige of Standard English, we have to postulate the existence of another set of norms – vernacular norms – which have covert prestige and which therefore exert a powerful influence on linguistic behaviour. In the light of Trudgill's self-evaluation tests and the examples of male/female differences given earlier in the chapter, it seems reasonable to infer that vernacular forms have covert prestige not just for the working class but also for *men*. Under-reporting is equally common among middle-class men as among working-class men in Norwich. It looks as if many Norwich men are actually aiming at non-standard working-class speech.

This also seems to be the case for the male adolescents in Sydney, Australia, studied by Eisikovits (see section 4.3.4). Female speakers self-correct towards the standard, as in the following example:

(1) me an' Kerry – or should I say, Kerry and I – are the only ones who've done the project

But the self-corrections of male speakers are *from* standard *to* non-standard forms:

(2) I didn't know what I did – what I done

(3) we were skating around – we was skating along an' someone walked bang in front of me.

A study of language attitudes in Kentucky (Luhman 1990) also provides evidence that male speakers place high value on non-standard varieties (in this case, Appalachian English).

We see here the development of a stronger explanatory model. Early work on gender differences in language emphasised women's apparent sensitivity to prestige forms. The concept of prestige as a force which attracts different speakers more or less powerfully depending on their gender is supported by the sociolinguistic evidence: men do indeed use fewer prestige forms than women. But the introduction of the concept of covert prestige strengthens the model, by postulating the existence of two opposing sets of norms competing for speakers' loyalty: Standard English with its overt prestige, and vernacular norms with covert prestige. It is claimed that women are attracted by the norms of Standard English while men respond to the covert prestige of the vernacular. This model is also used to explain social class differences – in other words, it is argued that social class differences in language exist because middle-class speakers give allegiance to the institutionalised norms of Standard English while working-class speakers reject these norms and instead give allegiance to the vernacular.

This suggests an interesting parallelism between women and the middle class, on the one hand, and men and the working class, on the other (Figure 4.14).

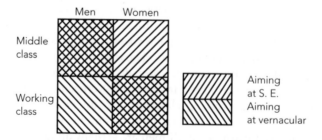

Figure 4.14 The intersection of social class, gender and language

Middle-class *women* and working-class *men* have no conflict of interests. Both their gender and their social class point to the same affiliation. For middle-class men and working-class women, however, there is a conflict of interests: the behaviour predictable on the basis of their social class will be incompatible with the behaviour predictable on the basis of their gender. A case in point is Eckert's study of Belten High students (see section 4.3.5). The linguistic choices of the jock girls are what their social class and their gender predict; whereas the linguistic choices of the burnout girls show that they have resolved the tension between their gender and their burnout status in favour of the latter, which means they lead even burnout boys in their use of (uh) and (ay).

The ambiguity of the position of middle-class male speakers and working-class female speakers is nicely pinpointed by the results of the following experiment (Edwards 1979a). Adult judges were presented with tape recordings of twenty middle-class and twenty working-class children and asked to identify whether children were male or female from their speech. In a minority of cases, the judges were not able to do this accurately. As Figure 4.15 shows, the judges did not make random mistakes; they made mistakes about two sets of children: middle-class boys and working-class girls. Some of the middle-class boys sounded like girls to the judges, while some of the working-class girls sounded like boys.

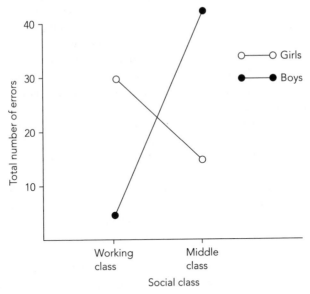

Figure 4.15 Interaction between gender and social class of children in terms of errors of gender identification (Edwards 1979b: 93)

4.4.4 Status and solidarity

These explanations themselves require explanations. If we accept that, in speech communities such as those described in this chapter, speakers choose between opposing sets of linguistic norms, we still have to explain why it is that women are more likely to be influenced by the publicly legitimised standard norms, and that men are more likely to be influenced by vernacular norms which are not publicly recognised. In this section, I shall look at the explanatory framework provided by social psychology, while the following section (4.4.5) will describe an explanation which draws on the notion of the linguistic marketplace.

Social psychologists have studied attitudes to speech in some detail. Their research confirms that RP has more prestige than regional accents in Britain. One of the 'rewards' (to use the social psychologists' term) for speakers who use speech closer to standard norms is that they acquire greater **status**. Another reward seems to be that RP speakers are perceived as being more ambitious, more intelligent and more self-confident. However, while RP speakers are rated highly in terms of competence, regionally accented speakers are rated highly in terms of personal attractiveness: they are perceived to be serious, talkative, good-natured, and as having a sense of humour. This suggests that there are also rewards, though of a different kind, for those speakers who choose non-standard forms.

Most social psychological studies are designed to explore attitudes to different varieties of English without considering gender as a variable. A rare study (Elyan et al. 1978) designed to test reactions to women speaking with standard and non-standard accents (RP and Lancashire) revealed that women using an RP accent were rated by judges as being more fluent, intelligent, self-confident, adventurous, independent and *feminine* than women with a regional accent. In addition, RP-accented women were also rated as being more *masculine* (judges had to rate each speaker for both masculinity and femininity on a nine-point scale). This may seem contradictory, but if masculinity and femininity are seen as two independent dimensions, then individuals have the choice of both characteristics. American research shows that between 30 per cent and 45 per cent of American women college students score high on both feminine and masculine dimensions: this is called **psychological androgyny** (Bem 1974, 1975). It is suggested that androgynous behaviour offers many rewards for women in contemporary society, allowing them a broad repertoire of behaviour to cope with the wide variety of social roles they have to take on. We can argue that, in Britain, RP is part of androgynous behaviour for speakers who are both female and middle class, because of these rewards.

Speakers, however, are not isolated individuals; they are members of social groups, and it is one of language's functions to act as a symbol of group identity. For all sorts of reasons, working-class speakers diverge linguistically from middle-class speakers, in order to mark the social distance between the two groups. At the same time, working-class speakers will converge linguistically with each other, in order to show **solidarity**, to mark their membership of the same social group. The conscious effort by members of the working class *not* to speak Standard English is well documented, as examples 2 and 3 above, from Eisikovits' research in Sydney, illustrated.

There are nowadays strong pressures on speakers who are *male* as well as on speakers who are working class to diverge from Standard English. Many high-profile men choose to adopt a non-standard accent: the violinist Nigel Kennedy is a well-known example, and the Prime Minister, Tony Blair, has been described as speaking 'Estuary English'. The following very brief extract comes from talk involving four young men in Manchester:

> *George:* we was playing naked football the other night, like it was only about half eleven, er-
>
> *Chaz:* play that often, do you?
>
> *George:* well I was- in our pants like, we were only kicking it about back I live off
>
> *Chaz:* what, in your duds or wi' fuck all?

Note the non-standard grammar (*we was playing*), the non-standard lexis (*duds*), the use of taboo words (*fuck all*). This extract comes from a conversation involving a sociologist and his friends. The talk was recorded because this researcher and his colleague (who was not present) wanted to carry out 'a detailed exploration of one all-male gathering and the ways in which four young white heterosexual men [. . .] negotiate and reproduce a range of masculinities whilst drinking alcohol' (Gough and Edwards 1998: 411). The extract appears as part of an article published in *The Sociological Journal* in 1998 entitled 'The beer talking: four lads, a carry out and the reproduction of masculinities'. By using non-standard forms, as well as by other linguistic signals such as swearing, these male speakers signal their solidarity with each other, even though it is unlikely that we would label university researchers as working class.

4.4.5 The linguistic market

A more recent explanation has been put forward by Penelope Eckert. Her research in Belten High, Detroit, revealed that there was not a simple male–female divide in the use of the phonological variables studied (see section 4.3.5). Rather, burnout girls emerged as the most advanced speakers in terms of new vernacular forms while jock girls were the most conservative. This is far from the tidy pattern we have observed in other sociolinguistic research, where female speakers tend to use forms closer to standard and male speakers tend to use less standard forms. At Belten High, it is female students who are associated with *both* the standard *and* the non-standard end of the scale. In other words, the girls' usage is more extreme than the boys'.

This clearly demands a different explanatory model: the explanations discussed so far in the chapter are inadequate to deal with Eckert's findings. (However, in some ways this new explanation could be said to be a re-working of the notion of women's sensitivity to linguistic norms, as discussed in 4.4.1.) Eckert develops the idea of 'symbolic capital' and of 'symbolic markets' from the French theorists Bourdieu and Boltanski (1975), to introduce the notion of 'linguistic markets'. In the wider world, men control material capital, but 'the only kind of capital a woman can accumulate is symbolic' (Romaine 2003: 104). Language use constitutes an important form of symbolic capital, and since educational level, employment and income are not reliable indicators of a woman's status (because women have not had the same educational and employment opportunities as men), language use becomes highly significant for women.

But women and men stand in very different relations to linguistic markets, and this includes both the standard language market and the vernacular market. Jock girls and burnout girls have to do more symbolically to establish their jock-ness or their burnout-ness because of their marginal status in the linguistic marketplace. As Eckert puts it, 'boys' actions and roles are defining of the jock and burnout categories, just as men's actions and occupations are defining of the adult professional and blue-collar worlds' (Eckert 1998: 70). Male speakers are at the centre of the marketplace, while female speakers are at the edge.

4.4.6 Summary

All these explanations seek to clarify our understanding of *why* male and female speakers use language differently. Some additionally try to clarify why many studies find a pattern of female speakers using linguistic forms closer to the standard. But this pattern is not fixed. And it is certainly not the case that male speakers invariably use vernacular forms more frequently than female speakers. Eckert's research shows the converse, as does work we shall look at in the next chapter.

4.5 Conclusions

In this chapter we have looked at some examples of sociolinguistic research which demonstrate gender differentiation, and we have discussed some of the reasons put forward to explain this phenomenon. In all known communities, male and female are important categories; that is, members of a community are distinguished from each other in terms of *gender*, as well as in other (more culture-specific) ways. Not surprisingly, in sociolinguistic research, gender has emerged as an important variable, and sociolinguists have found that gender differences in language often cut across social class variation. One robust finding of sociolinguistic research has been that women – like middle-class speakers – use proportionately more standard forms (those accorded overt prestige by society), while men – like working-class speakers – use proportionately more non-standard forms. Janet Holmes has even suggested that this finding could be considered a 'strong contender for the status of a sociolinguistic universal tendency' (Holmes 1998: 473). But as we have seen, recent work like Eckert's has uncovered patterns which do not fit such a 'universal tendency'.

The next chapter (Chapter 5) will look at work which explores the hypothesis that the level of integration of speakers in a community will be directly reflected in their language, and will show in what ways such work refines our understanding of male/female differences in language.

Notes

1   Note that, in order to pass public examinations, pupils need to internalise these concepts, and to acquire a facility in written Standard English.
2   The perceptive reader will have spotted that the term *vernacular* is used in this book – and in sociolinguistics generally – to mean both (1) non-standard varieties of a language; and (2) spontaneous speech between equals in private. Clearly these two senses are not coterminous: in particular, sense (1) excludes the informal talk of speakers of the standard variety, while sense (2) loses the contrast *vernacular-standard*. In practice, most sociolinguists slide without comment between the two senses, but readers need to be alert to the ambiguous nature of the term. (See Milroy 1987: 57–60 for further discussion of this point.)
3   See note 2.
4   This rests on the assumption that men's and women's social class has been accurately assessed. However, since Trudgill, like most other researchers, assessed women's social class partly on the occupation of their husband or father, it is not clear that this assumption is justified. (See Delphy 1981 for an incisive critique of stratification studies in relation to women.)
5   This account of Eckert's long-term research at Belten High is based on Eckert (1990, 1998, 1999) and Eckert and McConnell-Ginet (1995).
6   Note that the term *hypercorrection* is being used here in a different sense, since the variant is never used by UMC informants: it is a qualitative rather than a quantitative overshoot. Knowles (1974) and De Lyon (1981) both consider [ɛʊ] to be hypercorrect on Merseyside, but Newbrook (who refers to it as [ɐ̟ʊ]) feels it is not synchronically hypercorrect in West Wirral.

CHAPTER 5

Social networks

5.1 The concept of social network

One of the most fruitful explanations of linguistic variation in recent years has been the concept of social network. This concept has been current in the social sciences for some years, but was not mentioned in sociolinguistic analysis until Blom and Gumperz (1972), and not well known before publication of the Milroys' Belfast study (Milroy and Milroy 1978; Milroy 1980).

Members of a given speech community – such as Belfast – can be seen as being connected to each other in social networks which may be relatively 'closed' or 'open'. An individual whose personal contacts all know each other belongs to a closed network. This is shown diagrammatically in Figure 5.1. The arrows represent mutual knowing.

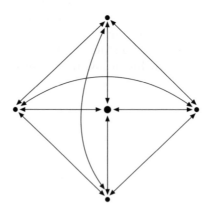

Figure 5.1 A closed network

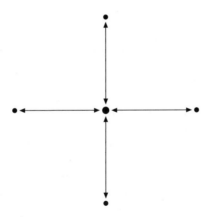

Figure 5.2 An open network

An individual whose personal contacts tend not to know each other belongs to an open network (see Figure 5.2).

Closed networks are said to be of **high density**; open networks are said to be of **low density**. Moreover, the links between people may be of different kinds: people can relate to each other as relatives, as neighbours, as workmates, as friends. Where individuals are linked in several ways, for example, they live in the same street, work in the same factory and share leisure activities, then the network ties are said to be **multiplex**.

It seems that the networks typically found in socially mobile, highly indus-trialised societies are of low density and **uniplex** (i.e. individuals are not linked in more than one way). In rural village communities and in traditional working-class communities, on the other hand, the networks typically found are of high density and multiplex.

Relatively dense networks, it is claimed, function as norm-enforcement mecha-nisms. In the case of language, this means that a closely knit group will have the capacity to enforce *linguistic* norms. Lesley Milroy, working in Belfast, showed that in the working-class communities (both Catholic and Protestant) there is polarisation of gender roles, with men's and women's activities being sharply distinguished. Such polarisation is typical of communities with dense networks. What Milroy established was that the men's networks are denser and more multiplex than the women's, and that this difference in network strength is matched by linguistic differences.

Let's now look at two pieces of sociolinguistic research where network strength is shown to be a significant factor in predicting male/female differences, starting with Lesley Milroy's work on Belfast, and then considering Jenny Cheshire's study of adolescents in Reading.[1]

5.1.1 Belfast

Milroy investigated three working-class communities in Belfast: Ballymacarrett (a Protestant area in East Belfast), the Hammer (a Protestant area in West Belfast) and the Clonard (a Catholic area in West Belfast). All three areas are poor working-class districts with a high incidence of unemployment.

Milroy's analysis of these communities was based not on interviews but on **participant observation**. Through informal contacts with core members of these communities, she was able to approach them in the capacity of 'a friend of a friend'. This role meant that she was accepted with friendliness and trust; it also enabled her to observe and participate in prolonged and informal inter-action. Her tape recorder was soon accepted in the various households she visited, and she could be reasonably confident that the conversations she recorded were representative of the vernacular.

She observed not only the language of the people she contacted, but also their social networks. Because all three communities revealed dense and multiplex networks, she decided to give each individual a Network Strength Score, de-pending on five factors. Scores for each individual were calculated by assigning one point for each condition fulfilled. The five factors were as follows:

1. Belonging to a high-density, territorially based group.
2. Having substantial ties of kinship in the neighbourhood (more than one household in addition to the nuclear family).
3. Working at the same place as at least two others from the same area.
4. Working at the same place as at least two others of the same sex from the area.
5. Associating voluntarily with workmates in leisure hours.

The total score was designed to reflect the individual's level of integration into localised networks.

Individual scores, then, ranged from 0 to 5. As will be apparent, factors 3, 4 and 5 will give high scores to men in traditional employment. In Ballymacarrett, where traditional employment patterns still prevail to some extent (the men working in the shipyards), the men typically had high scores. In the Hammer and Clonard, on the other hand, which are both areas of high *male* unemploy-ment, individual women often scored as high as or higher than men.

The value of the social network as a concept, and of the Network Strength Score as an analytical tool, lies in their ability to demonstrate a correlation between the integration of an individual in the community and the way that individual speaks. Individuals who participate in close-knit networks are also those who most consistently use vernacular forms in speech. It would be a common-sense assumption that the speech of members of a close-knit group would tend to be more homogeneous than that of members of a loosely knit group; the Network Strength Scale allied with linguistic analysis allows the assumption to be examined more closely.

The variable (th)

One of the variables examined by Milroy was the interdental voiced fricative (th) occurring intervocalically in words such as *mother, bother, together*. Vernacular speakers in Belfast delete (th) in such words; they pronounce *mother*, for example, as [mɔ.ər]. In Figure 5.3, a score of 0 represents consistent pronunciation of (th) intervocalically, while 100 represents consistent deletion of (th). (Note that a score of 100 now represents consistent *vernacular* pronunciation.) Both studies described in this chapter focus on working-class communities and their speech. Their scoring is therefore the inverse of that used in Chapter 4: speakers are measured against the set of norms which constitute the vernacular, not against the set of norms known as Standard English. Figure 5.3 shows the distribution of (th) by age, gender and area.

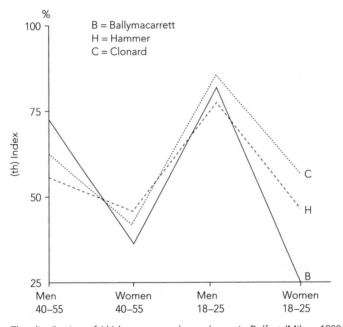

Figure 5.3   The distribution of (th) by age, gender and area in Belfast (Milroy 1980: 128)

This variable shows the pattern typical of stable sociolinguistic markers. All three communities are revealed as sharing the same attitude to (th). The gender differences are very marked, particularly in Ballymacarrett, the most traditional of the three areas. The two generations are shown to pattern similarly, though men's and women's pronunciation is more polarised in the younger generation, with higher scores for 18–25-year-old men and low scores for 18–25-year-old women (particularly Ballymacarrett women).

It's important to consider individual scores as well as group scores. In the three communities, individual scores confirm the striking gender differentiation of intervocalic (th) – the men's and women's scores do not overlap at all.

Even the men with the lowest scores (the men who delete (th) least) score more than the women with the highest scores. In other words, even the men whose pronunciation is furthest from the vernacular norms delete (th) intervocalically more than any woman.

The variable (a)

This pattern is not found with all variables, however. Consider Figure 5.4, for the variable (a).

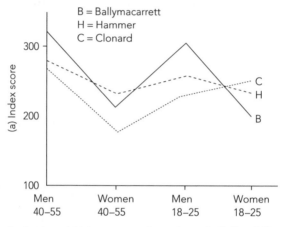

Figure 5.4 The distribution of (a) by age, gender and area in Belfast (Milroy 1980: 124)

This is a much more complex variable, since it cannot be scored in the simple binary fashion that (th) was. A five-point scale was used to measure the degree of retraction and back-raising of (a) in words like *hat, man, back*, with a score of 1 for [æ] ranging through [a], [ä], [ɑ] to a score of 5 for [ɔə]. (The higher the score, the greater the backing of (a).) First, consider the pattern for Ballymacarrett. As we saw with (th), there is clear gender differentiation in this community, with the same zig-zag line as before. The Hammer and the Clonard, however, do not show this pattern. In the Hammer, the difference between men and women for (a) is insignificant, while in the Clonard the *young women* use *more* backed variants of (a) than the young men (quite unlike the older women, whose scores are significantly lower than those of the men of their generation, following the usual pattern).

So what do the data on these two variables in Belfast tell us? First, for certain stable variables such as (th), there is clear differentiation between the sexes. As earlier sociolinguistic studies had established, this difference is the result of the men using variants consistently closer to the vernacular norms, and of the women using variants consistently less close. Milroy suggests as an explanation of this difference that men in working-class inner-city areas belong to denser, more multiplex networks than women. By using her Network Strength Scale, she was able to show that a high Network Strength Score was clearly correlated with use of the vernacular. In most cases, this meant that men whose speech revealed high usage of vernacular forms were also found to belong to tight-knit social networks. If it is accepted that social networks operate as important norm-enforcing mechanisms, then it would seem to be the case that, in inner-city Belfast, with stable linguistic variables such as (th), the tight-knit social networks in which most of the men participate serve to enforce the vernacular speech norms. Conversely, vernacular forms are less evident in women's speech in these communities because the women belong to less dense, less multiplex social networks, which therefore have less power to enforce norms.

The second variable above, however, does not follow this pattern. While the women and men in Ballymacarrett differ in their use of (a) in the expected way, this pattern is not found in the Hammer or in the Clonard. It is the Clonard findings which are particularly interesting: while the older generation conform to the expected pattern, the younger generation reverses it. How can we explain the high scores of the young Clonard women for this variable? It seems that Ballymacarrett as a community differs from the other two: it suffers little from male unemployment, largely because of its location by the ship-yards. The Hammer and the Clonard both had unemployment rates of around 35 per cent at the time of Milroy's research, which clearly affected social rela-tionships. Men from these areas were forced to look for work outside the community, and also shared more in domestic tasks (with consequent blurring of gender roles). The women in these areas went out to work and, in the case of the young Clonard women, all worked together. This meant that the young Clonard women, by contrast with all the other female groups, belonged to a dense and multiplex network; they lived, worked and amused themselves together. The young Clonard women have the highest network score of any sub-group (mean = 4.75); the mean for the young Clonard men is 3.0. This is in complete contrast with the scores for Ballymacarrett, where the mean network score for men is 3.96, compared with 1.33 for the women. The contrast is between a traditional working-class community (Ballymacarrett) and a working-class community undergoing social change because of severe male unemploy-ment (Clonard). The tight-knit network to which the young Clonard women belong clearly exerts pressure on its members, who are linguistically homo-geneous. Because of their social circumstances, the young Clonard women are linguistically more like the young Ballymacarrett men than like the other women in the three communities. Social networks in this case help to explain not only linguistic differences between the sexes, but also the seemingly divergent beha-viour of the younger Clonard women.

5.1.2 Reading

It seems to be the case that social networks are most close-knit around the age of 16. This means that adolescents will be more consistent vernacular speakers than adults. Labov's famous study of Black English Vernacular focused on adolescent peer groups in New York (Labov 1972b), and Cheshire's more recent work in Reading was based on three groups of adolescents. While Labov studied only male peer groups, Cheshire studied both boys and girls, which enabled her to examine gender differentiation in vernacular usage.

Cheshire, like Labov and Milroy, gained her data through long-term participant observation. That is, having decided to analyse the speech of working-class adolescent peer groups, she located three groups (two of boys, one of girls) in two adventure playgrounds in Reading, and was gradually accepted by them. (She told the first group that she had a vacation job, finding out what people in Reading thought of the town. They sympathised with her need to earn some money and accepted the tape recorder as an aid to her supposedly poor memory.) She visited the playgrounds two or three times a week for nine months, and was soon on very friendly terms with the adolescents. She took care, through details like informal dress and riding a motorbike, to reduce the social distance between the adolescents and herself as far as possible.

Cheshire examined non-standard morphological and syntactic features in the speech of the adolescents. Examples of eleven of these variables are given below.

1. Non-standard -s
   'They calls me all the names under the sun, don't they?' (Derek)

2. Non-standard has
   'You just has to do what the teachers tell you.' (Mandy)

3. Non-standard was
   'You was with me, wasn't you?' (Ann)

4. Negative concord
   'It ain't got no pedigree or nothing.' (Nobby)

5. Non-standard never
   'I never went to school today.' (Lynne)

6. Non-standard what
   'Are you the little bastards what hit my son over the head?' (Nobby)

7. Non-standard do
   'She cadges, she do.' (Julie)

8. Non-standard come
   'I come down here yesterday.'

9. Ain't = auxiliary have
   'I ain't seen my Nan for nearly seven years.' (Tracey)

10. Ain't = auxiliary be
    'Course I ain't going to the Avenue.' (Mandy)

11. Ain't = copula
    'You ain't no boss.' (Rob)

Table 5.1 gives percentage scores for male and female speakers for these eleven variables. A score of 100 represents consistent use of the non-standard forms.

Table 5.1: Gender differences in non-standard features of Reading speech
(Cheshire 1998: 38)

| | Frequency indices | |
	Boys	Girls
non-standard -s	53.16	52.04
non-standard has	54.76	51.61
non-standard was	88.15	73.58
negative concord	88.33	51.85
non-standard never	46.84	40.00
non-standard what	36.36	14.58
non-standard do	57.69	78.95
non-standard come	100.00	75.33
ain't = aux have	92.00	64.58
ain't = aux be	74.19	42.11
ain't = copula	85.83	61.18

The non-standard forms are all used less often by the girls than by the boys, apart from non-standard *do*, a feature which seems to be involved in linguistic change. These findings, then, conform to the expected pattern, with female speakers adhering more closely to standard norms, while male speakers use non-standard forms more consistently.

In terms of the social networks they belong to, it seems that the boys belong to structured peer groups of the kind described by Labov in his work with black adolescents in New York, while the girls belong to a much less tightly knit group. The sociometric diagram (Figure 5.5) shows the friendship patterns

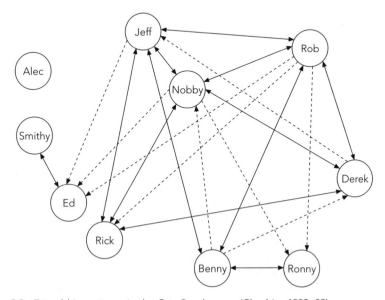

Figure 5.5 Friendship patterns in the Orts Road group (Cheshire 1982: 89)

obtaining between the boys in the Orts Road group. Each boy was asked which friends he spent most of his time with; solid lines represent reciprocal naming and thus the main social links within the group.

On the basis of the boys' responses, Cheshire divided them into three groups: core members, secondary members and non-members. Cheshire investigated the relationship between use of non-standard linguistic features and peer group status. She found some positive correlations: of the nine most frequently occurring non-standard features in the boys' speech, six were used more by core members than by others, and four of the features (non-standard present tense forms, *has*, *was*, and *never*) were used most by core members and least by non-members. But this correlation is not as regular and systematic as that found by Labov in his work on black adolescent peer groups. It seems that adolescent peer groups in Britain have a more flexible structure. The hierarchically structured and tight-knit adolescent groups in New York show a corresponding high correlation between peer group status and use of non-standard language. Cheshire also suggests that not *all* the non-standard features of Reading English necessarily serve as markers of peer group status. In order to investigate *which* variables function as markers of vernacular loyalty, she constructed a vernacular culture index, based on the following six factors:

1. Skill at fighting.
2. Carrying of weapons.
3. Participation in minor criminal activities.
4. Sort of job preferred.
5. Style (i.e. dress, hairstyle).
6. Swearing.

Each boy was given a score for each of these factors, and on the basis of their total scores the boys were divided into four groups: group 1 boys are those who adhere most closely to the norms of vernacular culture, and group 4 boys are those who do not adhere to these norms. Cheshire was able to show that six of the non-standard features of Reading English seem to be closely linked to the speaker's involvement in the vernacular culture. Table 5.2 gives the scores for these six variables. As the table shows, the four variables in class A are very sensitively linked to vernacular loyalty, while those in class B are less sensitive markers.

Cheshire found that the girls did not form structured peer groups like the boys. All the girls in the group studied by Cheshire knew each other, but they tended to break up into pairs of 'best friends', and these pairings would be intense but short-lived. In terms of their main friendship patterns, the girls can be divided into three separate sub-groups, as shown in Figure 5.6. When asked who they spent most of their time with, each girl named her 'best friend' (double lines in Figure 5.6). When asked who else they spent time with, they named all the other girls in the group, except for the three 'outsiders', Lynne,

Table 5.2: Adherence to vernacular culture – scores for frequency of occurrence of six non-standard forms (based on Cheshire 1998: 32)

		Group 1	Group 2	Group 3	Group 4
	non-standard -s	77.36	54.03	36.57	21.21
Class A	non-standard has	66.67	50.00	41.65	(33.33)*
	non-standard was	90.32	89.74	83.33	71.43
	negative concord	100.00	85.71	83.33	71.43
Class B	non-standard never	64.71	41.67	45.45	37.50
	non-standard what	92.31	7.69	33.33	0.00

* Number of occurrences of this variable was low, so the index score may be unreliable.

Marlene and Sharon, who form a separate sub-group. Valerie and Christine are also peripheral and spend less time at the playground: Valerie is older and gave her boyfriend's name in answer to the first question; Christine is younger and named a schoolfriend.

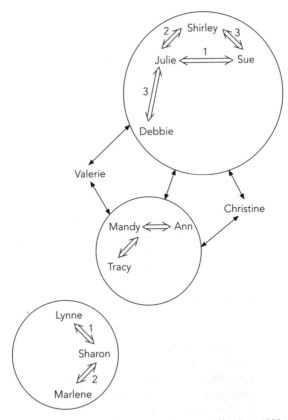

Figure 5.6 Friendship patterns in the Shinfield girls' group (Cheshire 1982: 93)

Cheshire found no systematic pattern of variation in language correlating with this rather unstructured pattern of relationships. Moreover, she decided that the vernacular culture index which she had used to measure the boys' adherence to vernacular values could not be used for the girls. Although the girls took part in activities which could be called delinquent, such as stealing and setting fire to the playground, their attitude to such activities differed from the boys'. They did not boast about what they had done, and although they had fights from time to time, they did not value certain girls as 'good fighters'. In other words, they did not seem to value the vernacular norms of toughness and violence in the same way the boys did. In some ways – in terms of their interest in pop music, films, television and boyfriends – they were closer to mainstream culture. But they also clearly rejected many of the values of mainstream society; most of them, for example, did not attend school regularly.

Cheshire finally made a simple binary distinction between those girls who seemed in part to adhere to the vernacular norms defined earlier and those who did not. The three 'good' girls in the latter group did not swear, steal, set fire to the playground or play truant from school. Table 5.3 shows a comparison between the scores for the two groups.

Table 5.3: Frequency indices for eight variables for two groups of girls (Cheshire 1998: 39)

	'Good' girls	'Bad' girls
non-standard -s	25.84	57.27
non-standard has	36.36	35.85
non-standard was	63.64	80.95
negative concord	12.50	58.70
non-standard never	45.45	41.07
non-standard what	33.33	5.56
non-standard come	30.77	90.63
ain't = copula	14.29	67.12

As Table 5.3 shows, there are five features which are used more by the 'bad' girls than by the 'good' ones: non-standard -s, was, come, negative concord, and ain't as copula. Three of these, as we saw earlier, function as markers of vernacular loyalty for boys too: non-standard -s suffix, was and negative concord. Non-standard come is, however, invariant for the boys (they all use it 100 per cent of the time) whereas it clearly functions as a marker of vernacular loyalty for the girls, being almost categorical for 'bad' girls, but occurring much less frequently in the speech of the three 'good' girls (30.77 per cent). Ain't too seems to function as a marker of vernacular loyalty for girls, but not for boys, who all use it with relatively similar frequency. Non-standard never and what function only loosely as markers of vernacular loyalty for the boys; for the girls they seem not to be markers at all, since the 'good' girls use them more.

Cheshire concludes that different speakers exploit the system in different ways. While some non-standard linguistic features act as markers of vernacular loyalty for both male and female adolescents in Reading (non-standard present tense verb forms, non-standard *was*, and negative concord), there are other non-standard features which act primarily as gender markers: that is, they function as markers of vernacular loyalty only for girls (non-standard *come* and *ain't* as a copula) or only for boys non-standard *never* and *what*). These results implicitly challenge the notion that members of a speech community can be defined in terms of shared norms.

5.2 Explanation in the light of social network theory

The concept of the social network, which enables us to see the individual in relation to the group, clearly refines our understanding of gender differences in language. The evidence is that a tight-knit network structure is an important mechanism of language maintenance. Men's speech in many speech communities is closer to the vernacular than women's, and we can see that it is the close-knit social networks to which men have traditionally belonged which serve to maintain vernacular speech norms. Women's speech, then, is closer to the standard not because women are deliberately aiming at Standard English but because the less tight-knit networks to which women belong are less efficient at enforcing vernacular norms. In other words, women may use forms closer to Standard English for the negative reason that they are relatively less exposed to vernacular speech and more exposed to Standard English.

Cheshire's examination of style-shifting in the speech of her informants gives us additional information on the nature of peer group pressure. She made a set of recordings in the schools attended by the adolescents in her groups, and she used this material to see whether the speech of the adolescents was affected by the more formal school context. She found that all three groups in her study used fewer non-standard verb forms in school (i.e. non-standard -*s*). Interestingly, it emerged that the girls' use of non-standard verb forms decreased more sharply than the boys'. We can infer from the fact that the girls were not part of a cohesive peer group, and that their friendships fluctuated frequently, that they are less under pressure from the group to use vernacular forms, and consequently more exposed to the prestige norms of Standard English valued by institutions such as schools. In other words, the girls are more likely to see non-standard forms as being inappropriate in the school context, and to style-shift accordingly.

Not all the boys used fewer non-standard verb forms in school (as would be predicted by the Labovian model, with non-standard features reducing as the situation becomes more formal). The boys' speech in school is shown to be linked to their relationship with their teacher. Where they have a good relationship with the teacher, they use fewer non-standard present tense verb forms; that is, they adapt their speech in the direction of school norms. Where they have a poor relationship with their teacher, on the other hand, they either maintain their vernacular usage or actually increase the proportion of non-standard forms in their speech. One of the boys studied by Cheshire used non-standard speech in this way to mark his hostility to the school: he diverged from Standard

English more in school than in the adventure playground, presumably to mark his loyalty to the vernacular culture. (*All* of the boys in Eisikovits' study (see section 4.3.4) used *more* non-standard forms when interacting with an adult in the school context than when interacting with each other.)

Milroy suggests that a status-based model of the kind initially developed by Labov in New York City (and described in section 4.2.1) is inadequate to deal with the language patterns of urban populations such as Belfast. She asserts the importance of **solidarity** as a factor in influencing patterns of language use. The status-based model would predict that speakers who belong to relatively loose-knit networks will change their speech in the direction of publicly legitimised norms (Standard English). However, in Belfast, speakers from the Hammer, with more loose-knit networks resulting from re-housing and unemployment, are *not* more standardised than Ballymacarrett or Clonard speakers. The change in their speech patterns shows a drift away from the focused vernacular norms of more tight-knit groups, but not a drift towards the prestige norms of Standard English. In these working-class communities, then, it is more accurate to say that men's speech differs from women's because men's tight-knit networks exercise control over their members and maintain vernacular norms. It seems that working-class women are not aiming at prestige norms; they belong to relatively loose-knit networks which have less capacity to enforce focused linguistic norms, and they therefore use vernacular forms less consistently than men. This is quite different from claiming that women and men are aiming at different norms.

5.3 Woman as lames?

In his work on the speech of black adolescent peer groups in New York, Labov introduces the term *lame* to refer to isolated individuals on the fringes of vernacular culture: 'To be lame means to be outside of the central group and its culture' (Labov 1972b: 258). Labov demonstrated that lames differ systematically in their use of language from full members of the peer group: while their speech is non-standard, it is much less close to the vernacular than is the speech of central members of the street culture. For example, if we look at one grammatical feature of Black English Vernacular – negative concord – we find that the adolescent peer group known as the Thunderbirds uses negative concord 98 per cent of the time, while the lames use it only 76 per cent of the time. (Note, however, that 76 per cent as a score for the use of negative concord is still very high: the lames are certainly not approximating to (white) prestige norms.)

Can we describe women as lames? The work of both Milroy and Cheshire demonstrates that female speakers are less closely integrated into vernacular culture, that female speakers use vernacular norms less consistently than male speakers, and that these two findings are interrelated. In this respect, women are like Labov's lames. But Labov used the term to refer to isolated individuals. Most women are not isolated: among the women in Belfast studied by Milroy only three had a Network Strength Score of 0; among the Reading adolescents, only two of the girls are clearly peripheral (see Figure 5.6). Women do belong to social networks, but these seem to be less dense and multiplex than those of men.

There are other reasons for pausing before labelling women as lames, that is, describing women as deviant. The Androcentric Rule (see p. 10) predicts that commentators will describe the linguistic behaviour of men as 'normal' and the linguistic behaviour of women as deviating from that norm. Is it possible that sociolinguistic research has an androcentric bias?

Certainly, conventional criteria for network strength may be less applicable to the particular circumstances of women's lives. Out of the five criteria used by Milroy, for example (see p. 72), the third, fourth and fifth are male-oriented because they relate specifically to waged work. While it is true that women do participate in waged work (especially in working-class communities like those studied by Milroy), they also have domestic responsibilities which these criteria do not recognise.

Secondly, we need to beware of defining the vernacular in such a way that it excludes female speakers. Sociolinguists frequently write of working-class vernacular culture and male culture as if they were one and the same thing. It is important to stress the fact that vernacular norms are features which mark a speaker's loyalty to a particular network. Women's loyalty to vernacular norms is not always marked with the same linguistic features that mark men's identification with vernacular culture. Cheshire's work in Reading (see section 5.1.2) showed this clearly: some non-standard features functioned as markers of vernacular loyalty only for the girls, while others functioned as markers of vernacular loyalty only for the boys.

Finally, the claim that women in general belong to less dense and multiplex networks than men is controversial. Work in other cultures suggests that this is not always the case. In her study of Tenejapa (a Mayan community in Mexico), Penelope Brown observes that 'where men dominate the public sphere of life and women stick largely to the domestic sphere, it seems likely that female relationships will be relatively multi-stranded, male ones relatively single-stranded' (Brown 1998: 134).

In the final section of this chapter, I shall examine two counter-examples, both involving communities in Britain. In both examples, it is women, not men, who use a higher proportion of non-standard forms, and women who belong to dense, multiplex networks.

5.4 Women and vernacular speech

The sociolinguistic studies described in Chapters 4 and 5 found that, in Norwich, Glasgow, West Wirral and Ballymacarrett in Belfast, men consistently used more non-standard speech. Using the social network approach, Milroy and Cheshire concluded that dense multiplex social networks have the capacity to sustain vernacular norms and that it is working-class *male* speakers who typically belong to such networks. However, such patterns are not immutable, nor are they found in all communities – Eckert's research on adolescent speakers in Detroit found female, not male, speakers at both ends of the standard-non-standard continuum (see section 4.3.5). The two examples to be described in this section demonstrate that in some communities it is women who are closer to the vernacular.

As we saw in section 5.1.1, recession and growing male unemployment in parts of Belfast are coinciding with new patterns of interaction and employment for women. The Clonard community in Belfast shows that, where men lose their interaction patterns and women live as neighbours and work and amuse themselves together, then it is *women* who display consistent usage of vernacular forms.[2] The young Clonard women have the highest Network Strength Score of any sub-group studied by Milroy. The strength of their network ties is reflected in the homogeneity of their linguistic forms. In other words, the tight-knit network to which they belong acts as a powerful norm-enforcing mechanism.

The second example comes from Wales. Beth Thomas (1989) studied the East Glamorgan dialect of Welsh in the small community of Pont-rhyd-y-fen and discovered that only older *women* retained the local vernacular variant [ɛː]. The social networks of both men and women of the older generation in Pont-rhyd-y-fen are dense, multiplex and localised, but those of the women are even more community-based than those of the men. Their lives revolve around the home, the immediate neighbourhood and the chapel. Use of the [ɛː] variant is confined to those women who have networks based on the two chapels at the eastern end of the village.

Thomas's study shows that the fact that women have a traditional domestic role does not necessarily correlate with weaker networks and more standard pronunciation. Her findings indicate how important it is to examine the conditions of people's lives at a very local level. While employment opportunities were crucial factors in the formation of social networks in Belfast, involvement in the chapel was crucial in shaping interaction patterns in Pont-rhyd-y-fen.

It is one of the strengths of the social network approach that it is sensitive to both individual and small group differences. Sociolinguistic work using the social network approach provides us with valuable insights into why individual speakers use vernacular forms with greater or less consistency. At the same time, the approach helps us to understand linguistic differences between male and female speakers.

Notes

1 The Belfast material is based on Milroy and Milroy (1978) and Milroy (1980, 1982). The Reading material comes from Cheshire (1978, 1982, 1998).

2 It should be noted that the Clonard young women's use of other variables was in line with 'normal' female usage, but Lesley Milroy points out that (a) is a particularly important variable in Belfast and is currently undergoing change (see section 10.3.3).

CHAPTER 6

Gender differences in conversational practice

6.1 The concept of communicative competence

So far I have used the term *language* in the narrow sense of grammar and phonology, the formal structure of language. The gender differences in language described in Chapters 4 and 5 were differences in women's and men's syntax, morphology and pronunciation. This focus on linguistic form, with the sentence as the highest unit of structure, was established in linguistics and has been carried over into sociolinguistics: there are many sociolinguists who consider studies of social variation in grammar and phonology to be 'sociolinguistics proper'. It is becoming more and more apparent, however, that this view of language is far too narrow. The sociolinguist has to deal with real language data from a wide variety of situations; you will know if you have ever studied conversational interaction that you cannot deal adequately with it if you restrict yourself to sentence grammar.

In response to the growing awareness that the study of language should be more than the study of grammar and phonology, new disciplines have emerged such as discourse analysis and pragmatics, while others, such as ethnomethodology, conversation analysis (CA) and speech act theory, have experienced a revival of interest. The concept which marks the beginning of this revival of interest in language in its broadest sense is **communicative competence**. The term was first used by Dell Hymes (1972). He argued that it was essential to incorporate social and cultural factors into linguistic description. In his view, the Chomskyan notion of the child internalising a set of rules which enable her or him to produce grammatical sentences doesn't go far enough: the child learns not just grammar but also a sense of **appropriateness**. It is not sufficient for the child to be linguistically competent; in order to function in the real world, she or he must also learn when to speak, when to remain silent, what to talk about – and how to talk about it – in different circumstances. Imagine someone who speaks at the same time as others, who doesn't respond to questions, who looks away when addressed, who stands embarrassingly close to others, who doesn't laugh when someone tells a joke, etc. Such a person might use well-formed sentences, but we would all recognise that she or he was *incompetent* in an important sense. It is this knowledge of how language is used in a given society which constitutes communicative competence.

6.2 The communicative competence of women and men

In this chapter I shall look at ways in which women and men seem to differ in terms of their communicative competence. Our knowledge as members of a speech community of how to pay a compliment or how to apologise is part of our communicative competence, but the research evidence suggests that women and men develop differentiated communicative competence: in other words, women's and men's behaviour in conversation suggests that they have a different understanding of how a compliment or an apology is done. Such differences have led some researchers to talk of different female and male 'styles' in conversation (e.g. Maltz and Borker 1982). (The notion of gender-differentiated conversational styles will be explored further in Chapter 8.)

Gender differences in communicative competence are part of folk knowledge (as we saw in Chapter 2). In Britain, for example, we all grow up to believe that women talk more than men, that women 'gossip', that men swear more than women, that women are more polite, and so on. Research in this area often directly challenges cultural stereotypes, since much of the folklore associated with male/female differences turns out to be false.

The main section in this chapter will focus on gender differences in communicative competence, presenting evidence from a range of studies where male and female speakers differ in their use of particular conversational strategies. I will then look at language choice in bilingual communities, at gossip and whether or not it is a gendered activity, and at politeness and its linguistic correlates. The chapter will end with an examination of the question, 'Is women's language really powerless language?'

6.3 Gender and conversational strategies

This section will explore the way in which women and men characteristically draw on different strategies in conversational interaction. I shall concentrate on the following aspects of conversational practice: minimal responses, hedges, tag questions, questions, commands and directives, swearing and taboo language, and compliments.

Minimal responses

Minimal responses – sometimes called 'back-channels' – are forms such as *yeah* or *right* or *mhm*. The following extract illustrates the way they are used by listeners in conversation (listener's responses in brackets):

(1) and this put her into a bit of a flap (*mhm*) so before she could do anything about this she had to pull forwards (*mhm*) in order to er to open the gates so she took the car out of reverse, put it into first gear (*yeah*) and pulled forward very gently (*yeah*).
(Crystal and Davy 1975: 44)

Research on the use of minimal responses is unanimous in showing that women use them more than men, and at appropriate moments, that is, at points in conversation which indicate the listener's support for the current speaker (Strodtbeck and Mann 1956; Hirschmann 1974; Zimmerman and West 1975; Fishman 1980a; Coates 1989a, 1991, 1994; Holmes 1995). Holmes (1995: 55) asks rhetorically whether minimal responses are 'a female speciality'. She gives the following example, from a conversation where two women are talking about a good teacher. Lyn's use of minimal responses throughout this extract illustrates women's sensitive use of minimal responses in talk. Notice how skilfully placed the minimal responses are – not overlapping what Tina is saying, nor interrupting the flow of Tina's talk. [This example is transcribed using stave notation, like a musical score. The contributions of Tina and Lyn can then be seen in relation to each other.]

(2) *Tina:* she provided the appropriate sayings for
    Lyn:

    Tina: particular times   and and so on
    Lyn: right   right

    Tina: she didn't actually TEACH them but
    Lyn:

    Tina: she just   provided a model
    Lyn: provided a model

    Tina: you know you- you must refer to this
    Lyn: yeah mhm   mhm

    Tina: and this   and she actually produced a book
    Lyn: mhm mhm

    Tina: that set out some of these ideas at the very
    Lyn: mhm

    Tina: simplest level
    Lyn: yeah
    (from Holmes 1995: 55)

This extract comes from same-sex conversation. In *mixed* interaction, Fishman (1980b) describes women's skilful use of minimal responses as 'interactional

WOMEN, MEN AND LANGUAGE

shitwork'. She concludes that there is a division of labour in conversation which supports men and women in positions of power and powerlessness respectively. As we will see in the next chapter (section 7.3), when men *do* use minimal responses, these are often delayed, a tactic which undermines the current speaker and reinforces male dominance.

Hedges

Women's speech is often described as 'tentative', and this assertion is linked to the claim that women use more **hedges**. Hedges are linguistic forms such as *I think*, *I'm sure*, *you know*, *sort of* and *perhaps* which express the speaker's certainty or uncertainty about the proposition under discussion. A recent newcomer to the class of hedges is the word *like*, which is used by younger speakers all over the English-speaking world to mitigate the force of utterances (see, for example, Underhill 1988; Andersen 1997; Irwin 2002). Robin Lakoff explicitly linked women's use of hedges with unassertiveness. She claimed that women's speech contains more hedges (a claim based on no empirical evidence), and argued that this is because women 'are socialised to believe that asserting themselves strongly isn't nice or ladylike, or even feminine' (Lakoff 1975: 54).

Surprisingly few researchers have carried out empirical work designed to investigate Lakoff's claims. The few studies there have shown that in some situations women *do* use more hedges, but suggest that we need to be sensitive to the different *functions* of hedges, and also need to query the (androcentric) assumption that more frequent use of hedges is a weakness.

One relatively straightforward piece of research focusing on the expression of tentativeness was carried out by Bent Preisler (1986). He recorded groups of four people (some single-sex, some mixed) discussing controversial subjects such as violence on television or corporal punishment for children. His sample consisted of women and men from two different age groups (20–25 and 45–50) and from three occupational groups. All the informants lived and worked in Lancaster (northern England). His analysis showed that the women in his sample used significantly more hedges than the men.

Janet Holmes's analysis (based on a corpus consisting of equal amounts of male and female speech) is more delicate than Preisler's, because she distinguishes between the different functions served by hedges (Holmes 1984, 1987). Instances of *you know* in her data, for example, are categorised into two broad groups: one where *you know* expresses the speaker's confidence or certainty, as in the following example (examples from Holmes 1987):

(3) and that way we'd get rid of exploitation of man by man all that stuff/
     you knòw/ you've heard it before
     [*radio interviewee describing past experience*]

and one where *you know* expresses uncertainty of various kinds (note the rising intonation here):

(4)   and it was quite// well it was it was all very embarrassing *you knów*
       [*young women to close friend*]

Table 6.1 summarises the distribution of these two different functions in
women's and men's speech.

Table 6.1: Distribution of *you know* by function and speaker's gender (Holmes 1987: 64)

Function of *you know*	Female	Male
Expressing confidence	56	37 (p = 0.05)
Expressing uncertainty	33	50
Totals	89	87

This table shows that the women recorded by Holmes use *you know* more
frequently than men when it expresses confidence, but less frequently when it
expresses uncertainty. Holmes's sensitive analysis demonstrates that hedges are
multifunctional, and that any analysis of gender differences needs to allow for
this. Moreover, her findings challenge Lakoff's blanket assertion that women
use more hedges than men, as well as Lakoff's claim that women's use of
hedges is related to lack of confidence, since female speakers used *you know*
more in its confident sense.

Research focusing on adolescent speakers claims that young people use *like* as
a hedging device 'to partially detach themselves from the force of utterances
that could be considered evaluative, either positively evaluative of self or negatively evaluative of others' (Irwin 2002: 171). The following example shows
how Anna uses *like* to avoid boasting:

(5)   [*Context: Anna, Cassie, Emma and Jill talking during a break at their drama
       group*]
       Anna: Josephine used to come here and I was her *like* really good
                 friends with her she was *like* my best friend [italics added]

She uses *like* to hedge her potentially boastful claim to have been 'really good
friends' with Josephine and that Josephine was her 'best friend'. By contrast,
when she talks about neutral facts, she does not use *like*, as example (6) shows
(this example follows straight on from the previous one):

(6)   *Anna*:   so I decided to come [to drama group] one day and it was quite
                 good

Compare this with the possible utterance 'so I decided to like come one day
and it was like quite good'. Cassie in the next example uses *like* and *kind of* to
hedge her remarks which deal with the clearly controversial topic of going out
with a much older boy:

(7)   [Context: Cassie talking to Lana about boyfriends and parents]

    Cassie: if it's one of those boys who kind of *like* you meet somewhere
                and you're kind of going out with them and they're *like* (.)
                they're *like* twenty-one or something [italics added]

Note how Cassie repeats *like* in the final clause here – *and they're like (.) they're like twenty-one or something.* This repetition seems to mark even more clearly that she wants to distance herself from what she is saying. Irwin, like other researchers, notes that *like* is more frequently used by girls than by boys, and more by middle-class girls than by working-class girls.

A possible reason for male speakers' apparently lower usage of hedges is their choice of topics: unlike female speakers, male speakers on the whole avoid sensitive topics. They only rarely self-disclose and prefer to talk about impersonal subjects (see section 8.2.2 for further discussion). When sensitive topics are under discussion, then hedges become a valuable resource for speakers, because they mitigate the force of what is said and thus protect both speaker's and hearer's face.

Tag questions

Lakoff (1975) nominated the tag question as one of the linguistic forms associated with tentativeness, but provided no empirical evidence to show that women use more tag questions than men. According to Lakoff, tag questions decrease the strength of assertions. Compare the two sentences below:

(8a)   The crisis in the Middle East is terrible.

(8b)   The crisis in the Middle East is terrible, isn't it?

Lakoff claims that women use sentences like (8b), which contains the tag question *isn't it*, more often than men, who are supposed to favour (8a).

Siegler and Siegler (1976) presented students with sixteen sentences, four of which were assertions with tag questions like (8b) above. The students were told that the sentences came from conversations between college students, and for each sentence were asked to guess whether a woman or a man produced it originally. The results of this test supported Lakoff's hypothesis: sentences with tag questions were most often attributed to women, while strong assertions, like (8a), were most often attributed to men (the difference in attributions was statistically significant). This, however, only confirms what speakers' *attitudes* are; it doesn't prove that women actually use more tag questions.

While several studies have confirmed that English speakers *assume* a connection between tag questions and female linguistic usage (see O'Barr and Atkins 1980; Jones 1980, to be discussed in sections 6.7 and 8.1 respectively), one of the rare studies which set out to test this assumption empirically found it unproven. Dubois and Crouch (1975) used as their data the discussion sessions following various formal papers given at a day conference. They listed all examples of formal tag questions (such as 'Probably industrial too, isn't it?') as well as 'informal' tags (such as 'Right?', 'OK?' as in 'That's not too easy, right?'). A total of thirty-three tag questions was recorded (seventeen formal and sixteen informal) and these were *all* produced by men. By contrast, Preisler's (1986) research reveals that tag questions, in *combination with* other linguistic forms (e.g. certain modals and other stressed auxiliaries), are used significantly more by women than by men.

All this work is based on the questionable assumption that there is a one-to-one relationship between linguistic form (tag question) and extra-linguistic factor (tentativeness). Refreshingly, Holmes (1984) analyses tags according to whether they express primarily **modal** or **affective** meaning. Tags with primarily **modal** meaning signal the speaker's degree of certainty about the proposition expressed:

(9)   She's coming around noon isn't she?
      (Husband to wife concerning expected guest)

Such tags can be described as **speaker-oriented** since they ask the addressee to confirm the speaker's proposition. Tags whose primary function is **affective** express the speaker's attitude to the addressee (and are therefore **addressee-oriented**). They do this either by supporting the addressee (facilitative tags):

(10)   The hen's brown isn't she?
       (Teacher to pupil)

or by softening the force of negatively affective speech acts:

(11)   That was pretty silly wasn't it?
       (Older child to younger friend)

Table 6.2 shows the overall distribution of tags in a 60,000-word corpus consisting of equal amounts of female and male speech in matched contexts.

Table 6.2: Distribution of tag questions according to speaker's gender and function of tag in discourse (based on Holmes 1984: 54)

	No. of tag questions	
Type of meaning	Female	Male
Modal meaning		
Expressing uncertainty	18	24
	(35%)	(61%)
Affective meaning		
Facilitative	30	10
	(59%)	(25%)
Softening	3	5
	(6%)	(13%)
Total	51	39

Women and men do not differ greatly in total usage (but note that women do turn out to use more tags). However, the important point to notice is that 59 per cent of the tags used by women are facilitative (compared with 25 per cent for men) while 61 per cent of the tags used by men are modal, expressing uncertainty (compared with 35 per cent for women).

When the relationship between the participants in the interaction is taken into account, it emerges that **facilitators** are more likely to use tags than non-facilitators (Holmes uses the term *facilitator* to refer to those responsible for ensuring that interaction proceeds smoothly, for example, interviewers on radio and television, discussion group leaders, teachers, hosts). Moreover, women are more likely than men to use tags when acting as facilitators. The significance of Holmes's findings will be taken up in the discussion of women and politeness (section 6.6) and of women and powerless language (section 6.7).

Cameron, McAlinden and O'Leary's (1989) study of tag questions supports Holmes's findings. They looked at gender differences in tag usage in both symmetrical and asymmetrical discourse. In asymmetrical discourse (i.e. in discourse where participants are not equal in status), the striking finding was that powerless participants *never* used affective tags. Table 6.3 gives the details.

Table 6.3: Tag questions in unequal encounters (Cameron, McAlinden and O'Leary 1989: 89)

	Women		Men	
	Powerful	Powerless	Powerful	Powerless
Modal	3	9	10	16
	(5%)	(15%)	(18%)	(29%)
Affective				
Facilitative	43	0	25	0
	(70%)	–	(45%)	–
Softeners	6	0	4	0
	(10%)	–	(7%)	–
Total		61		55

It seems that affective tags are associated with *powerful* speakers, a finding which challenges Lakoff's assumption that tags are intrinsically weak. This finding will be discussed further in the following section on questions.

Questions

Fishman (1980a) analysed her transcripts of couples in conversation for questions as well as for *you know*. She looked at yes/no questions such as 'Did you see Sarah last night?' as well as at tag questions. The women in her sample used three times as many tag and yes/no questions as the men (87:29). During the 12.5 hours of conversation transcribed, a total of 370 questions was asked, of which women asked 263 (2.5 times as many as the men). A survey of the linguistic behaviour of people buying a ticket at Central Station in Amsterdam also established that women ask more questions than men, especially when addressing a *male* ticket-seller (Brouwer et al. 1979). Why should this be so? Are men seen as repositories of knowledge and women as ignorant? Perhaps women feel less inhibited about asking for information, since this does not conflict with the gender-role prescribed by society. Fishman prefers to explain women's question-asking in linguistic terms. Questions are part of the conversational sequencing device Question + Answer. Questions and answers are linked together in conversation: questions demand a response from the addressee. In interactive terms, then, questions are stronger than statements, since they give the speaker the power to elicit a response. In the following extract (taken from Harold Pinter's *The Birthday Party* (1960)) note how Petey is forced to participate in conversation by Meg's use of questions:

(12)   (*Meg gives Petey a bowl of cornflakes. He sits at the table, props up his paper and starts to eat*)

   Meg: Are they nice?

   Petey: Very nice.

   Meg: I thought they'd be nice. You got your paper?

   Petey: Yes.

   Meg: Is it good?

   Petey: Not bad.

   Meg: What does it say?

   Petey: Nothing much.

Research findings so far suggest that women use interrogative forms more than men and that this may reflect women's relative weakness in interactive situations: they exploit questions and tag questions in order to keep conversation going.

However, as Cameron et al.'s (1989) research on tag questions demonstrates, some kinds of question are associated with *powerful* speakers. Sandra Harris, in her study of the language of magistrates' courts, established that questions are a crucial resource for powerful participants, since questions oblige the addressee both to produce an answer and to produce an answer that is conversationally relevant. In other words, questions control what the next speaker is able to say. Not only do powerful participants use many questions, but also participants *without* power are explicitly prohibited from using them in this situation:

(13) *Magistrate*: I'm putting it to you again – are you going to make an offer – wh–wh– to discharge this debt?

Defendant: Would you in my position?

Magistrate: I – I'm not here to answer questions – you answer *my* question

(Harris 1984: 5)

Research into other sorts of asymmetrical discourse, such as doctor–patient interaction (Todd 1983; West 1984; Fairclough 1992), teacher–pupil interaction (Barnes 1971; Stubbs 1983), or talk between host and callers on radio phone-ins (Barnard 2000; Thornborrow 2002) confirms this finding: questions are overwhelmingly used by more powerful participants.

In contexts where men and women are supposedly status equals but where the context has high status, men ask far more questions than women. This finding emerges in several studies: in a study of academic seminars at Durham University (Bashiruddin et al. 1990), in research analysing questions following formal presentations at conferences (Swacker 1979; Holmes 1988b), and in research analysing questions and other elicitations following public meetings (Holmes 1995). Moreover, if questions in such contexts are categorised as supportive, critical or antagonistic, analysis revealed that male and female speakers asked a similar proportion of supportive and critical questions. What varied was their use of antagonistic questions, with men challenging the presenter twice as often as women (Holmes 1995).

Thus, while it seems that in some situations women use more questions than men, in others it is men who ask more questions, while sometimes the relevant variable is occupational status not gender. If we are to make sense of the way questions are used in speech, we have to distinguish between the different functions of questions, and we have to keep symmetrical and asymmetrical discourse separate. It is certainly true that questions are powerful linguistic forms: they give the speaker the power to elicit a response from the other participant(s). This characteristic of questions is exploited by powerful participants in asymmetrical situations; it is also exploited by women speakers – relatively powerless participants in many contexts – to keep conversation going.

Commands and directives

We can define a directive as a speech act which tries to get someone to do something. Goodwin (1980, 1990, 1998) observed the group play of girls and boys in a Philadelphia street, and noticed that the boys used different sorts of directives from the girls. The boys used explicit commands:

(14) *Michael*: <u>Gimme</u> the pliers (*Poochie gives pliers to Michael*)

(15) *Huey*: <u>Get off</u> my steps (*Poochie moves down steps*)

Michael, the leader of the group, often supported his commands with statements of his own desires:

(16)   *Michael:* <u>Gimme</u> the wire . . . Look man, <u>I want</u> the wire cutters right now.

Goodwin calls examples like these 'aggravated' directives. The boys tended to choose aggravated directives and used them to establish status differences between themselves. The girls, by contrast, typically used more 'mitigated' directives such as the following:

(17)   *Terry:* Hey y'all <u>let's</u> use these first and then come back and get the rest cuz it's too many of 'em.

(18)   *Sharon:* <u>Let's</u> go around Subs and Suds.
       Pam: <u>Let's</u> ask her 'do you have any bottles?'

The form *let's* explicitly includes the speaker together with the addressee(s) in the proposed action; *let's* is hardly ever used by the boys.

The girls' use of *gonna* (as in (19) below) is another form of mitigated directive, one which makes a suggestion for future action:

(19)   *Sharon:* We <u>gonna</u> paint 'em and stuff.

The modal auxiliaries *can* and *could* are also used by the girls to suggest rather than demand action:

(20)   *Pam:* We <u>could</u> go around looking for more bottles.

(21)   *Sharon:* Hey maybe tomorrow we <u>can</u> come up here and see if they got some more.

Note the use of the adverbial *maybe* in (21) to further soften the directive.

While Goodwin demonstrates convincingly that the girls and boys use quite different linguistic means to express directives when playing in same-sex groups, she stresses that this does not mean that girls are incapable of using more forceful directives in other contexts (such as in cross-sex arguments or when taking on the role of mother while playing house). She argues that the linguistic forms used reflect and at the same time reproduce the social organisation of the group: the boys' group is hierarchically organised, with leaders using very strong directive forms to demonstrate control, while the girls' group is non-hierarchical with all girls participating in decision-making on an equal basis.

Engle's (1980) study of the language of parents when they play with their children revealed that fathers tend to give directions:

(22)   Why don't you make a chimney?

(23)   Off! Take it off!

Mothers, on the other hand, are more likely to consult the child's wishes:

(24)   Do you want to look at any of the other toys over here?

(25)   What else shall we put on the truck?

Not only were the fathers more directive than the mothers, they were also more directive with their sons than with their daughters. These linguistic differences again reflect a difference in organisation: mothers view interaction as an occasion to help children learn how to choose; fathers were less concerned with the children's desires and introduced new ideas. Differences in parents' speech to children will be taken up in Chapter 9.

Using Goodwin's definition of aggravated and mitigated directives, West (1998a) looked at the directives used by male and female doctors to their patients. Male doctors preferred to use aggravated forms, such as imperatives:

(26) (a) Lie down

(b) Take off your shoes and socks

(c) Sit for me right there

They also used statements in which they told patients what they 'needed' to do, or what they 'had to' do. Female doctors, on the other hand, preferred more mitigated forms, phrasing their directives as proposals for joint action:

(27) Okay? well let's make that our plan

(28) So let's stay on what we're doing

They also used the pronoun *we* rather than *you* in their directives:

(29) Maybe what we ought to do is, is to stay with the dose . . . you're on

When a woman doctor used the pronoun *you*, the directive was typically mitigated by the addition of modal forms such as *can* or *could*:

(30) and then maybe you can stay away from the desserts and stay away from the food in between meals

The female doctors' mitigated directives are very similar to those used by the girls in Goodwin's Philadelphia study. Just as in example (21), the addition of the adverbial *maybe* in the two examples above softens the force of the directive.

West's discovery that male and female doctors issued directives in very different ways was followed by the discovery that patients reacted differently to these different directives. If the aim of giving a directive is to get someone to do something, then the directives used by women doctors were far more successful than those used by male doctors. Male doctors' bare imperatives (e.g. *lie down!*) elicited compliant responses in 47 per cent of cases, while their statements of patients' needs elicited only 38 per cent compliant responses. As West puts it, 'the more aggravated the directive, the less likely it was to elicit a compliant response' (West 1998a: 349). Female doctors' proposals for joint action (using *let's*) elicited compliant responses in 67 per cent of cases, while suggestions for action (e.g. *you could try taking two every four hours*) had a 75 per cent success rate. Overall, the women doctors used far fewer aggravated directives than the male doctors, and their overall rate of compliant responses was 67 per cent, compared with the male doctors' 50 per cent.

Swearing and taboo language

As we saw in Chapter 2, the folklinguistic belief that men swear more than women and use more taboo words is widespread. Jespersen (1922) claimed (see section 2.3) that women have an 'instinctive shrinking from coarse and gross expressions and a preference for refined and (in certain spheres) veiled and indirect expressions'. In his preface to the *Dictionary of American Slang*, Flexner claims that 'most American slang is created and used by males' (Flexner 1960: xii). Lakoff (1975) also claims that men use stronger expletives (*damn, shit*) than women (*oh dear, goodness*), but her evidence is purely impressionistic.

Kramer (1974) analysed cartoons from the *New Yorker*. She found that cartoonists make their male characters swear much more freely than the female characters. She asked students to identify captions taken from the cartoons as male or female. For most of the captions there was a clear consensus (at least 66 per cent agreement) on the gender of the speaker, and the students commented explicitly on the way in which swearing distinguished male speech from female speech. A second study (Kramer 1975) used cartoons from four different magazines (*New Yorker, Playboy, Cosmopolitan, Ladies Home Journal*). Students correctly identified the gender of the speaker in 79 per cent of cases. Analysis of the captions showed that, among other things, women used fewer swear words. Both these studies confirm the existence of a cultural stereotype but provide no evidence as to whether or not men actually *do* swear more than women.

More recent sociolinguistic research is beginning to give us a clearer picture of the relationship between gender and swearing. Gomm (1981) recorded fourteen conversations between young British speakers: the participants were all female in five of these, all male in five, and mixed in four. An analysis of the transcripts of these conversations reveals no qualitative difference in the use of swear words, but Table 6.4 shows the difference in frequency between male and female usage. Clearly, the male speakers in Gomm's sample swear more often than the female speakers. Moreover, both women and men swear more in the company of their own sex; male usage of swear words in particular drops dramatically in mixed-sex conversations.

Table 6.4: Incidence of swearing in single-sex and mixed groups (based on Gomm 1981)

	Single-sex groups	Mixed groups	Total
Men	21	4	25
Women	7	2	9

Gomm's findings are supported by a small-scale study reported in Hudson (1992) and also by my own research on conversational narrative (Coates 2003). When men and women tell stories as part of everyday interaction, there are notable differences in their use of taboo language: the stories told in all-male groups contain a great deal of taboo language while the stories told by women to other women contain virtually none (a grand total of ten tokens of *bloody*, no examples at all of *fuck* or other 'four-letter words'). In mixed contexts, however, male and female speakers seem to accommodate to the perceived norms of the other gender: the narratives produced by male speakers in a mixed context contain far less taboo language than in a single-sex context, while the narratives produced by female speakers in a mixed setting contain far more.

Jenny Cheshire, in her research on adolescent talk in Reading, selected swearing as one of the measures to be included in her Vernacular Culture Index (see section 5.1.2), since 'this was a major symbol of vernacular identity for both boys and girls' (Cheshire 1982: 101). This index was applied only to the boys in her sample (since the girls were said not to have a clearly defined system of cultural values) and there is therefore no comparative data. But Cheshire's claim that swearing has symbolic value for this age group is confirmed by later research on adolescent speech. Young people, particularly those from working-class backgrounds, aim to be 'cool', and coolness includes the use of taboo language. Girls from these backgrounds also aim to subvert traditional gender roles (see, for example, Eder 1993; Eckert and McConnell-Ginet 1995; Pichler 2003, in press), which means that they adopt linguistic strategies traditionally associated with male speakers.

In research on adult conversational practice, there is evidence that female speakers are familiar with – and increasingly ready to use – a wide range of taboo words (De Klerk 1992). Moreover, research which moves the focus to *working-class* women in a deprived inner-city area (Hughes 1992) establishes that such speakers make frequent use of taboo language. As one of Hughes's informants said: 'It's not swearing to us, it's part of our everyday talking.'

So the stereotypes of the tough-talking male and the pure, never-swearing female are false. However, it does seem to be true that swearing is an integral part of contemporary masculinity: 'expletives . . . have become associated with power and masculinity in Western culture' (De Klerk 1997: 147), with the result that using taboo language has a symbolic association with masculinity, not femininity. Intriguing proof of this claim comes from Rusty Barrett's (1999) work on the language of African American drag queens. These are (male) performers who have to produce a convincing feminine speech style while *at the same time* signalling to their audience in some way that the performance is 'false', that they are in fact male. One of the ways they do this is through using taboo language.

Compliments

Research in New Zealand, the United States and Britain suggests that women both give and receive more compliments than men. Holmes (1988a) analysed a corpus of 484 compliment exchanges in New Zealand, and established that 51 per cent of these (248) were given by a woman to another woman, while only 9 per cent (44) were given by a man to another man; 23.1 per cent were given by a man to a woman, and 16.5 per cent by a woman to a man. This pattern has also been found in comparable American data (Wolfson 1983; Herbert 1998) and in comparable British data (Baptiste 1990).[1]

As Holmes (1995: 127) points out: 'Compliments are remarkably formulaic speech acts. Most draw on . . . a very narrow range of syntactic patterns'. Women and men in Holmes's data use these patterns with similar frequency, apart from 'What (a) ADJ NP!'[2] (e.g. *what lovely earrings!*) which is used much more by women, and the minimal pattern (e.g. *Great shoes!*) which men use significantly more than women. Herbert (1998) also found very high frequency of the 'I really like/love NP' in women's usage, which he explains in part by the sample being skewed to younger rather than older speakers who are native to the USA (where the use of 'I love NP' seems to be more common than in Britain or New Zealand).

Compliments can be analysed in terms of personal focus (Herbert 1998: 56):

1st person focus:	*I like your hair that way*
2nd person focus:	*your hair looks good short*
3rd person focus: [= impersonal]	*nice haircut!*

Herbert found that women preferred more personalised forms (compliments with first or second person focus) while men preferred impersonal (third person) forms. Approximately 60 per cent (290 out of 486) of the male-offered compliments in his corpus were impersonal expressions versus 20 per cent of the female compliments (114 of 576).

The compliments given by women to other women differ both in tone and topic from those given by men to other men. For women in the company of other women, giving and receiving compliments is unremarkable, an everyday occurrence. Women tend to compliment each other on appearance:[3]

(31) [*in college*]
     Hi, Joanna, you look nice – your eye make-up is brilliant

(32) [*in the office*]
     you've got such lovely eyes

Men, by contrast, prefer to compliment each other on possessions or skill:

(33) [*on top deck of bus, South London*]
     Rasclat, man, your boots are wicked, know what I mean?

(34) [*in pub*]
     you're very quick with witty one-liners – I would imagine you must have a very high IQ

Men tend to avoid complimenting each other on appearance. As David Britain comments: 'To compliment another man on his hair, his clothes or his body is an *extremely* face-threatening thing to do, both for speaker and hearer. It has to be very carefully done in order not to send out the wrong signals' (Britain, personal communication, quoted in Holmes 1995: 133), that is, to avoid being seen as gay.

Cross-sex compliments can also be problematic, as the following examples illustrate. In example (35), the man's 'compliment' amounts to sexual harassment:

(35)   [in office]
       you look so sexy today, Faye – I must remember to have a cuddle with you later

Example (36), on the other hand, illustrates male uneasiness with a compliment from a woman:

(36)   [in pub]
       Woman: the thing I really like about you and the thing that makes our relationship into a special kind of friendship above all else is that you're always prepared to listen

       Man: pardon? (sarcastic)

In some situations, compliments seem to function as **positive** politeness strategies, that is, they attend to the positive face needs of the addressee. As examples (31) and (32) illustrate, women tend to use compliments as signals of positive politeness. In other situations, however, as illustrated in example (35), compliments can be face-threatening, because they ignore the **negative** face-needs of the addressee. (See section 6.6 for further discussion of the role of face.) Cross-sex compliments are clearly more face-threatening than same-sex compliments, and compliments seem to be more face-threatening to men than to women.

Among English speakers, it is generally agreed that the polite thing to do is to accept a compliment. In practice, however, as the last two examples illustrate, compliments are not always accepted. Pomerantz (1978) argues that this is because compliments place addressees in a difficult position: they have to juggle two conflicting conversational rules: 'Agree with the speaker' and 'Avoid self-praise'. Herbert's (1998) analysis of 1,062 compliments and compliment responses found that only about one-third of responses could be categorised as acceptances. And sometimes acceptances indicated that the addressee was uncomfortable:

(37)   Male 1: nice tie

       Male 2: [look of dismay; checks tie] thankyou

(Herbert 1998: 62)

Where speakers are status equals, responses which are not acceptances are common and include examples like *I bought it for my holiday in France* or *it really knitted itself* or *it's really quite old*. In effect, such responses say, 'I recognise that your compliment was intended to make me feel good; I choose to avoid self-praise and thus assert that we are equal'. However, a surprising finding of Herbert's analysis is that, overall, compliments given by female speakers tended not to be accepted, whereas compliments given by male speakers, particularly to females, tended to be accepted. This suggests that, all other things being equal, women and men are not seen as status-equals. Where two people are not status-equals, then the expected pattern is that the person with higher status pays the compliments, while the lower status participant accepts such compliments. Such an interpretation would explain Holmes's (1988a) finding that higher-status females were almost twice as likely to be complimented as higher-status males. In other words, such women, *because* they are women, end up on the compliment-accepting rather than the compliment-giving side of the equation. Their apparent 'high status' is worth less than that of their male 'peers'.

6.4 Language choice

I shall now look at a very different aspect of communicative competence: our competence in switching between different languages and the links between language choice and gender. When speakers are bi- or multilingual, then language choice can have a key role in the construction of gendered identities. A good example of this is given by Joan Pujolar, in his investigation of language choice in post-Franco Catalonia (Pujolar 1997). During General Franco's dictatorship (1939–75), the use of Catalan was forbidden. But since Franco's death, Catalan has been re-introduced into schools as a medium of instruction. Pujolar observed that young men (aged 17–23) living in working-class districts of Barcelona made choices about Spanish or Catalan which were crucially linked to their sense of themselves as particular kinds of men. For some of them, Spanish monolingualism represented authentic masculinity, to the extent that they did not speak Catalan and claimed to hate it. Catalan, according to Pujolar, 'was constructed as conveying unspontaneous, inauthentic or "unmasculine" voices' (1997: 103) – these connotations were in conflict with the way the men wanted to present themselves. But another, more politicised group, was making the effort to challenge these connotations. They chose to speak Catalan as well as Spanish, in part to signal their support for Catalonia's self-determination, though they tried to avoid the highly standardised form of Catalan taught in school. This research demonstrates how powerfully language and gender can be entwined: for some of these men, bilingualism itself was seen as effeminate.

Susan Gal (1979, 1998) investigated language shift in the bilingual town of Oberwart, in eastern Austria, which until 1921 was part of Hungary. In this community a shift is occurring from German-Hungarian bilingualism to the exclusive use of German. Since the Second World War, there has been a change in the connotations of the two languages. Hungarian, the national language until 1921, used to have great prestige as the language of intellectuals and the upper classes, while German used to be a language of outsiders, associated with merchants, bureaucrats, and people from other villages. Now, Hungarian is increasingly associated with peasant status, while knowledge of German is an economic necessity for anyone wanting employment of any kind apart from

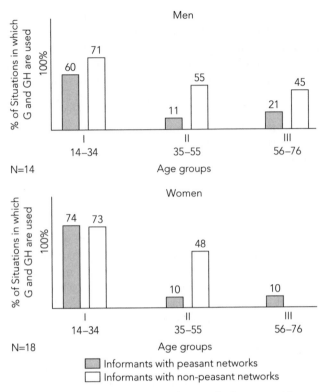

Figure 6.1 Percentage of G and GH language choices of informants with peasant and non-peasant social networks in three age groups (Gal 1998: 155)

working on the land. (Since the war, the proportion of adult males working in full-time agriculture has dropped from 100 per cent to 19 per cent.)

Gal carried out a survey to establish patterns of linguistic usage. For example, she asked people which language they would use at the doctor's, in the post office, at work, with their friends, with their brothers and sisters, with their grandparents. She established that the shift from Hungarian to German is being led by the young *women*. Figure 6.1 gives the results of her survey (answers were coded G for German, H for Hungarian, and GH for where people said they could use either language). This figure shows that for men there is a regular pattern: use of G increases as the sample gets younger, but in all three age groups, speakers with peasant networks use more H than speakers with non-peasant networks. For women, the pattern is different. In the older group, there are no women with non-peasant networks, a reflection of women's limited lives before 1945. The middle group of women gives responses which match those of the men; those with peasant networks prefer Hungarian, while those with non-peasant networks increasingly choose German. The youngest

Table 6.5: Endogamous* marriages of all bilingual Oberwarters and bilingual male peasant Oberwarters (Gal 1998: 157)

	Endogamous* marriages of all marriages (%)	Endogamous* marriages of male peasants (%)
1911–40	71	87
1941–60	65	54
1961–72	32	0

Source: Marriage Register, City of Oberwart.
*Endogamy means marriage within the tribe.

group of women is unlike all other groups: first, they use more German and less Hungarian than any other group; secondly, their language choice is not influenced by whether or not they belong to peasant networks.

How do we explain this pattern? Gal argues that the young women's rejection of Hungarian represents a rejection of peasant life. They have observed the lives of their mothers and grandmothers: they have seen that the life of a peasant wife is hard. So they are consciously choosing *not* to marry peasant men (see the revealing zero at the bottom of the last column in Table 6.5), and this choice is reflected in their choice of language. Ironically, this means that young peasant men have been forced to marry women from other towns and villages, and these women are frequently monolingual German speakers. So the Oberwart women's rejection of peasant life has both a direct *and* an indirect impact on the shift from Hungarian to German.

6.5 Gossip

The speech activity commonly labelled 'gossip' has been subject to re-evaluation by sociolinguists in recent years. It is conventionally accepted that gossiping is something that women do. In everyday talk, 'gossip' is a term used almost exclusively of women's talk and it is a term which usually has pejorative connotations ('idle talk . . . tittle-tattle', *Concise Oxford Dictionary*). In 1980, Deborah Jones published a paper which looked at the kind of talk normally labelled 'gossip' from a non-androcentric perspective. In other words, she used the term 'gossip' in a *positive* sense. She accepted it as a term describing women's talk, but redefined it in a non-pejorative way as 'a way of talking between women in their roles as women, intimate in style, personal and domestic in topic and setting' (Jones 1980: 194). Using a term such as *gossip* (rather than 'all-female talk', for example) draws attention to the fact that the language women use when talking to each other has not traditionally been treated as serious linguistic data. By contrast, men's talk is seen as 'real' talk and has always been taken seriously.

Jones's use of the term *gossip* was not original: it is used in anthropological work to refer to informal communication between members of a social group. Anthropologists stress, among other things, the social function of gossip – it maintains 'the unity, morals and values of social groups' (Gluckman, as quoted in Jones 1980: 194). This is clearly an important function. According to Emler (2001, forthcoming), gossip is, perhaps, *the* basic process in the social psychology of everyday life, since gossip 'provides people with information essential to their capacity to cope with their social worlds, to solve the various problems they face, and to deal with the people around them' (Emler forthcoming). Robin Dunbar, a biological anthropologist, has published a provocative book entitled *Gossip, Grooming and the Evolution of Language* (1996), in which he argues that gossip has evolved to replace physical grooming among apes, and that it is vital in terms of maintaining the cohesiveness of the social group.

It is clear that anthropological researchers see gossip as a process vital to everyday life and not restricted to women. Sociolinguists, too, are beginning to explore the notion of gossip as a more general phenomenon. Sally Johnson and Frank Finlay explicitly ask the question 'Do men gossip?' in the title of their (1997) paper on the subject. While they do not deny that gossip is an intrinsic part of the female subculture, they argue that men also participate in gossip. 'The main difference is that the seemingly casual, superficial talk of men is rarely defined as such' (Johnson and Finlay 1997: 131). They focus on men's talk about football, making the following claim: 'If female gossip is a way of talking which solidifies relationships between women, then talking about football would appear to serve a very similar purpose for men' (1997: 137).

Deborah Cameron (1997) suggests that 'sportstalk' is a typically masculine conversational genre. She analysed the conversation of a group of male students to show how gender is performed through talk (see section 8.3 for a discussion of performativity). The group was recorded while they watched sport on television (one of their commonest shared activities): their comments on the basketball game they are watching are an intrinsic part of their gossiping. They also gossip about non-present others: they discuss in great detail certain males of their acquaintance, accusing them of being gay. This talk constructs solidarity: the five friends are bonded by their shared denigration of the supposedly gay outsiders. Interestingly, Cameron shows how the men's gossip involves several features normally associated with 'cooperative' women's talk – hedges, overlapping speech, latching. But it also displays more competitive features – two speakers dominate the talk, and speakers vie for the floor.

What emerges from this research is that there are aspects of men's talk which can be labelled 'gossip', but there are differences. First, certain elements of competition enter into all-male talk, alongside cooperative elements (the issue of competition and cooperation will be pursued in 8.2). Secondly, whereas personal experience is at the heart of women's gossip, men's sportstalk seems to function in part to marginalise such experience: interest in other's lives and experience is displaced into a 'reified world located firmly within the public sphere' (Johnson and Finlay 1997: 142).

6.6 Politeness and language

It is part of folklinguistics, and has also been asserted by linguists, that women are more polite than men. In order to examine this claim, we need to look at what politeness is, and how it is realised linguistically in different societies.

Brown and Levinson (1978, 1987) define politeness in terms of the concept of face. The term *face* is used as in everyday phrases such as *to lose face*. Respecting face is defined as showing consideration for people's feelings. We show consideration by respecting two basic human needs: (1) the need not to be imposed on (this is called **negative face**); and (2) the need to be liked and admired (this is called **positive face**). In British society, we try to satisfy the negative face wants of others by, for example, accompanying requests with apologies for the imposition: 'I'm awfully sorry to bother you but I've run out of milk – could you possibly lend me half a pint?' A request phrased like this makes it possible for the addressee to say no without appearing rude, that is, without losing face. We try to satisfy the positive face wants of others by greeting them when we see them, asking them how they are, expressing admiration and approval for what they've been doing and for what they feel about things: 'You're looking marvellous!'; 'I know exactly how you feel'. To ask for something baldly, for example, 'Give me some milk', or to ignore someone we know in any social setting, is to act impolitely in our culture. Politeness, then, can be defined as satisfying the face wants of others (while protecting our own), and linguistically this can be carried out in many different ways.

A good example of cross-cultural research testing the hypothesis that women are more polite than men is Brown's (1998) study of the language of women and men in a Mayan community in Mexico. She argues that the level of politeness appropriate to a given interaction will depend on the social relationship of the participants. This means that linguistic markers of politeness are a good indication of social relationships. If women *do* use more polite forms than men, what does this indicate? That women treat men as socially superior? That women treat men as socially distant? That women are involved in more face-threatening acts (i.e. that when women address men, their requests etc. impose on men's negative or positive face)?

In Tzeltal, the language spoken by the Mayans, there is a class of particles which operate as adverbials and modify the force of the speech act. To put it simply, they either strengthen or weaken the force of what is said. Roughly translated, speakers can either add strengtheners: *I emphatically/sincerely/really assert/request/promise* . . . or they can add weakeners: *I tentatively/maybe/perhaps assert/request/promise.* . . . In all languages, you can emphasise the force of your speech act to be positively polite, or hedge the force of your speech act to be negatively polite.

Brown tested three hypotheses: (1) women use more strengthening particles when speaking to women (i.e. pay a lot of attention to women's positive face wants); (2) women use more weakening particles when speaking to men (i.e. pay a lot of attention to men's negative face wants); (3) women speaking to women use more particles than men speaking to men. She compared the speech of male and female speakers in mixed and single-sex pairs (her data consisted of spontaneous conversation). She matched these pairs as far as possible for familiarity of participants, status of participants, and speaker's knowledge of the topic (all speakers hedge more when they know less about a topic). The analysis of particles used by members of same-sex pairs showed that Brown's third hypothesis was confirmed: women do use more particles (Table 6.6).

Table 6.6: Average number of particles for 100 speech acts in same-sex pairs (based on Brown 1998: 89)

	Strengtheners	Weakeners	Total particles
Mean for female pairs	25.2	34.1	59.3
Mean for male pairs	14.4	18.1	32.6

However, her data did not confirm her other two hypotheses, as Table 6.7 (for mixed-sex pairs) shows.

Table 6.7: Average number of particles for 100 speech acts in mixed-sex pairs (based on Brown 1998: 89)

	Strengtheners	Weakeners	Total particles
Mean for women speaking to men	35.7	24.4	60.2
Mean for men speaking to women	24.1	33.1	57.2

Tables 6.6 and 6.7 show us that the women did not use more strengthening particles when speaking to women; in fact, they used more when speaking to men (a ratio of 35.7:25.2). Nor did women use more weakening particles when speaking to men; a comparison of the two tables shows, on the contrary, that women used more weakening particles when speaking to other women (34.1:24.4). Why is this?

Brown argues that conversation between two men in her Mayan community differs in terms of topic so much from conversation between two women that the two are not strictly comparable (gender differences in topic choice will be discussed further in section 8.2.1). She emphasises, however, that on the crude measure of gross use of particles women clearly use more, and thus particle-usage in this community is a crude index of politeness. It emerges, as expected, that women are more polite than men.

It seems to me that the most interesting fact thrown up by Tables 6.6 and 6.7 is the particle usage of men talking to men. For the other three possible combinations (men to women, women to women, women to men), the averages, in terms of total particles used, are not strikingly dissimilar as Table 6.8 shows. But the men, as this table shows, use a different style with each other, a style

Table 6.8: Average usage of particles in different groupings, with male–male average emphasised

	Speaking to women	Speaking to men
Women	59.3	60.2
Men	57.2	**32.6**

Adapted from Brown, P. (1998), ed. J. Coates, p. 89. Blackwell Publishers.

characterised by low particle usage; this style differs from that used when they talk to women, or when women talk to women, or when women talk to men.

Brown examined particle usage in Tzeltal to establish the full range of expression available to the individual speaker. She came to the conclusion that the usage of women and men differs systematically. Women seem to be alert to the fact that what they are saying may threaten face. This sensitivity to the face needs of others results in different linguistic usage. Women use the extremes of positive and negative politeness; men's speech is more matter-of-fact. Moreover, certain usages – such as the women's use of the diminutive [ʔala], or the men's use of the strengthening particle [melel] in public speaking – result in recognisable 'feminine' and 'masculine' styles.

Holmes's (1995) comprehensive account of gender differences in the expression of politeness confirms Brown's findings. Holmes focused on the language of women and men in New Zealand, and overall she observes that 'women are more orientated to affective, interpersonal meanings than men' (Holmes, 1995: 193) while men are more oriented to the referential functions of talk. What concerns Holmes is 'the overt disvaluing of women's politeness norms in public spheres' (1995: 197). Holmes argues that women's politeness patterns could be a valuable asset in many public contexts, such as the workplace and the classroom. The problem lies in society's labelling of women's linguistic patterns as weak or ineffective. This is the subject of the next section.

6.7 Powerful and powerless language

Brown argues that negative politeness – where the speaker apologises for intruding, uses impersonal structures (such as passives) and hedges assertions – is found where people are in an inferior position in society. This deduction is also made by O'Barr and Atkins (1980) in their study of courtroom language. O'Barr and Atkins observed that manuals for lawyers on tactics in court often treated female witnesses as a special case. This led them to wonder if female witnesses differed *linguistically* from male witnesses. They analysed transcripts of 150 hours of trials in a North Carolina superior criminal court, looking at features which they call Women's Language or WL (and which are largely based on Lakoff 1975). These ten features are listed below.

1. Hedges, e.g. *sort of, kind of, I guess.*

2. (Super) polite forms, e.g. *would you please . . . ; I'd really appreciate it if. . . .*

3. Tag questions.

4. Speaking in italics, e.g. emphatic *so* and *very*, intonational emphasis equivalent to underlining words in written language.

5. Empty adjectives, e.g. *divine, charming, sweet, adorable.*

6. Hypercorrect grammar and pronunciation.

7. Lack of a sense of humour, e.g. poor at telling jokes.

8. Direct quotations.

9. Special vocabulary, e.g. specialised colour terms.

10. Question intonation in declarative contexts.

Each witness was given a score arrived at by dividing the total number of WL features used by the number of utterances. Scores varied from 1.39 (indicating an average of more than one WL feature per utterance) to 0.18 (indicating very infrequent use of WL features). The following is an example of speech high in WL features:

(38) *Lawyer:*   What was the nature of your acquaintance with the late Mrs. E.D.?

Witness A: Well, we were, uh, very close friends. Uh, she was even sort of like a mother to me.

This witness gained an overall score of 1.14. The following is an example of speech low in WL features:

(39) *Lawyer:*   And had the heart not been functioning, in other words, had the heart been stopped, there would have been no blood to have come from that region?

Witness C: It may leak down depending on the position of the body after death. But the presence of blood in the alveoli indicates that some active respiratory action had to take place.

Witness C gained an overall score of 0.18.

Both these examples are taken from the speech of *female* witnesses, and they show that the use of WL features (as defined by O'Barr and Atkins for this study) does not correlate with speaker's gender. They found that not only did some female witnesses use very few WL features, but also some male witnesses used a high proportion of WL features. The example below comes from the speech of witness D, a man:

(40) *Lawyer:*   And you saw, you observed what?

Witness D: Well, after I heard – I can't really, I can't definitely state whether the brakes or the lights came first, but I rotated my head slightly to the right, and looked directly behind Mr Z, and I saw reflections of lights, and uh, very, very,

> very instantaneously after that, I heard a very, very loud
> explosion – from my standpoint of view it would have been
> an implosion because everything was forced outward like
> this, like a grenade thrown into a room. And, uh, it was,
> it was terrifically loud.

Witness D's score for WL features was 1.39 – higher than that of witness A. O'Barr and Atkins' findings can be summarised as follows:

1. WL features are not characteristic of the speech of all women (see, for example, witness C).

2. WL features are not restricted to the speech of female speakers (see, for example, witness D).

3. The scores of speakers can be placed on a continuum (from high to low) – more women have high scores while more men have low scores.

O'Barr and Atkins argue that Lakoff's description of such features as 'Women's Language' is inaccurate. They show that the frequency of WL features in the speech of the witnesses in their study correlates not with gender, but with two other factors: first, with the speaker's social status; and secondly, with the speaker's previous courtroom experience. Witness C is a pathologist who often has to appear in court as an expert witness; she is a highly educated, professional woman. Her low score for WL features correlates with her high social status and her courtroom experience. Witnesses A and D, on the other hand, who both have high scores, have low social status and little courtroom experience (A is a housewife; D is an inexperienced ambulance attendant).

On the basis of this correlation, O'Barr and Atkins rename the linguistic features normally associated with women's speech as **Powerless Language**. They argue that powerless language has been confused with women's language because, in societies like ours, women are usually less powerful than men. Many women therefore typically use powerless language, according to O'Barr and Atkins, but this is the result of their position in society rather than of their gender.

O'Barr and Atkins' findings are not supported by more recent sociolinguistic work which keeps the non-linguistic variables of gender and social status apart. Both Candace West and Nicola Woods investigated whether women in powerful positions in society take on a dominant role in interaction. West (1984, 1998b) analysed doctor–patient interaction in a local clinic and discovered, among other things, that doctors regularly interrupt their patients, except when the doctor is female and the patient white and male (when it is the doctor who gets interrupted). This unexpected finding suggests that, even when a woman is in a position of power (in the role of doctor), it is her gender, not her status, which enables us to predict who interrupts whom. The finding that gender overrides status is confirmed by Woods (1989), who made recordings of three-party conversations between work colleagues of differing occupational status. In some cases, a male speaker held the 'boss' position, and in others, a female speaker was the most powerful. While occupational status did have some influence on floor-holding, it was men who dominated, whether they were boss or subordinate; being the boss did not lead to women holding the floor more than men.

O'Barr and Atkins claimed that low-status speakers with little courtroom experience used 'powerless' language. West's and Woods' studies, on the other hand, show that low-status *males* do not use powerless language but, on the contrary, try to dominate interaction through the use of powerful forms such as interruptions. These latter two studies show that, where status and gender are in conflict, as in the case of female doctors or women 'bosses', then gender seems to override status.

One of the problems with O'Barr and Atkins' work is their unquestioning acceptance of Lakoff's claims. In particular, their re-labelling of Lakoff's 'Women's Language' features as 'Powerless Language' perpetuates the myth of the intrinsic *weakness* of women's language. As we have already seen in this chapter, some of these linguistic features can be very powerful. We must avoid labelling linguistic forms in a simplistic manner as 'powerful' or 'powerless'. We must also fight against the androcentric tendency to assume that, because certain linguistic forms are characteristic of women's talk, they must inevitably be weak. As Chapter 8 should make apparent, this is far from the case.

6.8 Conclusion

In this chapter we have looked at work which reveals gender differences in conversational practice. The evidence at present suggests that women and men do pursue different interactive styles: women use more hedges and pay more compliments to other speakers, while men talk more, swear more and use aggravated directives to get things done. Women also use more linguistic forms associated with politeness. These clusters of linguistic characteristics are sometimes termed 'men's style' and 'women's style'. This terminology is disputed by O'Barr and Atkins, who claim that the linguistic features found in the speech of many women are typical of people of low status in society, both women and men, and should more accurately be called 'Powerless Language'. Subsequent studies of asymmetrical discourse, however, have shown that low-status *men* do not use powerless language, but attempt to dominate interaction.

Dominance in interaction is the focus of Chapter 7.

Notes

1   It should be noted that in all these studies female fieldworkers outnumbered male. An empirical study of compliments carried out by a male fieldworker (Bevan 1990) found a higher proportion of male–male compliments, a result which suggests that the gender of the fieldworker is a significant variable.

2   ADJ stands for adjective and NP for Noun Phrase.

3   All the examples are taken from Baptiste (1990).

CHAPTER 7

Conversational dominance in mixed talk

7.1 The concept of conversational dominance

The last chapter focused on gender differences in conversational practice. In this chapter, I shall concentrate on the way certain conversational strategies can be used to achieve dominance in talk. 'Conversational dominance' is the phrase used to refer to the phenomenon of a speaker dominating others in interaction. Research focusing on mixed talk in a variety of social contexts has revealed asymmetrical patterns, with men's greater usage of certain strategies being associated with male dominance in conversation.

Interruptions are perhaps the most unambiguous linguistic strategy which can achieve dominance, since to interrupt someone is to deprive them – or at least to attempt to deprive them – of the right to speak. But there are many linguistic strategies which can be used to achieve dominance, as the contents of this chapter will show. However, before we can investigate conversational dominance, we need to examine the way talk is organised, to establish some norms of conversational behaviour.

7.2 Turn-taking in conversation

The organisation of talk is often referred to as turn-taking. When we are young, we learn how to participate in a multitude of shared activities, and one aspect of this is learning how to take turns. As speakers, we learn as part of our everyday communicative competence to orient to certain norms which guarantee that talk is distributed on a turn-by-turn basis. We do this in order to achieve a speech event that can be called conversation, not chaos. Figure 7.1 is a flow chart which represents the way turns are taken in conversation. It is

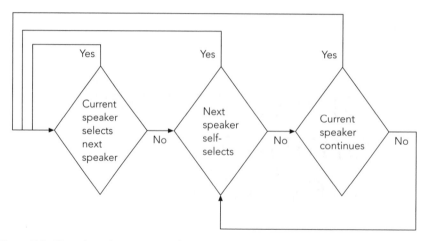

Figure 7.1 Flow chart showing turn-taking in conversation (based on Zimmerman and West 1975: 110)

based on Sacks, Schegloff and Jefferson's (1974) model of turn-taking in natur-
ally occurring conversation. This is the model of conversational turn-taking
most widely used in discourse and conversation analysis. In Figure 7.1, the
diamonds represent decision points. What this diagram tells us is that the
current speaker in conversation may select the next speaker (by asking them a
question, for example, or addressing them by name), in which case the person
selected must speak next. If the current speaker does not select the next speaker,
then one of the other participants in the conversation can opt to speak next. If
none of them does so, then the current speaker has the option of continuing to
speak. This third option – where the current speaker continues to speak – is the
default option.

The turn is the fundamental unit in this turn-taking model and turns are
conceptualised as tied to individual speakers. As the well-known dictum
says: 'One speaker speaks at a time, and speaker change recurs'. Because turns/
speakers follow each other in an orderly fashion, with no gap and no overlap
between them, the model is sometimes known as the 'no gap, no overlap'
model. This name – 'no gap, no overlap' – draws attention to two important
claims made by the model. 'No gap' refers to the claim that participants in
conversation interpret syntactic, semantic and prosodic clues so well that they
can accurately predict the end of the current speaker's turn. As a result, there is
no perceptible gap between the end of one turn and the beginning of the next.
The 'no overlap' claim complements this by asserting that the next speaker
predicts the end of the current speaker's turn so accurately that she or he starts
to speak just when current speaker stops and not before.

When a speaker is described as 'dominating' conversation, it usually means
that she or he is in some way breaking the underlying rules of this turn-taking

model. First, a speaker may break the 'one speaker speaks at a time' rule by interrupting the current speaker and **grabbing the floor**. Secondly, a speaker may contravene the norm of 'speaker change recurs' by taking a very long turn, ignoring other speakers' bids for the floor, and **hogging the floor**. Thirdly, and paradoxically, a speaker may talk too little, in effect withdrawing from conversational interaction; such non-cooperative behaviour will often lead to the breakdown of conversation. I shall examine the research evidence for each of these disruptions of the normal conversational pattern, and will show how it is most commonly male speakers who are responsible for such disruption.

7.3 Grabbing the floor: interruptions

If all conversation matched the ideal described by Sacks, Schegloff and Jefferson (1974), then there should be no instances of overlap. However, in spontaneous conversation, speakers do not always keep to the 'one-at-a-time' rule. Zimmerman and West (1975; West and Zimmerman 1983), using Sacks et al.'s model of turn-taking, taped thirty-one conversations involving two participants 'in coffee shops, drug stores and other public places' on the campus of the University of California; ten conversations took place between two women, ten between two men, and eleven between one woman and one man.

Zimmerman and West focused on *irregularities* in the transcribed conversations, that is, points in the conversations where turn-taking did not follow the smooth pattern predicted by the model. They found profound differences between the same-sex conversations and the cross-sex conversations. They labelled the two sorts of irregularity they identified as **overlaps** and **interruptions**.

Overlaps are instances of slight over-anticipation by the next speaker. Instead of beginning to speak immediately following the current speaker's turn, the next speaker begins to speak at the very end of the current speaker's turn, overlapping the last word (or part of it). Example (1) is an illustration of an overlap: Jo's *when* is uttered at the same time as Ruth's last word *early*. [In examples using the stave notation, any word appearing vertically above or below any other word is to be read as occurring at the same time as that word.]

(1) [*Jo complains to her friend Ruth that she is feeling very tired*]

Jo:	⌈when you say early
Ruth:	so you'd better go to bed ⌊early/
Jo:	tell me what you mean/
Ruth:	

Note that Jo's slight over-anticipation does not prevent Ruth from finishing her turn. **Interruptions**, on the other hand, are violations of the turn-taking rules of conversation. The next speaker begins to speak while the current speaker is still speaking, at a point in the current speaker's turn which could not be defined as the last word. Interruptions break the symmetry of the conversational model: the interruptor prevents the speaker from finishing her or his turn, at the same time gaining a turn for her or himself, as in the following example.

(2) [a brother and sister are discussing wild rice]

Anna:	wild rice is nice/ you've never tasted it ⌈so ((xx)) –
Bill:	⌊well the Indians
Anna:	
Bill:	don't eat it so why the bloody hell should you?
Anna:	they probably do/
Bill:	they don't/

Bill's utterance *well the Indians don't eat it so why the bloody hell should you?* effectively cuts Anna off and takes over the floor. (The symbol ((xx)) in the transcription means that Anna's words at this point were impossible to decipher.)

Tables 7.1 and 7.2 show the number of overlaps and interruptions occurring in the conversations analysed by Zimmerman and West. Table 7.1 deals with the conversations which took place between speakers of the same sex (two women or two men). Here, in twenty conversations, there were twenty-two overlaps, divided twelve and ten between the participants, and there were seven interruptions, of which three involved the first speaker and four the second. (For the purposes of the analysis, the person speaking first in a given stretch of conversation was labelled 'first speaker'; this does not mean that this speaker initiated the conversation.)

These results are in complete contrast to those given in Table 7.2, where the conversations involved one woman and one man. In these eleven conversations there were nine overlaps and forty-eight interruptions. All of the overlaps were caused by the male speaker, and forty-six of the forty-eight interruptions

Table 7.1: Turn-taking irregularities in twenty same-sex pairs (based on Zimmerman and West 1975: 115)

	1st speaker	2nd speaker	Total
Overlaps	12	10	22
Interruptions	3	4	7

Table 7.2: Turn-taking irregularities in eleven mixed-sex pairs (based on Zimmerman and West 1975: 116)

	Male speakers	Female speakers	Total
Overlaps	9	0	9
Interruptions	46	2	48

were cases of the man interrupting the woman. These results were checked to see that they weren't caused by one abnormal conversation: the interruptions occurred in every conversation except one. Note that the number of interruptions is very high when we consider that there were only seven altogether in the twenty same-sex conversations. The ratio of interruptions to conversation is 0.35:1 (seven out of twenty) for same-sex conversations, and 4.36:1 (forty-eight out of eleven) for mixed-sex conversations. Secondly, note that Table 7.1 shows us that men rarely interrupt one another; it is only when they are talking to women that they use interruptions. These results indicate that in mixed-sex conversations men infringe women's right to speak, specifically women's right to finish a turn. Conversely, the fact that women used no overlaps in conversation with men (while they did use some in same-sex conversations) suggests that women are concerned *not* to violate the man's turn but to wait until he's finished. West and Zimmerman (1998) claim that women in contemporary American society, like children, have restricted rights to speak, and that interruptions are used both to exhibit and to accomplish socially sanctioned relations of dominance and submission.

These results are confirmed by other research looking at interruptions (e.g. Eakins and Eakins 1979; Leet-Pellegrini 1980; Mulac et al. 1988; Schick Case 1988; Holmes 1995; Gunnarsson 1997). Male speakers were found to be more likely to interrupt others disruptively; they were also much more likely to interrupt women than women were to interrupt men. The following example, from a meeting of colleagues in a government department, shows how men's use of this strategy can make it difficult for women to get their points across in public arenas:

(3) *Peter*:   what has your section done in this area for instance?

　　 Judith: well we have begun thinking about it/ we've been holding regular

　　 Judith: review ⌈sessions on–

　　 Peter: 　　　⌊it'll take a lot more than that I can tell you/ this is a

　　 Peter: serious matter/

(from Holmes 1995: 51)

As we saw in the last chapter (section 6.7), this tendency for women to be interrupted by men is found even where the woman has high status. West (1998b) found that, in doctor–patient interaction, the norm is for doctors to interrupt patients rather than for patients to interrupt doctors, *except* where the doctor is a woman. In doctor–patient interaction involving male doctors, the doctors' interruptions outnumbered those of the patients (in fact there were twice as many interruptions by doctors). In doctor–patient interaction involving female doctors, by contrast, the interruptions made by male patients outnumbered those of the doctors. Similarly, Nicola Woods showed that, even where a woman has a high-status position in the workplace, she is more likely to be interrupted by a male subordinate than to interrupt him (Woods 1989).

Woods showed that men used interruptions as a way of getting the floor, and succeed in this 85 per cent of the time.

This pattern is found again in a study of broadcast interviews on Australian TV (Winter 1993). Joanne Winter compared two political interviews, one involving a male interviewer and the other a female interviewer. The interviewees were both high-ranking figures in the Australian government of the time: the Prime Minister and the Chancellor of the Exchequer (Treasurer). Winter's analysis revealed that the male interviewer adopted a belligerent style: he interrupted his interviewee more than the interviewee interrupted him (4:1) whereas the female interviewer did not interrupt at all but was interrupted five times by her interviewee. (It is instructive to listen to radio discussion programmes such as BBC Radio 4's *Start the Week*: even now in the early years of the twenty-first century, male participants dominate discussion and women participants are regularly interrupted by the male host.)

Interruptions seem to function as a way of controlling topics. Topic choice is normally shared equally between participants in a conversation, but Leet-Pellegrini (1980) found that, in conversations where one speaker is male and one female, male speakers tend to dominate. Leet-Pellegrini looked at the interaction of the independent variables of the speaker's gender and expertise (expertise refers to the speaker's level of knowledge of the topic under discussion). By examining linguistic features such as talkativeness, interruptions, overlaps and minimal responses, Leet-Pellegrini was able to establish that *in conjunction* the variables of gender and expertise were a good predictor of dominance. In other words, speakers who were both male *and* well-informed tended to dominate conversation. They talked more and infringed the other speaker's turns more. On the other hand, speakers who were both female and uninformed talked less and used more minimal responses and other supportive linguistic behaviour. Male speakers who were well-informed dominated conversation because they used a style of interaction based on power (asserting an unequal right to talk and to control topics) while well-informed female speakers preferred an interactional style based on solidarity and support. These findings will be taken up in Chapter 8.

7.4 Hogging the floor: talking too much

The model of turn-taking outlined in section 7.2 above assumes that participants in conversation are equals and that they have equal rights to the floor. This means, among other things, that talking time is normally shared among participants. As competent speakers, we all know this, and will be aggrieved if someone talks non-stop and gives us no chance to speak. But we are also able to judge when a situation is exceptional – say if a friend is having a crisis – and can choose to give someone a larger share of talking time.

Talking a lot, or talking too much, is an aspect of conversational behaviour that needs to be very carefully defined, and we need to be very sensitive to context. Are we talking about same-sex talk or mixed talk? Are we talking about number of turns or number of words, or both? As far as mixed talk is concerned, there is a widespread belief in our society that women talk more than men, yet research findings consistently contradict this. In fact, research on amount of talk establishes unambiguously that, in the public sphere, that is, in public contexts which have high status, it is men who do the talking. Men have been shown to talk more than women in settings as diverse as staff meetings (Eakins and Eakins 1978, 1979), seminars (Swacker 1979; Bashiruddin et al. 1990), television panel discussions (Bernard 1972; Edelsky and Adams 1990), mock jury deliberations (Strodtbeck and Mann 1956), and experimental pairs (Argyle et al. 1968). When asked to describe three pictures, male subjects took on average 13.00 minutes per picture compared with 3.17 minutes for female subjects – more than four times as long (Swacker 1975). A study of media interaction assessed the amount of talking time taken by interviewers in a series of television interiews with well-known men (Franken 1983, quoted in Holmes 1995). Each programme involved three interviewers: the 'host' interviewer (female) and two guest interviewers (one male, one female). Figure 7.2 shows the distribution of talk among these three. You would expect the amount of talk to be evenly distributed among the three interviewers – after all, each of

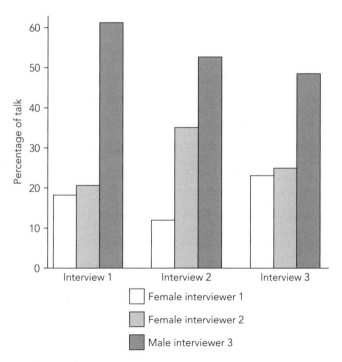

Figure 7.2 Distribution of talk in three television interviews (Holmes 1995: 34)

From Holmes, J. (1995), p. 34. Pearson Education Ltd.

them has the same task, to draw out the interviewee through questions – but as Figure 7.2 shows, in every programme the male interviewer talked more than his female peers.

Spender (1980a) explains the persistence of the myth of the talkative women in the face of evidence to the contrary by suggesting that we have different expectations of male and female speakers: while men have the right to talk, women are expected to remain silent. Talking at any length, then, will be perceived as talkativeness in women (see section 2.7). In an academic setting, for example, Spender (1979) claims that women are normally allowed no more than 30 per cent of talking time. This seems to be the upper limit before men feel that women are contributing more than their share. Interestingly, Herring, Johnson and DiBenedetto (1998) found that this same statistic applies to women's speaking roles in commercials on television. Spender (1990) estimates that, in the school classroom, teachers normally give two-thirds of their attention to boys. This is confirmed by Joan Swann's (1998) research on classroom interaction (to be discussed in Chapter 11).

Spender's hypothesis is borne out by a study of electronic discourse (discussion via computer) among academics in the United States. Susan Herring had observed (Herring 1992) that participation on the e-mail discussion list known as Linguist (subscribed to by professional linguists world-wide) was highly asymmetrical, with male participants contributing 80 per cent of the total discussion. Herring, Johnson and DiBenedetto (1998) therefore undertook an investigation of a smaller, more woman-friendly list: they hypothesised that, in a less adversarial environment, women would be more likely to participate equally in discussions. However, this was not what they found. During a discussion of 'men's literature' which lasted five weeks, the men contributed 70 per cent of the total words, as Table 7.3 shows. They also used more words per contribution than female participants did.

Table 7.3: Gender-based inequality in contributions made to the 'men's literature' discussion

	Female speakers	Male speakers
Number of contributors	18 (30.5%)	41 (69.5%)
Number of contributions	87 (36%)	155 (64%)
Average words per contribution	162	211.5
Total words contributed	14,114 (30%)	32,774 (70%)

From Herring, S., Johnson, D. and DiBenedetto, T. (1998), ed. J. Coates, p. 199. Blackwell Publishers.

What was particularly interesting – and alarming – was that during these five weeks there were two days when women's contributions exceeded men's. The effects of this brief period of dominance by women were significant: men became distressed and angry, claiming they were being 'silenced' and threatening to 'unsubscribe' from the network. These reactions suggest that women and men do not have equal rights to speak. '[B]y contributing more, even temporarily, ... women in the group violated the unspoken convention that control of public discourse belongs rightfully to men' (Herring et al. 1998: 198).

Nicola Woods (1989) showed how holding the floor was connected with gender more than with occupational status. She recorded nine triadic conversations between work colleagues of differing status (three involved two women and a man, ranked F–M–F; three involved two men and a woman, ranked M–F–M, and three were same sex). She hypothesised that powerful speakers would hold the floor disproportionately in these conversations. However, her analysis shows that, while male bosses spend more time holding the floor than subordinates, females bosses do not. Table 7.4 shows the results for the six mixed groups.

Table 7.4: Floor-apportionment (measured in seconds) in six mixed workplace conversations

	A			B		
Ocupational status	1	2	3	1	2	3
Gender	F	M	F	M	F	M
Floor holding (in seconds)	117	**173**	70	**168**	93	99

From Woods, N. (1989), eds. J. Coates and D. Cameron, p. 155. Pearson Education Ltd.

Table 7.4 shows how gender rather than relative rank seems to dictate how much talk a speaker engages in. The speakers who talk most (shown in bold) are male, either males in the top-ranking position in the three B groups, or the males in second position in the A groups. The following extract comes from one of the A group conversations and involves two women and a man: note how the male speaker dominates the floor by continuing to speak at points where speaker change could occur:

(4) *Male*:   the way he starts the meeting is he comes in and he blathers for about two minutes in Irish, err Scots Gaelic, and then he turns round and says to them 'do you repeat?'

Female 1: =mhm

Male: =err and then asks 'what is that?', err, and then somebody will say 'Irish' and he'll say 'oh very clever' and then go on from that= so you

Female 1:   =mhm

Male: won't have missed much=

Female 1: =no

Female 2: does somebody always say Irish?

Male: err, no Gaelic you usually get and . . . (Woods 1989: 155–6)

One of the female speakers here (Female 1) is the male speaker's boss, but it is not possible to tell from this extract which of the female speakers it is, since both female speakers use conversational strategies such as minimal responses and questions which support the current speaker and keep the conversation moving. In doing the 'conversational shitwork' (Fishman 1980b) in the work context, women could be seen to collude in undermining their own status.

7.5 Strategies of non-cooperation

A third way in which conversational dominance is achieved is through non-cooperation in talk. Interruptions and talking too much could both be described as uncooperative, but in both cases the dominant speaker is fully engaged in conversation. What I am calling 'non-cooperation' in this section involves interaction where one participant displays a lack of commitment to having a conversation at all. This 'non-cooperation' strategy seems to be used by speakers in informal talk in the *private* sphere, in contexts where, unlike the public sphere, being seen to talk does not signal the importance of the speaker.

The following is an extract from a malfunctioning conversation recorded in the home, where the woman is struggling to keep the conversation going, but is receiving no support from the male participant. Note the frequent silences (figures in brackets indicate length of pause in seconds):

(5) in other words black women are white (2) *y'know* it's really a simplistic article (0.5) *you know* he starts off saying – this – (1) *y'know* (0.8) sort of this gross indiscriminate black versus white (1) vision and . . .
(Fishman 1980a: 130)

This example comes from data collected by Pamela Fishman (1980a), who taped the daily conversations of three young American couples (a total of fifty-two hours of speech). She found that the women used *you know* five times more than the men in the 12.5 hours of conversation which she transcribed (women 87: men 17). In example (5), note how the *you knows* occur immediately before or after pauses, at points where the woman might expect (but doesn't get) some response from the man. *You know* reveals malfunction in turn-taking: change of speaker is not occurring because the man is not participating in the conversation (he rejects the topic under discussion). This use of *you know* by women in mixed-sex conversation is evidence of the work they have to do to try to keep conversation going. Women use *you know* more than men because it is men rather than women who fail to respond minimally or with a full turn at appropriate points. (In the cases where Fishman *did* find men using *you know*, it was doing the same work.)

In a study which extends Fishman's work, Victoria DeFrancisco (1998) got seven married couples to tape themselves at home for a week or more. She subsequently interviewed each of the participants on their own and asked them to comment on extracts from their recorded conversations. Her overall finding was that the women worked harder than the men to keep conversation going, but were less successful at achieving this. In contrast to Leet-Pellegrini's findings (see section 7.3 above), DeFrancisco found that, although the women in her study talked *more* than the men, and introduced more topics, this was not associated with dominance. In fact, the women were less successful than the men in getting their topics accepted. The following is an extract from DeFrancisco's data (figures in brackets represent pauses in seconds).

(6) *Mary*: I've got this all figured out (3) I talked to Doyle today? (4) and (4) you know explained to him the fact that you know, come April I'll probably have to (1) ahm (#)

   Bud: Excuse me, open the back door, I'm gonna give this to ((the dogs)) (8)

   Mary: I'll probably have to terminate my appointment

Note how the man fails to give any responses, not even *mhm* or *yeah*, at appropriate moments during his wife's story, and how he interrupts her story by leaving the room. When he was interviewed by DeFrancisco, he said he didn't feel like talking at the time the conversation was recorded, and anyway he'd 'heard it all before'. His behaviour was typical of the men in this study. The men were responsible for more turn-taking violations across all categories studied; Table 7.5 gives the detailed results. The clearest asymmetries are in the two top categories, 'no response' and 'delayed response'. Both these signal a lack of commitment to ongoing conversation.

Table 7.5: Turn-taking violations in the daily interaction of seven couples (based on DeFrancisco 1998: 179)

	Women (%)	Men (%)
No response	32	68
Delayed response	30	70
Inadequate response	40	60
Interruption	46	54

Nearly half the violations identified by DeFrancisco were no-response violations. In other words, this strategy seems to play a particularly important role in domestic interaction. Overall, DeFrancisco concluded that the men's strategies allowed them control over interaction. They defined the day-to-day reality of each couple's communication patterns, while the women had to adapt to the patterns imposed. This finding is supported by Sattel (1983), who argues that no response, or silence, is used by men as part of male dominance. He claims that male inexpressiveness is a method for achieving control in both mixed and all-male conversation.

Lack of response is also a strategy employed by male participants in inter-action on the Internet. During the Internet discussion on 'men's literature' analysed by Herring, Johnson and DiBenedetto (1998) (see section 7.4 above), female participants initially had a hard time getting men to acknowledge their contributions. After nearly two weeks, a female participant who was also a full professor and one of the more outspoken members of the discussion group, posted a message which talked explicitly about the issue of silencing:

> I am fascinated that my thoughtful [. . .] response on the 'men's literature' thread was met with silence [. . . M]y own fledgling analysis of MBU[Megabyte University] discourse from last summer suggests that there is a real pattern of male response to males and lack of response to females in *important* topics on MBU (Here I mean socially important). *When threads initiated by women die from lack of response that's silencing.* (Herring et al. 1995: 77, my italics).

This professor's analysis was correct: during the early part of this discussion, men's messages received an average response of over 100 per cent (i.e. there was more than one response for each message posted), whereas women's mess-ages only received a 64 per cent average response rate.

7.6 Silence: symbol of power or powerlessness?

Silence, then, is frequently the outcome of the violation of turn-taking norms. Speakers tend to fall silent after interruptions; there are long pauses at points where no response occurs; and when a speaker talks for a long time, other speakers are forced to be silent. Silence, in other words, is often a sign of malfunction in conversation. Under the ideal conditions displayed in the turn-taking model described at the beginning of the chapter (see Fig-ure 7.1), participants in conversation alternate their turns smoothly, with little or no gap between turns. Sacks (1995: 497) claimed that, 'it's a non-rare, really common occurrence that . . . there's no gap beween the end of a last [turn] and the beginning of a next [turn]'. However, Zimmerman and West (1975) found that the average silence in *mixed-sex* conversations lasted for 3.21 sec-onds, significantly longer than the average silence in *single-sex* conversations (1.35 seconds).

The following example from their data shows clearly the effect of interrup-tion on a speaker, and demonstrates why interruptions can be viewed as dis-plays of dominance. (Figures in brackets indicate seconds and tenths of seconds between turns; (#) indicates a silence of one second or less.)

(7) | 1 *Female*: | how's your paper coming? =
     | 2 *Male*: | = alright I guess (#)
     | 3 *Male*: | I haven't done much in the past two weeks
     | 4 | (1.8)

```
 5  Female:   yeah, know how that ⌈can
 6  Male:                        ⌊hey ya' got an extra cigarette?

 7            (#)

 8  Female:   oh uh sure ((hands him the pack)) like my

 9  Female:   ⌈pa-
10  Male:     ⌊how 'bout a match?

11            (1.2)

12  Female:   ere ya go uh like my ⌈pa-
13  Male:                          ⌊thanks

14            (1.8)

15  Female:   sure (#) I was gonna tell you ⌈my –
16  Male:                                   ⌊hey I'd really

17  Male:     like to talk but I gotta run (#) see ya

18            (3.2)

19  Female:   yeah
```

The pauses between turns in this conversation are very unlike the pattern found in a smoothly running conversation. In this brief extract, the 'no gap' pattern predicted by the model is consistently broken, with silences resulting both from the male's interruptions (lines 7, 11, 14 and 18) and his uncooperativeness (particularly apparent after line 17).

Silences in Zimmerman and West's data resulted not just from interruptions and overlaps, but also from **delayed minimal responses**. Minimal responses, such as *mhm* or *yeah*, are a way of indicating the listener's positive attention to the speaker, as was pointed out in the previous chapter (section 6.3). The listener has an active, not a passive, role in conversation, and minimal responses (as well as paralinguistic features such as smiling, nodding, grimacing) signal active attention. Zimmerman and West found that in mixed-sex conversations male speakers often delayed their minimal responses. In other words, they said *mhm* or *yeah* at an appropriate point but only after a pause. It seems that a delayed minimal response may function to signal a lack of understanding or a lack of interest in what the current speaker is saying. Just as a well-placed minimal response demonstrates active attention on the part of the listener and support for the speaker's topic, so a delayed minimal response signals a lack of interest in and lack of support for the speaker's topic.

Adversarial behaviour of any kind in interaction typically renders women silent. Sutton (1994) observes men's use of adversarial language in Internet discourse, and notes that this results in women's silence. This silence 'could be interpreted as the silence of disapproval, the silence of being fed up, the silence women use when something offensive or threatening is said' (Sutton 1994: 517). It is claimed that women sometimes avoid contributing to discussion because of their fear of unsupportive or critical responses from men. Such fears again result in women being silenced. To avoid male discussants' adversarial behaviour, many women retreat to 'the margins of cyberspace': women-only Internet discussion groups (Herring et al. 1995). Interestingly, men-only groups are virtually non-existent on the Internet, while women-only groups are a growing phenomenon (Herring et al. 1995: 69).

What this chapter shows is that silence cannot be interpreted as having one simple meaning. Depending on the circumstances – who is speaking, who they are speaking to, in what social context, and so on – silence can be interpreted as both powerful and powerless. When a man does not cooperate in talk with his partner, then his lack of talk, his silence, demonstrates his power to choose whether or not to participate in talk. When women fall silent after being interrupted or after delayed minimal responses, or after any of the non-cooperative moves described above, then their silence is a sign of power-lessness. As we saw in the last chapter, no linguistic form ever has only one meaning. Silence, or lack of talk, can have different meanings depending on context. But whether it denotes power or powerlessness, silence in conversation is always (in English-speaking westernised societies) a sign of malfunction: when conversation runs smoothly, there are no gaps. This is what the turn-taking model predicts. Long pauses, or silences, are a sign that conversational interaction is not working properly.

7.7 Conclusion

The research referred to in this chapter presents a consistent picture of male–female relations, with men dominating talk in a range of environments. It would not be true to say that all conversations involving both women and men display the patterns described here: in some settings, participants converse as equals for at least some of the time (see Tannen 1984; Edelsky 1993). However, by and large, sociolinguistic research into mixed talk exposes the fact that women and men do not have equal rights to the conversational floor. West and Zimmerman (1998), investigating the similarities between male–female interchanges and parent–child interaction in the United States, make the controversial claim that women in contemporary American society, like children, have restricted rights to speak, and that interruptions are used both to exhibit and to accomplish socially sanctioned relations of dominance and submission.

If West and Zimmerman's claim has any basis in fact, then the consequences for society are serious. Such consequences will be explored further, in relation to both the school classroom and the workplace, in Chapter 11.

CHAPTER 8

Same-sex talk

8.1 Women and men in same-sex groups

By contrast with the previous chapter, which focused on interaction involving both women and men, this chapter deals with women's and men's talk in same-sex groups. This is an important and still developing area of language and gender research: it allows researchers to look at women's and men's linguistic usage outside a dominance framework. In other words, it allows women's talk to be examined outside a framework of oppression or powerlessness, and it allows men's conversational strategies to be assessed in terms other than dominance. (These issues will be discussed again in Chapter 12.)

As I said in Chapter 1, gender was not a salient variable for early sociolinguists. Social class, ethnicity or age were the variables that interested sociolinguists at that point. Not only did sociolinguists not focus on gender in their research; there was a tendency to conflate 'speaker' with 'male speaker'. The androcentric bias of sociolinguistics was not challenged until the publication of Robin Lakoff's *Language and Woman's Place* in 1975. Even then, what Lakoff's book did was to foreground women's ways of talking – men's ways of talking remained, implicitly, the norm.

Same-sex talk was not explicitly addressed until Deborah Jones' paper, 'Gossip: notes on women's oral culture' (1980). Since then, a great deal of research has been carried out on same-sex talk. Nearly all of this research has had a comparative focus: for example, Deborah Tannen (1990b) compared the talk of same-sex pairs of friends at different ages; Jenny Cheshire (1982, see Chapter 5) compared the language used by adolescent single-sex groups in adventure playgrounds in Reading, England; and Marjorie Goodwin (1990, see Chapter 6) compared the language used by pre-adolescent single-sex peer groups in a Philadelphia street. All these papers focus on children or adolescents, and all investigate both female and male speakers.

There is now a growing body of research investigating women's conversational practices in a range of communities – white, African American, British Asian, deaf, hearing, gay, lesbian, straight, adult, teenage (see, for example, Coates 1996, 1999; Leap 1999; Morgan 1999; Wood 1999; Pichler 2000, 2003; Irwin 2002). Men remained invisible for longer, but in the last decade the whole issue of men and masculinity has been problematised. So we are now beginning to build up a picture of men's talk in all-male groups, though what we know is skewed to young men and adolescents and to non-domestic contexts such as the street, the pub, the sports changing room. In this chapter, I shall give an account of the findings from this research. This will involve some overlap with Chapter 6, but the focus here will be on same-sex talk. I shall also explore new understandings of the relationship between language and gender, in particular, the idea that language is a way of 'doing' gender. This **performative** approach to gender allows us to see the way speakers are 'doing' masculinity or 'doing' femininity when they talk.

8.2 Cooperative and competitive ways of talking

So what findings have emerged from research focusing on single-sex groups? Sociolinguists have investigated the talk of all kinds of single sex-groups, old and young, middle-class and working-class, from a variety of different cultures. One observation that has been something of a constant is that, while men tend to disagree with or ignore each other's utterances, women tend to acknowledge and build on them. It seems that men pursue a style of interaction based on power, while women pursue a style based on solidarity and support. Cheshire and Trudgill, summarising research on the links between gender and conversational discourse, come to the following conclusion:

> It seems clear that, other things being equal, women and men do have a preference for different conversational styles. Women – in most western societies at least – prefer a *collaborative speech style*, supporting other speakers and using language in a way that emphasizes their solidarity with the other person. Men, on the other hand, use a number of conversational strategies that can be described as a *competitive style*, stressing their own individuality and emphasizing the hierarchical relationships that they enter into with other people.
> (Cheshire and Trudgill 1998: 3)

In the next two sections I shall look at the evidence to support such a dichotomy in relation to same-sex talk. I shall also tease out some of the linguistic features said to characterise women's collaborative style and men's competitive style.

8.2.1 Women's collaborative style

In the 1970s and 1980s, several researchers claimed that the prime pattern of interaction in all-female groups is cooperative rather than competitive. Elizabeth Aries (1976) analysed the interaction patterns of six experimental groups: two all-female, two all-male, and two mixed. The all-male groups were concerned to establish where each member stood in relation to other members and in these groups a hierarchy emerged with some members holding dominant positions and others more submissive positions. The two women's groups, on the other hand, were more flexible: active speakers were concerned to draw out more reticent speakers and the women developed ways to express affection and interpersonal concern.[1]

Cooperative linguistic behaviour is the subject of Marie Wilson Nelson's (1998) study of five successive teams of teachers working at a university writing centre. The teams consisted almost entirely of female graduate assistants, and the working practices they established were explicitly collaborative. One of the rare male graduate assistants involved commented:

> I just love being in here with all you women. You make it such a nice place to work. You're so warm and supportive that I never feel stupid when I make a mistake. It's different in here from how I've seen people do things before. Most graduate students are so competitive.

These two studies were both based on white, more middle-class speakers. However, Goodwin's (1980) work on the street play of African American children in Philadelphia (described in section 6.3) could also be said to demonstrate a competitive–cooperative split. She established that the linguistic forms used by the children served to maintain the social organisation of their (very different) social groups: the use of cooperative rather than competitive forms served to construct and maintain the non-hierarchical nature of the girls' group. Wodak (1981) included working-class speakers in her work on the discourse strategies of women and men in group therapy. She noted interesting class differences: in particular, working-class *men* are considerably more emotional than many middle-class *women*, and working-class speakers in general differ significantly from lower middle-class speakers and from middle-class *men* in their presentation of their problems. However, she also noted significant gender differences. The men and women talked about their problems in different ways: the men tended to use circumstantial descriptions while the women were more personal.

The question we now need to ask is, can we pin down these vague but suggestive terms: cooperative and competitive? What are the linguistic characteristics of these two styles? In my own research (see Coates 1989, 1991, 1994, 1996, 1997), I have tried to answer this question. My data suggest that the following are some of the relevant categories for understanding how women's cooperative discourse is achieved: topic and topic development; minimal responses; hedges; questions; turn-taking patterns.[2]

Topic and topic development

There is considerable evidence that women and men tend to discuss different topics in same-sex groups (see for example Aries 1976; Aries and Johnson 1983; Seidler 1989; Pilkington 1998). Talk is central to women's friendships, and

WOMEN, MEN AND LANGUAGE

women typically choose to talk about people and feelings, rather than about things. Men in all-male groups are more likely to discuss current affairs, travel and sport. As one woman I interviewed commented: 'I think the friendships I've made have...always been around you know sort of <u>straight</u> talking, <u>vul</u>nerable talking, and it's ex<u>changed</u> vulnerable talking. It's just like you can say whatever you think or whatever you feel...' (underlining indicates speaker's emphasis). An example of 'exchanged vulnerable talking' taken from the all-female conversations I collected involves three women discussing relationships very openly with each other; another comes from a conversation involving four teenage girls when they share their experiences of mood swings and backache during their periods.

The following is the main topic sequence from a conversation involving five women friends: mothers' funerals; child abuse; wives' loyalty to husbands; the Yorkshire Ripper case; fear of men. Another sequence, from a conversation involving three women friends in their 30s, illustrates a less intense conversation, but one which still deals with personal matters: holidays; skiing; rabbits; piano lessons; musical instruments; relationships. These topics are developed slowly and accretively, with participants building on each other's contributions and arriving at a consensus. (For more on topics and topic sequences, see Coates 1996: 68–78.)

Minimal responses

Women use minimal responses to signal their active listenership and support for each other, as the following example from a conversation between two women shows (this example was first used in section 6.3, page 87, and comes from Holmes 1995: 55). In this conversation, two women are talking about a good teacher.

```
(1) Tina:  she provided the appropriate sayings for
    Lyn:

    Tina:  particular times      and and so on
    Lyn:                right                right

    Tina:  she didn't actually TEACH them but
    Lyn:

    Tina:  she just               provided a model
    Lyn:          provided a model

    Tina:            you know you- you must refer to this
    Lyn:   yeah mhm                              mhm

    Tina:  and this          and she actually produced a book
    Lyn:          mhm mhm

    Tina:      that set out some of these ideas at the very
    Lyn:   mhm

    Tina:  simplest level
    Lyn:            yeah
```

128

Lyn provides lots of minimal responses – *right, yeah* or *mhm* – to signal her attention to what Tina is saying. These are extremely well placed: Lynn produces them at the end of semantically and syntactically coherent chunks of speech, an achievement which demonstrates the work co-participants do in predicting how talk will develop. As the transcript shows, Lyn's minimal responses do not impede the flow of Tina's talk.

Female speakers also use minimal responses to mark their recognition of different stages of a conversation, for example, to accept a new topic, or to acknowledge the end of a topic. The following example comes at the end of a topic:

(2) [five women are discussing parents' funerals]

> Gina: there's two things aren't there/ there's the the other people like your mother or father who's left and or or siblings/ and there's also how you feel at that time about (.) the easiness

> Gina: of going [to the funeral]/
> Mary: mhm/
> Bea: mhm/
> Meg: mhm/
> Sally: yeah/

Note how Gina's friends only add their minimal responses after she has rounded off the topic. Here the minimal responses both demonstrate active support for the speaker, and also mark the group's acknowledgement that this is the end of the topic.

Hedges

Hedges are used to respect the face needs of all participants (see section 6.6), to negotiate sensitive topics, and to encourage the participation of others. Mitigated utterances (i.e. utterances involving hedges) encourage discussion because they prevent speakers taking a hard line. Women whose talk I have collected often discussed highly sensitive topics; the use of hedges prevents such talk from being too face-threatening. The two examples below illustrate this. In the first, Meg's description of an old friend enters the taboo area of (malicious) criticism. Note how the hedges become more frequent as the speaker becomes more embarrassed. Meg is rescued by Bea's jokey comment (hedges underlined):

(3) Meg: but I did see what amounted to <u>sort of</u> chest hair, black, she's a very dark <u>sort of</u> dark skinned and sallow complexion and a lo- <u>I mean</u> I – <u>I mean</u> I hope I'm <u>just</u> reporting this without any edge to it . <u>you know</u>, so <u>I mean</u> I <u>probably</u>-

> Bea: you mean you really feel that she's turning into a gorilla? <LAUGHTER>

The second example comes from a discussion of the Yorkshire Ripper case (a notorious murder case in Britain). After someone has raised the point that the police appealed to the public to consider men in their households, Sally reveals that she forced herself to consider her husband.

(4) *Sally:* oh god yes <u>well I mean</u> we were living in Yorkshire at the time
and I – <u>I mean</u> I . <u>I mean</u> I did/ I <u>sort of</u> thought <u>well</u> <u>could</u> it be
John?

The number of hedges present in this example is unsurprising, given the sensitivity of the topic. Self-disclosure of this kind can be extremely face-threatening and speakers need to hedge their statements.

Questions

Although questions often function as information-seeking devices, such questions are rare in all-female discourse. Women's avoidance of information-seeking questions seems to be related to their role in constructing a speaker as 'someone who knows the answer', an expert. In friendly conversation, women avoid the role of expert and therefore avoid forms which construct asymmetry. Instead, questions are used to invite others to participate, to introduce new topics, to hedge, to check the views of other participants, and to instigate stories. The following example is typical in showing how questions invite others to speak:

(5) [*Talking about doctors getting younger*]
Karen: I suppose if you're ill you don't care do you?
Pat: I suppose not, but there are um- there are limits aren't there?
Karen: there are

In this example, Karen and Pat use tag questions – *do you?, aren't there?* – to involve each other in the conversation. The next example shows how questions can be used to introduce a new topic, and thus involve others in talk:

(6) *Liz:* wasn't it terrible about that Oxford student? [*initiates discussion of recent murder in Oxford*]

In the next example, which comes from the discussion about the Oxford murder following Liz's question in (6), Sue's question is rhetorical – she doesn't expect an answer, but her question is a way of expressing not just her own incomprehension and horror but also that of the group:

(7) *Sue:* but how could you do that to somebody? [*i.e. murder someone and dispose of their body*]

In discussion, female speakers will often use questions like the one in example (7) as a way of checking that there is consensus in the group. Tag questions are also used to do this, as examples (8) and (9) show:

(8) [end of topic _Relationships_]

   Liz: it's strange <u>isn't it</u>? the life some people lead/

(9) [_gossip about school friends_]

   Claire: but they're so stupid <u>right?</u> cos then- cos Nina said . . .

In these two examples, the speaker's tag – whether it occurs at the end or in the middle of an utterance – does not produce a verbal response from other participants. The main function of these tags is to check the taken-for-granted-ness of what is being said, to confirm the shared world of the participants.

Turn-taking

As we saw in the last chapter (section 7.2), conversation is often organised in terms of speakers holding the floor in turn, with only one speaker speaking at any one time. Female speakers in all-female talk, however, often adopt a way of organising talk where the rule of one-person-at-a-time does not apply. This more collaborative mode of organising talk was first identified by Carole Edelsky (1993) who labelled it the **collaborative floor**. Edelsky was investigating the talk of a _mixed_ group, so it is potentially a way of talking available to all speakers, but women seem more inclined to use it than men. I call this way of talking a conversational **jam session** because, just like musicians playing jazz, women often get together 'for the spontaneous and improvisatory performance of talk, usually for their own enjoyment' (to adapt a dictionary definition). The defining characteristic of a conversational jam session is that the conversational floor is potentially open to all participants simultaneously.

Two key features of a conversational jam session are (a) that speakers co-construct utterances and (b) that speakers talk at the same time. The extract we looked at above in example (1) (of two women talking about a good teacher) contains a good example of a co-constructed utterance:

(10) | Tina: | she didn't actually TEACH them but | |
      | --- | --- | --- |
      | Lyn: | | |
      | Tina: | she just | provided a model |
      | Lyn: | provided a model | |

The clause _she just provided a model_ is co-constructed by Tina and Lyn, with Tina providing the subject (_she_) and Lyn the verb and object (_provided a model_). Tina then repeats Lyn's words, which functions as an acceptance of Lyn's contribution, and Lyn provides two minimal responses (_yeah mhm_) which function as an acceptance of Tina's acceptance. The same pattern occurs in the following, more complex example from my data:

(11) [talking about child abuse]

Bea:	I mean in order to accept that idea you're having to .		
Mary:			mhm . completely

Bea:	⌈completely change your view of your husband/
Mary:	review your ⌊view of your husband/

This example involves overlapping speech as well as co-constructon of an utterance. Mary's completion of Bea's words is overlapped by Bea's own completion which repeats Mary's words with a slight change from *review* to *change*.

Overlapping speech may occur in many different contexts. Co-conversationalists may ask questions or make comments *while another participant is speaking;* these questions and comments are, like minimal responses, signals of active listenership, but they contribute more substantially to the production of joint text. Simultaneous speech also occurs when speakers repeat or rephrase each other's words, as in the next example:

(12) [talking about aging parents]

Sue:		
Liz:	and I mean it's a really weird situation because	

Sue:	⌈you become a parent/ yeah/
Liz:	all of a sudden the ⌊roles are all reversed/

Finally, overlapping speech is found when two or more speakers pursue a theme simultaneously. In the following example, four teenage girls are talking about a chat show they had seen where a man was boasting about his promiscuity (square brackets indicate the extent of overlap):[3]

(13)

Nicky:	he can't understand it when his girlfriends leave him because		

Nicky:	he says ⌈it's in his genes ⌉ .hh ⌈he says it's
Jane:	⌊yeah he'll say you know⌋ obvious ⌊ly everyone

Nicky:	natural for him to be⌉ unfaithful
Jane:	wants to do that⌋

As this example demonstrates, simultaneous speech does not threaten comprehension, but on the contrary permits a more multilayered development of topics. Nicky and Jane are basically saying the same thing, but in slightly different ways. In a jam session, the different voices work *with* each other, not against each other, to construct meaning

8.2.2 Men's competitive style

It is a stereotype of male talk that it tends to be competitive rather than cooperative. What is the evidence for this? And is it oversimplistic to claim that women talk to each other one way while men talk to each other in a very different way? Some interesting observations on this question come from a man who chose to stay at home and look after his children, in effect taking over a role that is conventionally assigned to women. He commented that he had to learn a new way of talking, a way which was very much in contrast with his previous experience of talk. He argues:

> The constant care of children imbues those involved with . . . a need *to cooperate rather than compete*, . . . a willingness to accept confusion and speculation as an end rather than rely on the dogma of formulae. (Stone 1983, my italics)

In reflecting on his previous experience with other men, he says that what he misses is 'the stimulation of battling wit against wit', and he describes men's talk as follows:

> From football to sex, from politics to literature, talk had one thing in common; it knew where it was going. It wasn't baffled, it wasn't awed, it wasn't speculative . . . as a rule these conversations were gladiatorial, a contest in language with a familiar topic the arena.

These comments give us some insights into what is meant by 'competitive'. Images drawn on here to describe all-male talk include *contest*, *battle* and *gladiatorial*, all of which derive from an underlying metaphor which equates talk with conflict.[4]

So what are the characteristics of this more **adversarial** style of talk? I shall look in turn at topic choice; monologues and playing the expert; questions; verbal sparring; and turn-taking patterns.

Topic choice

It seems that, with each other, men avoid self-disclosure and prefer to talk about more impersonal topics such as current affairs, modern technology, cars or sport. The all-male conversations I've collected rarely involve self-disclosure of the kind found in women's friendly talk. For example, in one of these conversations three men friends discuss the 1960s at some length, and this topic can be divided into sub-topics such as Bob Dylan; revolution and why it hasn't happened in Britain; Marxism; students today. This contrasts with the topics found in conversations involving women of similar age and background (see section 8.2.1 above). When talk does become more personal, it deals with matters such as drinking habits or personal achievements rather than feelings. Topic choice is not a superficial matter: it has profound consequences for other linguistic choices. Hedging, for example, is closely correlated with more personal and/or sensitive topics. In terms of floor-holding patterns, non-personal topics encourage one-at-a-time floor-holding because these topics lend themselves to what I call 'expertism', which I shall describe in the next section.

Monologues and playing the expert

Monologues, that is, stretches of conversation where one speaker holds the floor for a considerable time, are characteristic of men's talk. They seem to be associated with playing the expert. By 'playing the expert', I mean a kind of conversational game where participants take it in turns to hold the floor and to talk about a subject on which they are an expert. This is a game which seems to be played most commonly by male speakers; women, by contrast, avoid the role of expert in conversation. Let's take as an example a conversation involving two men friends having lunch together.[5] The conversation ranges over a wide variety of topics, including the merits of Burger King vs McDonalds, mobile phones, work and plans for the future, computers. These topics tend to correlate with areas of expertise of the two friends, and mean that they both get a turn at being the expert, and a turn at 'doing' a monologue. A brief illustration from this conversation is given in example (14) below. Chris introduces the topic of mobile phones and proceeds to hold forth about mobile phone technology: here is an extract from his monologue (minimal responses from Geoff in italics):

(14)   cos you know we've got BT internet at home (*mhm*) and I've set it up so that . um through the BT internet WAP portal so that Kate can read . her email that she gets . um on her phone (*oh right*) which is qui- which is quite useful if you're kinda not behind a computer but I was musing the other day on . on how funny it is that the sort of graphics you get on WAP phones now . is like you used to get on the ZX81 (*yeah*) and every-everything's having to adapt to that kind of LCD based stuff (*that's right*) um computers have got to the point they've got to . and now we've gone all the way back with WAP technology . . .

This example illustrates very well how male speakers are happy to hold the floor for a considerable time. Note how this is achieved through the cooperation of the other speaker(s) present. In example (14), Geoff seems happy to be on the receiving end of Chris' monologue. His minimal responses function to show he is attending to what Chris is saying *and* to signal that he is content to go on listening.

Questions

Questions occur with some regularity in conversations such as these which encourage speakers to play the expert. For example, Chris's monologue about mobile phones in example (14) above comes in response to a question from Geoff:

(15)   So why are you so loyal to Nokia?

Such questions are used primarily to seek information (something women avoid – see section 8.2.1 above), and also invite the addressee to speak. As this example illustrates, addressees often provide long expert answers rather than short ones. Example (16) gives another illustration of an information-seeking question that potentially invites the addressee to to take up the role of expert. It comes from a conversation between two friends who are both linguists; the topic is speech synthesisers. Interestingly, as this example demonstrates, addressees are not always able to take up the role of expert:

> (16) *Peter:* what else do they use it for apart from the deaf? or do they have other applications- I don't mean the deaf, I mean the dumb, do they have other applications?
>
> *Rob:* well they didn't develop it for the dumb, I can't remember why they did develop it, um – I don't know

At other times, questions are used as a way of introducing a new topic which the *speaker*, rather than the addressee, can talk expertly about. The following example also comes from the conversation between two linguists:

> (17) *Rob:* do you know of the Pennsylvania experiment?
>
> *Peter:* no, tell me about it
>
> *[Rob proceeds to talk about the Pennsylvania experiment]*

Peter's answer – *no, tell me about it* – demonstrates that he interprets Rob's question not as a simple request for information but as having the pragmatic force of saying: 'if you don't know about this, I can talk about it at some length'. As this example shows, questions play a significant role in terms of turn-exchange. In other words, male speakers frequently use questions as a way of handing over the conversational floor to another speaker.

Verbal sparring

But all-male talk does not always consist of monologues, or of a series of long turns. Often, it takes the form of an exchange of rapid-fire turns, as in the following example, where Sam and Ray disagree over whether apples are kept in cases or crates:

> (18) *Ray:* crate!
>
> *Sam:* case!
>
> *Ray:* what?
>
> *Sam:* they come in cases Ray not crates
>
> *Ray:* oh same thing if you must be picky over every one thing
>
> *Sam:* just shut your fucking head Ray!
>
> *Ray:* don't tell me to fuck off fuck (. . .)
>
> *Sam:* I'll come over and shut yo-

> *Jim:* yeah I'll have a crate of apples thanks [*laughingly using a thick sounding voice*]
>
> *Ray:* no fuck off Jim
>
> *Jim:* a dozen . . .
>
> *Dan:* shitpicker! [*amused*]
>
> (from Pilkington 1998: 265)

Here we see Sam disagreeing with Ray, Ray disagreeing with Sam, Jim disagreeing with Ray, and Dan criticising Jim. But the participants here and in other similar exchanges seem to be enjoying themselves and their talk contains much laughter. It is friendly sparring, not a quarrel.

This example is reminiscent of the style of talking analysed by Labov in his famous chapter on the use of ritual insults among black teenagers in Harlem. In that culture, verbal duelling has evolved into a kind of art form, with young male speakers demonstrating their prowess on the street in what is known variously as 'sounding' or 'signifying'. Many of the insults involve obscenity and a large proportion insult the addressee's mother. The following is a (non-obscene) example from the group known as the Cobras:

> (19) *C1:* Your momma's a peanut man!
>
> *C2:* Your momma's an ice-man!
>
> *C3:* Your momma's a fire-man!
>
> *C4:* Your momma's a truck driver!
>
> *C5:* Your father sell crackerjacks!
>
> *C6:* Your mother *look* like a crackerjack!
>
> (Labov 1972b: 346–7)

Although these two examples come from very different contexts (a New Zealand workplace and a New York street), in both we see all-male groups organising talk in a stylised way which seems to relish conflict and where speakers limit themselves to a single utterance per turn.

Turn-taking

It should have become clear from the examples we have looked at so far that male speakers prefer a one-at-a-time model of turn-taking, in contrast with women, who often adopt the jam session model. Conversations involving long monologues give individual speakers privileged access to an (uninterrupted) floor, while the more gladiatorial style of talk, where males spar with each other, also depends on the well-timed exchange of speaker turns. This may explain the significance of questions in such talk: questions have the power to hand over the turn from one speaker to another, and also to invite someone to speak as an expert. Overlapping talk is rare in all-male talk. Because most men most of the time choose a one-at-a-time model of turn-taking, overlap is interpreted as deviant, as an (illegitimate) attempt to grab the floor. This means that, in mixed conversation, women and men may come into conflict over overlapping talk (which is a normal component of jam session talk). Mary Talbot (1992), for example, recorded a conversation involving two heterosexual couples having dinner. One of the men told a story about coming through customs and his partner joined in with collaborative comments and support for his story. Eventually the man said 'I wish you'd stop interrupting me!' – even though, as Talbot's transcript shows, the woman's contributions to the story did not actually overlap with her partner's words. But he experienced her collaborative mode of talk as intruding on his right to a solo floor.[6]

But overlapping talk does sometimes occur in all-male talk. While orientation to a one-at-a-time turn-taking model seems to be the norm in all-male talk, there are exceptions, for example, when friends become excited about a topic, or are gossiping (see Cameron 1997; Coates and Sutton-Spence 2001; Ryan 2003). The following example comes from a conversation involving a group of American college students talking about others whom they identify as 'gay':

(20)	Ed:	he's I mean he's like a real artsy fartsy fag (. . .)
	Ed:	and he sits next to the ugliest-ass bitch in the history
	Ed:	of the world ⌈and
	Bryan:	⌊and they're all hitting on her too, like
	Ed:	⌈I know it's like four homos hitting on her
	Bryan:	four guys ⌊hitting on her
	(from Cameron 1997: 56)	

This brief extract shows two of the men overlapping each other as they jointly construct an account of these 'gay' men, and this occurs at other points during this discussion, where they become 'noticeably excited' (Cameron 1997: 56). But although men's talk sometimes draws on these more collaborative features, note how the content of the talk displays a relatively aggressive masculinity (in this example an aggressively heterosexual and anti-gay masculinity).

8.2.3 Achieving solidarity in talk

It could be argued that men's competitive style is simply a different way of achieving solidarity. This is what Koenraad Kuiper (1998) argues in his research on the talk of men doing sport together. Kuiper demonstrates very clearly that men cooperate closely in certain interaction rituals, even though some of these rituals are highly competitive. The face-threatening strategies described by Kuiper for New Zealand males have been found in a range of societies in the talk of male speakers, for example, among black adolescents in New York (Labov 1972b), boys in south London (Hewitt 1997), adult males in Barcelona (Pujolar 1997). Insofar as such strategies are designed to create solidarity, they fit well with Wolfson's (1988) 'bulge' model, which predicts that speakers can afford to be less polite to people at the two extremes of a social distance continuum: strangers (people we don't know at all) and intimates (people we know very well indeed).

Jane Pilkington (1998) comes to similar conclusions. She recorded the talk of four same-sex groups, two all-female and two all-male, in Wellington, New Zealand. She shows how important overlapping turns, co-constructed talk and positive feedback are in women's friendly talk. By contrast, the all-male talk she recorded is characterised by silences, lack of verbal feedback, monologues, and the direct expression of disagreement, something women seem to avoid in talk. She concludes that the goal of friendly talk for both women and men is solidarity, but that women and men adopt very different strategies to achieve this. For many men, connection with others is accomplished in part through playful conflict and competition, in contrast to the mirroring self-disclosure more typical of women friends.

The all-male talk analysed by Deborah Cameron (1997) certainly functions to create solidarity. The five friends whose talk she examines are bonded by their shared denigration of others whom they label 'gay'. But Cameron argues that these men talk in a way that is simultaneously cooperative and competitive. We need, therefore, to acknowledge that cooperation and competition as talking styles cannot be simplistically separated out and attributed to one gender or the other. At one level, all speakers have to cooperate if conversation is to be sustained. But, as this section has illustrated, speakers in all-male talk often achieve solidarity through using conversational strategies which can be labelled competitive or adversarial.

8.3 Doing masculinity, doing femininity

In this final section I want to focus on the role of same-sex talk in constructing us as gendered beings. It is now considered more helpful to think of gender as something that is 'done' rather than something that just is. In other words, gender is no longer viewed as a static, add-on characteristic of speakers, but as something that is *performed* by speakers. Speakers are seen as 'performing' masculinity or femininity.

The expression 'performing masculinity/femininity' suggests that such a performance is a unitary and unified experience. However, the person we perform in interaction with others is not always the same: we have all had the experience of feeling like a different person when we are in a different situation. For example, the 'me' that has a drink at the pub with friends is a different 'me' from the one who participates in a committee meeting at work. Even in the same context we can change if something alters in that context. In the following example, Liz tells a story about her friend changing when her husband joined them for a drink:

(21) *Liz:* when I was at the Health Club the other night/ and this girl I went with her husband turned up to have a drink with us in the bar/ . and like the whole atmosphere changed when he arrived/ <LAUGHS> [. . .] and she changed/ she changed/ she- she- she suddenly went tense/ you know/

We change because different audiences require different performances – and also because we sometimes feel like playing a different role. Different 'selves' are possible because a range of alternative versions of femininity and masculinity are available to speakers. These alternative femininities and masculinities are in competition with each other, and speakers have to make choices which depend on their cultural understanding of prevailing norms. At any given time a particular version of femininity or masculinity will be dominant. This version is called the **hegemonic** form (see Connell 1995 for a full discussion of this concept).

8.3.1 Competing femininities

Dominant versions of femininity in play today position women as gentle, caring, maternal, attentive to their appearance and, above all, *nice*. The example below comes from a conversation where three 16-year-old girls are commenting on the appearance of the fourth, Sarah, who is trying on Gwen's make-up.

(22) *[Sarah tries on some of Gwen's make-up]*

Gwen:	doesn't she look really nice?		
Kate:		yes/	
Emily:		she DOES look nice/	
Gwen:		⌈I think with the lipstick	
Kate:	you should wear make-up ⌊more often . Sarah/		
Gwen:	it looks good/	[Sarah your lips . s- suit lipstick/	
Kate:			
Emily:	yeah looks [nice/		
Gwen:	((I'm saying)) what you said- big lips suit [lipstick/		
Kate:	oohh yes/	[share it/	
Emily:		[you should be [a model/	
Gwen:	yeah/ looks good to me/ Sarah you look really nice/		
Kate:	yeah/		
Emily:	models have big lips/		

In this talk, the girls are overtly complimenting Sarah. This is part of the routine support work that girls and women do with each other as friends. At the same time they are co-constructing a world in which the putting on and wearing of make-up is a normal part of doing femininity, and *looking nice/looking good* is an important goal. In this world, the size of your features – your eyes, your lips – is highly salient, and the fashion model is a significant figure, with high status.

The next example shows two women, Pat and Karen, aligning themselves with another dominant form of femininity, which asserts that all women are good mothers and love children.

(23) [*topic = end of term school plays*]

Karen:	did Peter do his song?	was he good?
Pat:		yes/	he was marvellous/
Karen:			oh the-
Pat:	he was marvellous/ every kid in it was marvellous/
Karen:	I think they always are/
Pat:	

Examples (22) and (23) both illustrate dominant or hegemonic femininity. But hegemonic femininity is always open to challenge from alternative femininities, as the next example demonstrates. This example comes at a moment in a conversation between Anna, Liz and Sue where they have been talking about a family they all know with difficult children. Their expression of negative feelings about these particular children (Anna refers to them as *ghastly children*) leads them to consider their attitude to children in general.

(24)

Anna:	
Sue:	
Liz:	I think it's a- . a fallacy as well that you like every child/
Anna:	no/ . that's right/
Sue:	mhm/ I still quite often don't like
Liz:	cos you don't/
Anna:	<LAUGHS>
Sue:	children/ <LAUGHS>
Liz:	actually I think you particularly dislike your own/

Here we can see the clash between the dominant discourse, which says that children are 'marvellous', and where all mothers take pride in their child's achievements, and an alternative discourse which asserts that not all children are likeable (in fact, some are *ghastly*) and that it is not compulsory for adults to like all children. For women speakers, particularly women who are themselves mothers (Sue and Liz), this is a very subversive discourse. Dominant ideas of femininity (and of motherhood) do not allow for the expression of negative feelings about children. Anna, Sue and Liz support each other in sustaining a radically different view, one which starts with the proposition 'you don't like every child' (Liz, supported by Anna), which moves on to 'I quite often don't like children' (Sue), and then to 'I think you particularly dislike your own' (Liz), a very strong position which directly challenges the idea of women as loving, caring, nurturing beings for whom having children is the ultimate experience of their lives.

It is often in private with trusted friends that women (and girls) explore alternative femininities and challenge the dominant norms. With each other, women have the possibility of celebrating their achievements ('boasting') or of expressing less 'nice' aspects of themselves (e.g. complaining about work or being rude about somebody). Through talk with each other, women can also reconcile conflicting aspects of themselves: for example, girls from the Bangladeshi community in London can align themselves both with Bangladeshi norms of femininity (which dictate that girls are modest and demure) and with contemporary street culture (through displaying knowledge about boys and dating) (Pichler 2003).

8.3.2 Competing masculinities

Male speakers also have the choice of a range of competing masculinities. Here are some examples of men performing hegemonic masculinity:

(25) [Max tells Rick about the state of his car – Rick's words are in italics]
can't believe my car, it's ((2 sylls)) [really] mhm, speedo's fucked [oh no] [. . .] wind[screen]wipers are fucked [oh right] and now the fucker won't start [oh no]

(26) [Rob tells his friends about a fight at work]
what he did was he threw this knife at me, this is honest truth, threw a knife at me, and then- and there was this cable [. . .] he fucking chased me with it, and I thought 'Fuck this', and he kept like having a go and teasing me, and I just smashed him straight round the face with a bell box in front of the boss

(27) [Julian tells a story of a sporting triumph]
so I took it on the half-volley, and it just went flying, [. . .] and it was just the most beautiful ball I've ever ever ever seen <EMPHATIC>

These men align themselves with hegemonic masculinity through their choice of topics (cars, fights, sport), through their emphasis on achievement (in fighting or sport), through their construction of a tough image through the use of swear words and (in the case of example (26)) the appeal to violence. These men also construct a masculinity characterised by emotional restraint. Male inexpressivity is recognised as a major feature of contemporary masculinity, and is increasingly seen as problematic: 'we have learnt to use our language to set a safe distance from our felt experience' (Seidler 1989: 63).

Not surprisingly, alternative masculinities represent a challenge to the hegemonic form. Some men in some conversations construct themselves as more reflective, as having experienced fear or pain. But there is a constant awareness that this exposes them to ridicule or to accusations of deviance, in particular, to the accusation of being gay. The two men in the next example met in the pub after work and began to discuss what it means to try to be more open with each other. This discussion began because one of their friends had talked about some difficult aspects of his life the previous week, and Pete and Tony agreed that this is something they admired. Tony says he is trying to be more like that:

(28) *Tony:* I think it's because I decided that- . that (1.0) I ((really)) didn't like this way of relating to people very much and that . life actually would be . improved by . people being more open with each other . not that I'm . brilliant at it <QUIET LAUGH>

Pete: makes you vulnerable though don't you think? . um don't- don't you feel vulnerable? . sometimes?

Tony: yeah but . I suppose that . that's a useful reminder really isn't it ((I mean)) vulnerability is er- (1.0) all the- all the- the- the masks and so on are supposed to keep vulnerability at bay but . .hh they only do this at a very high cost

Here we see an alternative masculinity being voiced: feeling vulnerable can be uncomfortable, yet wearing masks all the time is a much worse option. Tony here positions himself in an alternative discourse which challenges hegemonic masculinity and asserts the value of emotional honesty and openness.

But even when they do discuss more personal issues and thus potentially challenge masculine norms, in most contexts men will choose to use linguistic strategies that neutralise this by aligning themselves with conventional masculinity. The following exchange comes from a conversation between four male friends talking about a friend's girlfriend's infidelity:

(29) [*four men in a flat in Manchester, Northern England*]

Dave: fucking 'ell, harsh that . . .

Chaz: bit harsh that, innit?

Dave: yeah, it's a bit heavy innit?

George: blues big time

Ewan: I'd be fucking gutted . . .

(Gough and Edwards 1998: 419)

The young men's use of taboo words here performs dominant masculinity and thus maintains masculine norms, despite the (more sensitive) topic. But note the use of repetition and tag questions (*innit?*) in this brief exchange (linguistic strategies more often associated with all-female talk).

8.4 Conclusion

In this chapter I have summarised some of the research carried out on talk in same-sex groups. This research suggests that the linguistic characteristics of all-female talk and all-male talk differ, to the extent that some analysts have labelled all-female talk 'cooperative' and all-male talk 'competitive'. An understanding that these different ways of talking may share the goal of creating group solidarity suggests that it would be unwise to exaggerate male–female differences. However, even work which explores cooperation in all-male talk (e.g. Cameron 1997; Hewitt 1997) suggests that such cooperation either enables or accompanies competitive behaviour.

The final section of the chapter explores the notion of gender as performative. The idea that speakers 'do' gender rather than just 'being' men or women now informs much contemporary sociolinguistic work on gender. In their talk, men and women can be seen to align themselves with dominant norms of masculinity and femininity as they 'do' gender with one another. These dominant norms are always open to challenge, and masculinity and femininity need to be understood as plural rather than singular: speakers have a choice of a range of masculinities and femininities. These choices are, however, constrained by normative pressures – speakers are not free agents. It is more difficult to do masculinity or femininity in ways which challenge or subvert the dominant gender norms.

Notes

1 An unexpected finding of Aries' research was that the men she studied became less and less interested in attending the all-male sessions and looked forward to the meetings of the mixed groups; the women, on the other hand, preferred the all-female sessions. More recent research, looking at talk on the Internet, has discovered that women-only groups on the Internet continue to grow, while men-only groups are virtually non-existent (Herring et al. 1995: 69).
2 My database consists of recordings of spontaneous conversation between women and men friends in single-sex groups. These friendship groups represent a range of ages (from 12-year-old girls and 16-year old boys to speakers in late middle-age) and come from a range of social backgrounds and from a variety of regions (London, the Midlands, Belfast, Merseyside). My thanks yet again to all who participated for so generously allowing their talk to be used for research purposes. All names have been changed.
3 This example is taken from Pichler (2003).
4 This seems to be a more general version of the ARGUMENT IS WAR metaphor discussed by Lakoff and Johnson in their seminal book *Metaphors We Live By* (1980).

5   Thanks to Kate Segall for giving me access to this conversation.

6   Male irritation at, and incomprehension of, women's all-in-together style is nicely illustrated by this quotation from Kingsley Amis's novel *Stanley and the Women* (1984: 234): 'From the start she paid close attention to everything I said. . . . She . . . made some faces and a few noises at high or low points but *she came out with none of those dispensable prompts I had known females to hand out so as to stay in shot while someone else tried to talk*' (my italics).

Causes and consequences

CHAPTER 9

Children and gender-differentiated language

9.1 Children and gender identity

The last five chapters have established that women and men differ linguistically in a wide variety of ways. In this chapter I shall look at the way these different repertoires begin. Work on child language acquisition is relatively recent, and it tends to concentrate on how the (undifferentiated) child acquires his or her language. Language is often interpreted in the narrow sense of grammar, phonology and lexicon, with particular emphasis on the development of syntax. Classic studies in this field are Bloom (1975), Brown (1976), Dale (1976), Fletcher and Garman (1986), Ingram (1989). More recently, with increased awareness of language as social behaviour, researchers have widened the scope of their enquiries. They still aim to discover how a child becomes linguistically competent, but 'linguistically competent' has been redefined. As was pointed out in Chapter 6, a knowledge of grammar, phonology and lexicon is not enough – it does not make the child competent. Children need to master not only the formal rules of language, but also rules for the appropriate use of language. Linguistic competence is now taken to include a knowledge of the cultural norms of spoken interaction. An excellent example of work using this new framework is Ochs and Schieffelin's (1983) study of children's acquisition of conversational competence.[1]

Ochs and Schieffelin take the view that learning to speak is learning to be a member of a particular culture. The social order, in other words, is reproduced through speech. This being so, and since it seems to be common to all cultures that women's and men's roles are distinguished, it is reasonable to assume that when children learn to speak, one of the things they are learning is the cultural role assigned to them on the basis of their sex. This is a two-way process: in becoming linguistically competent, the child learns how to 'do' masculinity or femininity in a particular speech community; conversely, when children adopt particular linguistic behaviour as part of their performance of masculinity or femininity, they perpetuate the social order which creates gender distinctions.

Girls and boys learn during childhood to identify with either women or men. They demonstrate their membership of the group by their use of gender-appropriate behaviour, and this includes gender-appropriate *linguistic* behaviour. Social psychologists refer to this process (of learning how to 'do' being a girl or being a boy) as the acquisition of **gender identity**. This process will vary from culture to culture. It is relatively rigid in the USA, for example, where from infancy a child's clothes, toys, play activities, etc. are gendered (Kimmell 2000: 122–6). By contrast, in Vanuatu in the southwest Pacific, children are given a great deal of latitude in terms of gender to the extent that a 12-year-old girl commented to the sociolinguist Miriam Meyerhoff that her friend Vira 'used to be a girl but now he's a boy' (Meyerhoff 2003: 303). Nevertheless, by the time speakers on Vanuatu reach adulthood, they will have identified with the gender role conventionally associated with their sex.

In this chapter I shall describe work which demonstrates that gender differences are found in the speech of children. This work is of two kinds. First, there is work which aims to test the belief that girls acquire language at a faster rate than boys; this work will be described briefly. Secondly, there is work which explores children's use of gender-differentiated language in terms of both formal features and communicative competence; this work will be described in some detail. In this second group I shall include work which analyses the ways in which adults – particularly parents – interact with children, as well as work which analyses the ways in which children interact with each other in same-sex peer groups.

9.2 Gender differences in early language learning

One of the most well-known and best established generalisations in the area of gender differences is girls' superiority over boys in the acquisition of speech. On measures such as the onset of babbling, the first word, number of words used at 18 months, girls tend to do better than boys. This contrast between girls and boys seems to have been exaggerated in the past, although it has been suggested that differences between male and female children might be diminishing as a reflection of less polarised gender roles and less sexist modes of child care in contemporary societies. However, Maccoby and Jacklin's (1974) authoritative survey of all extant research in the area concluded that the generalisation still holds good. For pre-school children, the research findings indicate that, where a gender difference is found, it is nearly always girls who are ahead. Not all these differences achieved statistical significance, but the combined results of all the studies amount to a significant trend. For the early school years, on the other hand, no consistent differences emerge from the research literature, but from the age of 10 or 11 girls again outscore boys on a variety of measures of verbal competence. Some examples of these findings are described below.

Clarke-Stewart (1973) observed American mothers and first-born children for nine months, from when the children were 9 months old until they were 18 months old. She found that the language skills of girls in the sample in terms of both comprehension and vocabulary were significantly higher than those of boys; this was paralleled by the girls' more positive involvement with the mother. The girls' mothers differed from the boys' mothers in that they spent more time in the same room as their daughters, had more eye contact with them, used a higher proportion of directive and restrictive behaviours, and a higher ratio of social to referential speech. (Social speech includes greetings, *thank you*, apologies, etc. while referential speech, as its name implies, means speech which refers to things: *What's this?*; *Give me the red brick*, etc.)

Nelson (1973) studied the acquisition of vocabulary by eighteen children between 1 and 2 years of age (again in the USA). She divided her sample into two groups according to the rate at which they acquired vocabulary (the index was the age at which the child had acquired fifty words). All the boys fell into the group with a slower acquisition rate. The mean age for fifty words was 18.0 months for the girls and 22.1 months for the boys.

Perkins (1983) reports a study of modal expressions (*can, will, have to, probably*, etc.) used in spontaneous speech by children aged between 6 and 12. His subjects were the ninety-six children taking part in the Polytechnic of Wales Language Development project. All the children were monolingual English speakers, and the sample was balanced in terms of age, gender and social class. Perkins discovered that frequency of use of modal expressions varied in relation to the child's gender, with girls using modal expressions more frequently than boys (though this difference was too small to be statistically significant). Interestingly, Perkins found that social class was significantly correlated with modal usage: children from middle-class homes used modal expressions more frequently. This parallelism between girls and the middle class on one hand and boys and the working class on the other is something that has been noted earlier (see section 4.4.3).

In fact, linguistic gender differences seem to be more marked in poorer families: two studies of disadvantaged children (Shipman 1971; Stanford Research Institute 1972) found girls clearly ahead on a number of language measures. Gender differences are also more marked in children where language development is non-normal: the sex ratio of boys to girls in the population assessed as having specific language impairment (SLI) is 2.82:1 (Fletcher and Ingham 1995: 604).

These studies are representative of the many that have been carried out on child language and show a general pattern of girls acquiring language faster than boys. This means that, at any given age, girls will be found to be superior in terms of comprehension, size of vocabulary, reading ability, handling of complex expressions such as the modals, etc. While such findings are of interest, they are not necessarily relevant to the linguistic differences we find between women and men (many just reflect slower maturation). In the next section, I shall describe work which, it can be argued, shows children developing gender-differentiated language. The linguistic differences described below show girls and boys aligning themselves with the gender-roles prescribed by society.

9.3 The development of gender-appropriate speech

In this section I shall look first at work which describes gender differences in children's language which anticipate formal differences in adult language of the kind described in Chapters 4 and 5. Secondly, I shall look at work where children's language usage anticipates adult communicative competence differences of the kind described in Chapters 6–8.

9.3.1 Formal differences

Before puberty, children's vocal tracts differ only in relation to the child's size and not in relation to the child's gender. But children begin to 'sound like' boys or girls before there is any anatomical explanation for this difference: in other words, children learn to perform gender appropriately by manipulating the vocal tract in ways which mimic eventual anatomical differences. Liebermann (1967) suggests that, even before they can talk, babies alter the pitch of their voices depending on the gender of the addressee: their average fundamental frequency is lower when they 'talk' to their fathers than when they 'talk' to their mothers.

Several projects (e.g. Sachs et al. 1973; Meditch 1975; Fichtelius et al. 1980; Lee et al. 1995) have tested the ability of adult judges to identify a child's gender from recorded samples of speech. These projects find that adult judges identify children correctly as male or female with a success rate of around 70 per cent. Further analysis of the child speech samples suggests that it is **formant** patterns which identify speakers as male or female. (A formant is a concentration of acoustic energy, reflecting the way air vibrates in the vocal tract as it changes its shape; most sounds can be described on the basis of three main formants.) 'The child would be learning culturally determined patterns that are viewed as appropriate for each sex. Within the limit of his (*sic*) anatomy, a speaker could change the formant pattern by pronouncing vowels with phonetic variations, or by changing the configuration of the lips' (Sachs et al. 1973: 80). So even at an age when their articulatory mechanisms are identical, girls and boys are learning to perform gender appropriately, that is, to produce higher or lower formants respectively.

Fichtelius et al. (1980) showed that both adult and child judges could still guess the gender of a child speaker even when the tapes had been submitted to a process which affects the sound so that individual words and syllables are no longer discernible but rhythmic patterns and intonation are still apparent. Older children were more easily identified than younger ones, since as girls and boys get older, their speech becomes *prosodically* differentiated. Boys begin to employ a more rapid tempo, while girls use a greater variety of intonation patterns.

Children's acquisition of *intonation* has also been investigated by Local (1982) as part of the Tyneside Linguistic Survey. The children were aged between $5^{1}/_{4}$ and 6 by the end of the study. Taped extracts of their speech were abstracted from a larger corpus collected over a period of about a year. Adults on Tyneside use a system of nuclear tone which differs markedly in its frequency distribution from the system used by adult speakers of Standard English. Figure 9.1 pictures these differences and shows the gross percentage distribution of each tone in two samples (one of Tyneside speakers and the other of speakers of Standard English). Note especially the difference in the relative frequency of falls (\), rise-falls (/ \), and levels (—) between the Tyneside and Standard speakers. These differences reflect dialectal differences which enable us to say of a speaker using Tyneside intonation pattern 's/he comes from Tyneside'.

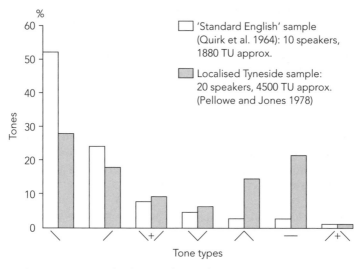

Figure 9.1 Gross percentage distribution of tones for two samples – Tyneside speakers and Standard English speakers (Local 1982: 89)

Local shows how the children's tone system altered over the period studied. Most importantly, there was a shift in the relative frequency of falls, rises and level tones in the children's speech. Further, there was a *decrease* in the frequency of nuclear falls, and an *increase* in the frequency of nuclear levels in the children's speech throughout the period studied. In other words, during the year all the children shifted their speech in the direction of adult Tyneside

English. However, the relative frequency of these tones was not the same for all children, and Local identified three different patterns:

Pattern 1:   More falls than rises and more levels than rises (Paul, Peter, James, Colin, Robert, Allan)

Pattern 2:   More falls than rises and more rises than levels (Keith, Derek, Cath, Eunice, Kate, Judith)

Pattern 3:   More rises than falls and more rises than levels (Claire, Angela, Sheila, Janice, Elaine, Anne)

These patterns reveal that the children's speech varies on the basis of speaker's gender. Pattern 3 (more rises than falls or levels) is typical of girls' speech; pattern 1 (falls and levels more frequent than rises) is typical of boys' speech; while pattern 2 is ambiguous, being realised by both girls and boys. Patterns 3 and 1 are also found in adult speech on Tyneside, with adult females using more rises than falls or levels and adult males using more falls and levels than rises. Thus Local's analysis reveals children acquiring not just Tyneside intonation, but Tyneside intonation appropriate to their gender.

Work on *phonological variation* in children's speech also confirms that gender differentiation is present from an early age. In the course of a study of child-rearing in a semi-rural New England village, Fischer (1964) was struck by differences between the pronunciation of girls and boys. Using his tapes of interviews with the twenty-four children in the sample, he carried out a quantitative analysis of the variable (ing). In this community, (ing) has two variants: the standard variant [ɪŋ] and the non-standard variant [ɪn]. The twenty-four children in the sample consisted of two equal age groups (3–6 year olds and 7–10 year olds), each group containing equal numbers of girls and boys. Fischer's analysis of his data revealed that the girls used the standard variant [ɪŋ] more frequently, while the boys preferred the non-standard variant [ɪn] (see Table 9.1). These differences are statistically significant. It seems likely that the children have learned that in their speech community [ɪŋ] is a marker of female speech and [ɪn] is a marker of male speech.

Table 9.1:   Gender differences in the use of (ing) (based on Fischer 1964: 484)

	More [ɪŋ]	More [ɪn]
Girls	10	2
Boys	5	7

In her study of primary school children in Edinburgh, Suzanne Romaine (1978) found that speaker's gender was the single most important factor correlating with use of the phonological variable (r). In a survey of gender differences in the language of children and adolescents, Romaine (1984) compares her results for 10 year olds in Edinburgh with Macaulay's results for 10 year olds in Glasgow (Macaulay's work on *adult* gender differences in Glasgow was discussed in section 4.3.2). Although the scoring procedures used in the two studies were slightly different, the results are very similar. Both Romaine and Macaulay investigated the variables (gs) (the glottal stop) as in *butter*, (i) as in *hit*, (au) as in *house*, and (a) as in *bag*. For all these variables, there is clear gender differentiation in both Edinburgh and Glasgow (though for (a) in Glasgow the differences in girls' and boys' scores is not large enough to be significant). In other words, girls obtained lower scores than boys for all these variables; their lower scores reflect less frequent use of non-standard variants.[2] The pattern of gender differentiation found among children in Edinburgh and Glasgow is the same as that found in the adult population: the girls consistently prefer forms which are closer to standard pronunciation, while the boys prefer forms which are more non-standard.

It's even possible that these findings greatly underestimate the variation in children's speech. The results discussed here are for 10 year olds; as children get older and move through primary school, their use of non-standard forms appears to diminish, so 10 year olds have lower scores on average than 6 year olds. If we look at the variable (au) in Edinburgh, as used by three different age groups, we can see how the scores get lower, apparently reflecting diminished use of the stigmatised non-standard variant [u:] (as in *hoos*) and increased use of the standard variant [au] (as in *house*) (see Figure 9.2). At the age of 6, the difference between boys' and girls' use of (au) is very marked – boys are shown to choose the non-standard variant [u:] more than 50 per cent of the time (i.e. they tend to say *hoos* rather than *house*). Girls at 6, on the other hand, use the non-standard variant less than 20 per cent of the time. As the children get older, both girls and boys are recorded as using fewer stigmatised forms, and the difference between girls' and boys' usage gets smaller.

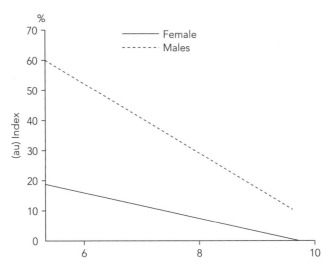

Figure 9.2 Percentage of non-standard [u:] in the usage of girls and boys in three age groups in Edinburgh (Romaine 1984: 101)

Romaine (1984) suggests that what these figures might actually show is children's growing ability to code-switch, that is, to use different forms in different contexts. She observes that, while use of the stigmatised variant certainly decreases in the interview situation as children get older, it is still much in evidence when children are talking among themselves in the playgrounds. So these children can be seen to be developing competence in style-shifting (they are learning which styles are appropriate in which contexts), as well as developing competence in gender-appropriate linguistic behaviour.

Eisikovits' (1987, 1998) study of adolescent speech in Sydney, Australia, which we looked at first in section 4.3.4, provides very interesting evidence of the way children's usage shifts as they develop gender-appropriate speech. She obtained data from two groups of working-class adolescents, interviewed in self-selected pairs (to reduce the formality of the situation). The twenty subjects in the first group had an average age of 16 years 1 month; the twenty subjects in the second group had an average age of 13 years 11 months. As we saw in section 4.3.4, the results for the 16 year olds showed the expected pattern, with male speakers using consistently more non-standard forms than female speakers. But if we compare these results with those for the 13 year olds, we can see that there are significant differences between the two: the younger speakers do not conform to the expected pattern. As Figure 9.3 shows, the younger girls use a *higher* proportion of non-standard past tense forms than any other group, while their use of multiple negation is very similar to that of the younger boys.

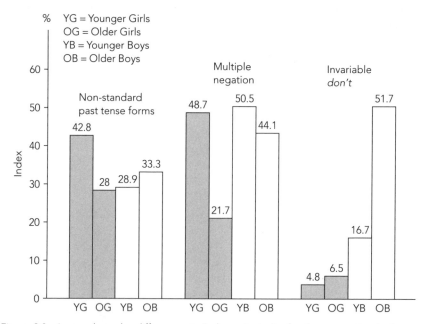

Figure 9.3 Age and gender differences in Sydney, Australia, for three non-standard grammatical features (based on Eisikovits 1998)

Invariable *don't* is the only non-standard grammatical feature which shows clear gender variation for both age groups; moreover, the boys increase their usage of this feature significantly as they get older.

What we see here is declining usage of non-standard forms among the girls, and stable or increasing usage among the boys. It looks as if many of the non-standard features of Sydney vernacular speech have prestige for young adolescents of both sexes. But as they get older, the girls learn to modify their speech in the direction of the standard, while the boys seem to consolidate their perception of non-standard forms as having positive value. In discussion with the interviewer, the older informants displayed divergent attitudes: the girls became increasingly conservative, the boys increasingly non-conformist. For example, the girls said they didn't like swearing any longer, and objected to their boyfriends swearing, while for the boys swearing is a normal part of every-day life: 'If I swear in front of me mother now, she don't say nothing'. It seems that a growing awareness of gender norms is matched by a shift in linguistic usage so that, by the age of 16, these speakers have adjusted their speech to be more congruent with dominant norms of masculinity and femininity.

Eisikovits' findings might help us to interpret those of Penelope Eckert (discussed in 4.3.5). Eckert's data revealed that the burnout girls were the most advanced speakers in terms of new vernacular forms. These girls, then, like their 13-year-old working-class peers in Sydney, display a preference for non-standard forms, a preference which upsets the expectation that female speakers will tend to choose more standard forms. What we need to ask is, what happens to burnout girls as they get older? Will they, like the working-class girls in Eisikovits' sample, begin to adjust their speech to conform to adult patterns?

9.3.2 Differences in communicative competence

So far I have looked at work which shows children acquiring the formal features of language. Now I shall examine the development of gender-differentiated communicative competence in children's speech. I shall look at work on verbosity and conversational dominance; interruptions and simultaneous speech; politeness; and the acquisition of folklinguistic beliefs.

Verbosity and conversational dominance

As far as verbosity is concerned, Smith and Connolly (1972) conclude that girls are both more talkative and more fluent. They talk more, both to their mothers and to other children, before the age of 4, but after that such quantitative differences disappear. These results could be the product of different expectations on the part of parents. Our culture expects girls and women to talk more and early research in this area, with crude measures and small samples, seemed to confirm the talkativeness of pre-school girls. However, as we saw in section 7.4, work on adult language indicates that women talk *less* than men in mixed company.

Certainly, recent research suggests that boys dominate mixed conversation from an early age. Adelaide Haas (1978, 1979) analysed the amount of speech produced by girls and boys aged 4, 8 and 12 in mixed-sex pairs: she found that boys produced longer utterances than girls. Joan Swann's (1998) analysis of classroom talk (using 9–11 year olds) showed convincingly that boys talked far more than girls, both in terms of the number of turns taken and the number of words uttered. (This research will be described in greater detail in section 11.2.) She also demonstrates that *all* participants in the classroom collaborate to achieve male dominance: the teacher by paying more attention to the boys; the boys by using the interactional resources available to contribute more; the girls by using the same resources to contribute less.

This pattern of differential usage of interactional resources can also be seen in the context of the family. Male children are socialised to dominate conversation with the active support of female participants. Frederick Erickson (1990) analysed the dinner-table conversation of a large Italian-American family: mother, father, four sons (aged 7–14 years) and a daughter (aged 9 years). A female researcher was also present at the meal. The conversation consisted of a series of narratives. One set of narratives focused on accidents or near-misses experienced by members of the family when riding their bikes. The initial story was told by the youngest boy. This was followed by stories from the older boys. Finally, the father told a dramatic story about his own experience of nearly crashing his motor-bike, which capped the previous stories. The stories were recounted almost exclusively by the male members of the family (the daughter started one but didn't succeed in sustaining it), and celebrate the bravery and skill of the riders. The mother, daughter and female guest acted as an attentive audience for the story-tellers. These stories not only establish the relative status of male family members; they also function as a display of male dominance which is achieved collaboratively by the whole family.

Ochs and Taylor's (1995) study of narrative roles at family dinnertimes comes to similar conclusions. Their starting point was that children come to understand family and gender roles through different ways of acting and expressing feelings in narrative activity. They show that mothers tend to introduce narratives, but fathers take on the even more important role of evaluating and judging the narratives, becoming the 'primary audience, judge and critic of family members' actions, conditions, thoughts and feelings' (Ochs and Taylor 1995: 99). This constructs a 'Father knows best' dynamic which contributes to the maintenance of traditional – and asymmetrical – family power structures.

Interruptions and simultaneous speech

Research on interruptions and simultaneous speech has found no significant differences between younger girls and boys. By the age of 15, however, boys are using interruptions to dominate talk (Gilbert 1990, cited in Holmes 1995: 53). Parents also differ significantly in terms of both interruptions and simultaneous speech. Greif (1980) studied sixteen middle-class children, aged between 2 and 5, in conversation with (1) their mothers and (2) their fathers. Her results show that fathers interrupted more than mothers (though this difference was not quite large enough to be statistically significant), and that both parents interrupted girls more than boys. In terms of simultaneous speech (i.e. both speakers starting to speak at the same time), parents were significantly more likely to continue talking than were children, father-and-child pairs were more likely to engage in simultaneous speech than mother-and-child pairs, and finally both fathers and mothers were more likely to engage in simultaneous speech with daughters than with sons.

As we have seen (section 7.3), the use of interruptions and simultaneous speech can be interpreted as a way of controlling conversation. It seems that fathers try to control conversation more than mothers (which fits the research results for adult conversations), and both parents try to control conversation more with daughters than with sons. The implicit message to girls is that they are more interruptible and that their right to speak is less than that of boys.

When equals, as opposed to asymmetrical pairs such as father–child, engage in simultaneous speech, then such linguistic behaviour is likely to symbolise solidarity and cooperation rather than dominance (see section 8.2.1). In his study of the gender politics of an elementary school classroom in San Diego, California, Jürgen Streeck (1986) describes an episode where the girls' ability to talk in unison becomes a powerful strategy for demonstrating to the boys the unity of the girls' coalition.

(1)   [*The teacher has given the group a task to do*]

    Leola: I know y-you gotta make some wo:rds out of these

    Wallace: you don't

    { *Leola*:   yes ⌈ you do

    { *Wallace*:   ⌊ you don't

    { *Leola*:   you see, here it s ⌈ ay–   how man–

    { *Carolyn*:   ⌊ it say–

    { *Leola*:   ⌈ how many words can you make out of those

    { *Carolyn*: ⌊ how many words can you make out of those

    { *Leola*:   ⌈ five letters

    { *Carolyn*: ⌊ five letters

Given that talk in unison is not easy to accomplish, we have to admire the girls' interactive skills, which clearly prefigure women's later skills in contrapuntal talk.

Politeness

Politeness is another dimension of communicative competence where we find gender differences (see section 6.6). Research on child language has concentrated on the way parents teach polite language, for example, formulae like greetings and *thank you*. Gleason (1980) studied parents and children in both natural and laboratory settings. She was interested in finding out how much *explicit* teaching of such formulae goes on. She found parents very consistent in prompting their children to respond with socially appropriate items, particularly *thank you*. Parents treated girls and boys similarly, but provided different models: the mothers used far more polite speech than the fathers. This was also the main finding of Snow et al. (1990) who studied the linguistic behaviour of parents in twenty-four families. Thus, while girls and boys are both urged to use polite forms, the children observe that it is predominantly adult females who use them themselves.

The one significant difference observed of the children in Gleason's study was that the boys were more likely than the girls to greet the researcher spontaneously (41 per cent:18 per cent). This may also result from the children's observation of adults: adult male speakers tend to take the initiative in conversation. Children's observation of adults is also behind the results of a study of family role-play. Aronsson and Thorell (1999) analysed the linguistic strategies chosen by children who role-played family conflict. They focused on controlling strategies, and concluded that the children enacted the father as 'the man of ultimate action' and the mother as 'compromiser and negotiator – the one who provides reasons, justifications and other mitigating accounts' (Aronsson and Thorell 1999: 43).

Politeness is a relevant dimension for the speech act of requesting. A request may vary from the blunt imperative *Give me a pound* to the more polite *Would you lend me a pound?* (more polite because it is sensitive to the face needs of the addressee – see section 6.6). Walters (1981) observed the requests of thirty-two bilingual children in four different contexts. He found no significant differences in terms of speaker's gender, but the gender of the addressee was significantly correlated with the politeness of the request. The children in the study were more polite when the addressee was female, and less polite when the addressee was male.

It seems that adult interaction with girls and boys may be significantly affected by *context*. In a long-term study of children in Bristol, Wells (1979) examined all conversations occurring when the children were $3^{1}/_{4}$ years old, and categorised them according to who initiated them (the child or the adult) and according to the context (mealtime, watching television, playing with another child, etc.). 30 per cent of conversation sequences were initiated by an adult (usually the mother), and an analysis of these revealed significant differences in the context in which adults addressed girls or boys. Table 9.2 gives the figures. This table shows that over half the sequences initiated with girls were in helping or non-play contexts – a ratio of 2:1 compared with the boys. Sequences initiated with boys, on the other hand, were overwhelmingly in the context of play. 'This suggests that adults emphasize more useful and domestic activities in their interaction with girls, whilst the emphasis with boys is towards a more free-ranging, exploratory manipulation of the physical environment' (Wells 1979: 392).

Table 9.2: Proportions of conversations initiated by adults with girls and boys in different contexts (based on Wells 1979: 391)

	Girls (%)	Boys (%)
Helping/non-play activity	56.8	28.8
Talking and reading	19.0	22.5
Playing with adult	5.2	18.1
Dressing, meals, toileting	12.1	14.4
Playing alone	3.4	8.1
Watching TV	0.9	5.4
Playing with another child	2.6	2.7
Total	100	100

Acquiring folklinguistic beliefs

Children are learning not only gender-appropriate behaviour, but also a knowledge of the folklinguistic beliefs of our society. At what age do children learn that in our culture swearing, for example, is seen as a way to do masculinity? Edelsky (1976) tested this by selecting twelve language variables conventionally associated with 'women's language' or with 'men's language' and presenting them, embedded in utterances, to adult and child judges. The judges were asked to rate each sentence as probably made by a woman, probably made by a man, or no preference. Her child judges (aged 7, 9 and 12 years) demonstrated a growing ability to recognise certain linguistic forms as appropriate to speakers of a particular gender. At 7 years, only two variables get a consistent response: *adorable* is judged to be female, and *Damn it!* is judged to be male. At 9 years, this has increased to eight variables: *adorable, oh dear, my goodness, won't you please* are judged to be female, and *damn it!, damn* + adjective, *I'll be damned* are judged to be male (tag questions get a neutral response). At 12 years, the child judges agree on assigning every one of the twelve variables to one sex or the other: tag questions, *so, very, just* are added to the female list, and commands to the male list.

We can see that children are gradually developing a knowledge of adult norms, and internalising the folklinguistic beliefs of our society (the fact that some of these beliefs are false – see section 6.2 – is irrelevant). Edelsky gives a more delicate analysis of her findings to show that there are two clear patterns of acquisition. Variables in her first group – *adorable, oh dear, my goodness, so, just*, tag questions – show a steady increase with age in the number of people able to interpret them as being appropriate to a particular sex. Variables in the second group – *I'll be damned, damn* + adjective, *damnit, won't you please, very*, command as male – show a different pattern: there is an increase in 'correct' answers peaking at 12 years old and decreasing in adulthood. It seems that the variables in this second group are features of language which are explicitly commented on through proverbs or admonishments. Expressions such as 'Little girls don't say that' mean that children are *taught* the gender-appropriateness of some linguistic terms. As happens with other features of child language, when a rule is learned it is frequently overgeneralised. Just as children add *-ed* to all verbs to form the past tense, once they've grasped this rule, producing forms like *goed, eated, singed* (even though they earlier used forms like *went, ate, sang* – and of course subsequently do so again), so it seems they overgeneralise the rule for gender-appropriate language and treat such differences as *gender-exclusive* rather than *gender-preferential* (see section 3.4). As a result, they have to modify their rules later to conform to adult norms.

9.3.3 Subculture and conversational style

The focus of much recent work on children's communicative competence is child–child talk rather than adult–child talk. It is now widely accepted that the peer group is of vital importance in a child's sociolinguistic development. Girls and boys tend to play in same-sex groups; gender is the organising principle that structures their activities. Streeck (1986), for example, describes the behaviour of the children he observed in primary school: the girls and the boys huddled on opposite sides of the table, their posture and position clearly signifying two separate camps; when joint activity was required, talk between the two groups was antagonistic. These findings are echoed by Barrie Thorne (1993) who carried out long-term fieldwork in two American primary schools. She describes the process whereby children are separated into two groups on the basis of gender as 'an intricate choreography' (1993: 36). This involves girls and boys sitting on different sides of the classroom, teachers pitting girls against boys in spelling and maths contests, girls and boys lining up for dinner in two separate lines, boys occupying nine-tenths of the playground, for example. As one 11-year-old girl said to Thorne, 'It's like girls and boys are on different sides' (1993: 63).

Collaborative vs competitive talk

One of the chief reasons that girls and boys develop different styles of talk is that the all-girls and all-boys groups to which they belong interact in vastly different ways. Boys play in larger, more hierarchical groups, while girls play in small groups, often in pairs. Boys' friendships tend to be based on joint *activity*, while girls' friendships are based on *talk*. In their influential article on gender-specific subcultures, Daniel Maltz and Ruth Borker (1982) argue that girls learn to do three things with words:

1. To create and maintain relationships of closeness and equality.
2. To criticise others in acceptable ways.
3. To interpret accurately the speech of other girls.

Boys, on the other hand, learn to do the following when they speak:

1. To assert a position of dominance.
2. To attract and maintain an audience.
3. To assert themselves when another speaker has the floor.

Maltz and Borker characterise girls' talk as **collaboration-oriented**, boys' talk as **competition-oriented**. This characterisation clearly prefigures adult patterns of talk in same-sex groups (see section 8.2).

These gender-specific patterns of interaction develop early. Farida Abu-Haidar (1995) observed groups of children aged 8–11 in a Lebanese rural community. She claims that the boys' talk is noticeably less fluent and articulate than the girls', and that the boys compete with each other whereas the girls construct talk in a mutually supportive way. The following brief extracts illustrate this contrast – a group of boys and a group of girls were asked to tell the researcher in their own words about a recent incident when a bus had been hit by a falling rock.

(2) Extract from boys' account

Boy 1: as it, the bus, was coming, turning the corner . . . crash!

Boy 2: no much earlier

Boy 1: it was at the corner . . . my uncle was there!

Boy 3: the rock came down, we heard it, like thunder . . .

Boy 4: before the corner

Boy 5: whoosh! [laughter]

[Abu-Haidar 1995: 191]

(3) Extract from girls' account

Girl 1: the rock came rolling down

Girl 2: just as the bus was coming up to the corner

Girl 3: you see, they'd been blasting on the other side of the valley . . . to build a road

Girl 1: yes and to widen the road leading to the village

Girl 4: they dug too deep . . .

Girl 2: they disturbed the soil, that's what my father said . . .

Girl 5: yes, so did my father . . .

Girl 1: that's right . . .

[Abu-Haidar 1995: 191]

The extract from the boys' talk shows that they dispute each other's account of the accident. Boy 1 says the bus was 'at the corner', while boys 2 and 4 claim it was 'before the corner'. They do not come to any agreement, their account is fragmentary and full of onomatopoeic utterances such as *crash* and *whoosh*. The girls, by contrast, work together to construct a coherent account of what

happened. Note how they design what they say to fit syntactically and semantically with the previous utterance, for example, *the rock came rolling down/just as
the bus was coming up to the corner*. They also make their acceptance of each
other's contributions explicit, by saying *yes* or *that's right*. The data that Abu-
Haidar collected suggest that the girls are more linguistically sophisticated than
the boys, while the boys already display 'the aggressive and competitive behaviour of males in a society where age-old patriarchal norms go unchallenged'
(Abu-Haidar 1995: 192).

Conflict talk

Research looking at conflict shows that girls and boys deal with it in very
different ways. In a study of quarrels between children aged 5–7, Miller et al.
(1986) found that boys used a more heavy-handed style, their priority being to
get their own way, while girls used more mitigating strategies (such as compromise, evasion or acquiescence) and were more concerned to maintain interpersonal harmony. Boys were more likely to resort to physical force to resolve
conflicts. Similar findings emerged from a study of talk among 3-year-old friends
in same-sex triads, carried out by Amy Sheldon (1990, 1996). She analyses in
detail two disputes over a plastic pickle which arose when the children were
playing in the home corner (with a toy cooker, pots and pans, a sink, and
plastic items of food). One of the disputes occurred in a group of girls, the
other in a group of boys. The girls succeeded in negotiating a resolution and
maintained interconnectedness among members of the group. They also sustained their fantasy play, pretending to prepare food for the dolls. The boys, by
contrast, adopted a more adversarial style and, since neither of the main prot-
agonists was prepared to give in, the conflict escalated (and lasted considerably
longer than the girls': 5 minutes compared with 1 minute 45 seconds for the
girls). Moreover, this conflict disrupted the boys' fantasy play.

Disputes between boys at nursery school in Italy (Corsaro and Rizzo 1990)
deal not only with issues of ownership and protection of territory, but also of
who is 'il capo', the boss. In the following example, Matteo and Luigi are
making a space ship; Nino approaches and tries to join in.

(4) *Nino*: Anch'io posso?
I can also?

Luigi: si, puoi giocare
yes, you can play

Matteo: no, io sono il capo
no, I'm the boss

Nino: si, e vero
yes, it's true

Luigi (to Matteo): Lui – puo giocare?
him – can he play?

(Nino reaches over and picks up some building materials near Matteo)

Matteo: no non puoi, ma, non puoi!
no you can't, but, you can't!

Girls in this nursery school also get involved in disputes over ownership and in excluding third parties from their play, but they demonstrate an ability to work *together* to achieve their aims. For example, in one incident observed by the researcher, Rosa and Grazia work as a team to get a piece of building material back from an intruder, Sara.

Goodwin's research on black children's street play was described in some detail in Chapter 6 (pp. 94–5). Analysis of the way *arguments* among the children were structured shows that girls and boys use many common strategies (Goodwin and Goodwin 1987). They organise their talk to emphasise disagreement or opposition. This is true both of same-sex and mixed talk.

(5) [*talking about Sharon's hair*]

Eddie: wet it!

Sharon: no, I don't *wanna* wet it

(6) [*talking about slings*]

Chopper: I don't want these big thick ones

Michael: you is crazy boy. I swear to god. You need that – thick like that.

However, there was one strategy which was used only by the girls, labelled 'he-said-she-said'. This strategy only indirectly challenges another participant, and opens the dispute to a wider group of participants. Examples (7) and (8) are typical he-said-she-said accusations:

(7) *Darlene*: and *Stephen* said that *you* said that *I* was showin off just because I had that *blouse* on

(8) *Pam*:   Terri said you said that. I wasn't gonna go around *poplar* no more

Framing accusations in this way allows both the accuser and the accused to save face. The accuser focuses attention on somebody not present (Stephen in example (7); Terri in example (8)). The accused can deny responsibility (*I ain't say anything*), or can blame someone else (*that was Vincent said*), or can blame the third party referred to by the accuser (*well I know that they telling a lie cuz I know I ain't say nothin about you*). The he-said-she-said strategy allows for much more complex talk, involving many speakers and a longer time-span than the two-party adversarial disputes typical of all-boy and of mixed talk.

Studies of older *male* children have found that most conflict exchanges are not resolved. In fact, resolution does not seem to be a primary goal. Some conflict is highly ritualised: what is most important is the display of verbal skill. The following example comes from Labov's famous study of pre-adolescent and adolescent boys in Harlem (Labov 1972b).

(9)   *C1:*   your mother got on sneakers!

      C2:   your mother wear high-heeled sneakers to church!

      C3:   your mother wear high-heeled sneakers to come out and play on the basketball court!

A second function of the exchange of ritual insults such as these is to create and maintain status differences among the boys. Girls are far less likely to engage in ritual exchanges of this kind (see Goodwin 1990, 2003). When they do, they seem more concerned with establishing normative behaviour than with status distinctions. Girls aged 10–14 were observed by Donna Eder (1990); in their conflicts they focused on resolving issues such as what does it mean to be someone's best friend, or what constitutes flirting. The trick is to respond to insults with a clever remark or a counter-insult, and not to take them seriously. The girls show some skill at defending themselves against insults from each other, but at other times their inability to joke about certain topics shows how significant such issues are for them.

An overview of all the work on conflict in children's interactions suggests that there is no simple dichotomy, with boys being 'competitive' and girls 'cooperative' (Goodwin 2003). Boys and girls of all backgrounds have to deal with conflict: 'conflict is as omnipresent in the interaction of females as in that of males' (Goodwin 2003: 243). Ritual insults may be more likely to occur in groups where 'toughness' is valued – in other words, this type of competitive linguistic behaviour may be associated as much with social class or with ethnic group as with gender. This is the view of some researchers who fear that the picture has been oversimplified. Others, however, argue that, while social class and ethnicity need to be considered, gender is an important factor in terms of conflict behaviour, and girls in many cultures seem to 'possess verbal negoti-ation skills that enable them to confront without being confrontational' (Sheldon 1996: 61).

Directives

Goodwin's work on directives has been described in 6.3. She showed how boys' strategies for getting someone to do something reinforce the hierarchical organ-isation of the boys' group. Dominant members use bare imperatives (*Gimme the pliers*), while subordinate members use mitigated requests (*can I be on your side Michael?*). Girls prefer to use forms such as *let's* which minimise status differences between participants and which emphasise joint action. Jacqueline Sachs (1987) looked at similar strategies in the talk of much younger children in a pre-school playgroup. Same-sex dyads were videotaped while they played at doctor-and-patient. Sachs analysed the use of 'Obliges', a category wider than directives which includes any utterance that demands a response from the addressee. The following are different sorts of Obliges:

1. Imperatives (a) positive, e.g. *bring her to the hospital*
   (b) negative, e.g. *don't touch it*
2. Declarative directive, e.g. *you have to push it*
3. Pretend directive, e.g. *pretend you had a bad cut*
4. Question directive, e.g. *will you be the patient?*
5. Tag question, e.g. *that's your bed, right?*
6. Joint directive, e.g. *now we'll cover him up*
7. State question, e.g. *are you sick?*
8. Information question, e.g. *what does she need now?*
9. Attention-getting device, e.g. *lookit*

Sachs used as her data the fantasy play of four 5-year-old girl dyads and four 5-year-old boy dyads. She found that girls and boys used roughly the same number of Obliges, but they varied significantly in terms of which type they preferred. Table 9.3 gives the results.

Table 9.3: Distribution of Obliges by category and gender (Sachs 1987: 182)

Category	Girls (%)	Boys (%)
Imperative	12	36
Declarative directive	5	6
Pretend directive	11	4
Question directive	2	0
Tag question	35	16
Joint directive	15	3
State question	2	11
Information question	16	22
Attentional device	2	2
Total	100	100

Notice the boys' preference for imperative forms, and the girls' for tag questions. Overall, the girls preferred more mitigated strategies than the boys: 65 per cent of the girls' Obliges were mitigated, compared with only 34 per cent of the boys'. These findings are summarised in Table 9.4. The girls softened their Obliges, and seemed more concerned to include the other child in planning what they were going to play.

Table 9.4: Distribution of mitigated and unmitigated Obliges (Sachs 1987: 183)

Category	Girls (%)	Boys (%)
Mitigated	65	34
Unmitigated	17	42
Other	18	24

Topic

The question of topic is addressed in Haas's (1978, 1979) study of child language. Adelaide Haas analysed the speech of 4-, 8- and 12-year-old children in same-sex and mixed-sex pairs. In same-sex pairs, the main difference between girls and boys was that boys talked significantly more about sports and location, while girls talked significantly more about school, identity, wishes and needs. Haas's comparison of mixed-sex pairs also found a difference related to topic – the subject of sport was significantly associated with boy speakers. This fits the observation that boys 'learn a masculinity which prescribes certain topics (sports, machines, competitions) and certain ways of speaking (jokes, banter and bravado)' (Tolson 1977: 32).

In Haas's study, boys also used more sound effects (e.g. *brrmm brrmm goes the car*) and more direct requests. The girls laughed more and used more compliant forms (e.g. *okay that's a good idea*). The girls' use of laughter was far more prominent in their interaction with boys than in same-sex interaction – they laughed only half as much when talking to each other. Haas comments that boys seemed to be the initiators of humour, and laughter was the girls' response to this. Laughter may also be seen as appropriately deferential behaviour by the girls, and therefore occurs more with the boys.[3] Both girls and boys adapted their linguistic behaviour when in mixed pairs, but girls accommodated to boys more than vice versa.

Tannen (1990a, 1990b) analysed the conversation of pairs of best friends (conversations which had been video-recorded for research purposes by a psychologist, Bruce Dorval). These children were asked by the researcher to talk about something serious or intimate, and were then left alone in front of a video camera. The youngest boys (8 years old) squirmed in their chairs, kicked their feet, made faces at each other and at the camera. Their conversation jumps from topic to topic, and consists of very short turns. They rebel against the researcher's instructions: they tell jokes, fool around in front of the camera, and conduct mock interviews. The following extract is typical of their conversation:[4]

(10) *Sam*: did you see Star Wars
      (0.8)
      Jeff: no, hey, guess *what*? (1.1) ahm=
      Sam: =you have HBO? (0.6) do you?=
      Jeff: =no [*shakes head*]
      (0.4)
      Sam: neither do we (1.5) you saw Star Track?
      (0.3)
      Jeff: yeah::= [*enthused tone, head motion*]
      Sam: =I like the part when they um, .hh when they
           ⌜were having that:: battle=
      Jeff: ⌞I, I, I,   =at the en', hah
      (0.5)

Sam: Un hn
(0.7)
Jeff: that's *goo::d*

Girls of the same age carried out the researcher's instructions to the letter, and talked seriously for twenty minutes with no sign of discomfort.

(11) *Ellen:* Remember what when I told you about my uncle?
He went up the ladder after my grandpa?
And he fell and um cracked his head open? He's and
you know what? it still hasn't healed

Jane: one time, my uncle, he was uh he has like this bull
ranch? in Millworth?
and the bull's horns went right through his head

Ellen: that's serious

Note how Ellen's comment on her friend's anecdote is supportive, and explicitly orients it to the instructions they've been given.

Pairs of male friends at all ages seemed less comfortable with the task assigned to them. They avoided eye contact and sat parallel rather than facing one another. Older pairs were able to sustain topics for longer, but preferred to remain at an abstract level of discussion and avoided personal details. The only pair who became involved in a personal discussion (16 year olds) did not respond to each other's revelation of anxiety or unhappiness with support, but played down the significance of what the other had said.

(12) [*talking about who to take to the dance*]

Tim: I don't want to ask Bar– , I just don't feel like asking anyone,
and I don't know why, and I don't want to ask Janet, and I felt
so bad when she came over and started talking to me last
night

(0.1)
Robert: why?
(0.9)
Tim: I don't know, I felt uncomfortable I guess
(2.3)
Robert: I'll never understand that <LAUGHS>
(0.7)
Tim: why?
(1.1)
Robert: ((x)) well I can't seem to just do that, ah, I mean, I know that's
what you do, but I mean, I just could never do that

The girls, on the other hand, sit closer to each other and look at each other directly. They talk about serious topics and self-disclose about feelings. Even the youngest girls can sustain a topic over several turns. Individual turns are longer, as the following example shows. It is taken from the conversation of the pair of 12-year-old friends.

(13) Susan: too bad you and Lesley are not good good friends anymore

 Jane: I know. God, it's – she's so *mean* sometimes because .h I mean–
she jus'gets you sta:rted in something nice, she says, um, she's
so *ni:ce* today, that's why I wanted to be her best friend, I mean,
I wasn't tryin' to to take her away from you or anything, .h but I
mean she's so ⌈*ni:ce*=

 Susan: ⌊*ni:ce*=

 Jane: =like I just couldn't (let) her down or anything, .h an' so I just wanted
to BE her friend, I mean – I wanted to be ⌈her best friend

 Susan: ⌊(I know)

 Jane: .h and then – what was so sad she just gets mad at you all of a
sudden .h an like if she does somethin *I* don't like (0.3) I mean,
I jist (0.5) I don't *li:ke* it, I mean I don't get *ma:d* at her!

 (0.7)

 Susan: she tries to upset people

 (0.5)

 Jane: she *doe:s*, and she just sees me crying an everything (0.5) she
just lets me suffer=

 Susan: =and she loves it

 Jane: I know

Note how the girls work together to try to understand a problem. Their talk involves longer turns than that of boys of the same age, and their turns follow very closely one after the other, with only occasional pauses. Moreover, when a girl told a story like this, her friend invariably responded with concern, rather than belittling the problem (compare Tim and Robert in example (12)). The girls' body posture, their patterns of eye contact, and the topics they choose, all emphasise closeness. The boys, on the other hand, choose patterns of physical alignment and eye contact which symbolise separateness, and their choice of impersonal topics and lack of engagement in each other's problems reinforce the impression of separateness.

All the studies referred to in this section demonstrate significant differences in the conversational strategies of girls and boys. Girls prefer a more mitigated style; they use linguistic forms which minimise differences between participants and which are sensitive to speaker's and hearer's face needs. Boys, on the other hand, prefer a more adversarial style and pursue their own agenda without reference to other participants. For boys, winning is all-important. Girls, by contrast, seem aware that where there are winners there are also losers; they prefer jointly negotiated outcomes. However, several of these studies show that, both when interacting with boys and when taking on roles such as mother in pretend play, girls are perfectly competent at the more adversarial style typical of boys (see Goodwin 1980, 1990, 1998, 2003; Maynard 1986; Miller et al. 1986; Goodwin and Goodwin 1987; Sheldon 1992; Sheldon and Johnson 1998). Girls, in other words, can style-shift to suit the sociolinguistic context.

These studies encompass children as young as 3 years old, and include both black children and white children, working-class children and middle-class children, in both natural and experimental situations. This research is unanimous in showing that the gender-specific subcultures which children belong to generate different linguistic subcultures. These anticipate the gender-differentiated talk of adult women and men.

9.4 Conclusion

As we have seen, various studies show differences in male and female children in a wide range of linguistic forms. What emerges is a picture of girls acquiring linguistic skills at a faster rate than boys (though this superiority is not as marked as was claimed in the past), and developing patterns which differentiate them from boys. In the past, researchers believed that such differences arose from innate biological differences, but now differences in linguistic usage are explained in large part by differences in the linguistic environment of girls and boys. Work on the development of differential communicative competence illustrates particularly clearly the crucial role played by environmental factors.

Language is an important part of the socialisation process, and children are socialised into culturally approved gender roles largely through language. Learning to perform masculinity or femininity in our society means among other things learning to use gender-appropriate language. This survey of work on children's acquisition of language suggests that socialisation is achieved in a variety of ways:

1. Through explicit comment on certain aspects of linguistic behaviour (e.g. swearing, taboo language, verbosity, politeness).

2. Through adults providing different linguistic models for children to identify with (see also Chapters 4–8).

3. Through adults talking to children differently depending on the gender of the child (e.g. adults are more likely to interrupt girls, and lisp more when talking to little girls).

4. Through adults having different preconceptions of male and female children (e.g. adults expect female infants to be more verbally able than male infants).

5. Through adults responding differently to girls and boys using the same linguistic strategy (e.g. boys arguing or talking assertively are more likely to get a positive response than girls).

6. Perhaps most importantly, through children's participation in gender-specific subcultures which create and maintain distinct male and female styles of interaction.

It is often suggested that child language may be the locus of linguistic change: that is, a comparison of the variety of language used by children with the variety used by adults of the same ethnic group, social class, etc. will reveal linguistic change in progress. I shall turn now from this survey of child language and the development of gender-preferential differences to an examination of the role these gender differences play in the process of linguistic change.

Notes

1 Other good work using this framework includes Ochs and Schieffelin (1979), McTear (1985), Foster (1990), Schieffelin (1990).
2 Both Romaine and Macaulay adopted scoring procedures which represent RP with a score of 0.
3 See Pizzini (1991) for an analysis of the way humour is used to reinforce existing power relationships between women and men in the obstetrical/gynaecological setting.
4 Examples (10), (12) and (13) are taken from transcripts given in the Appendix of Dorval (1990). Example (11) comes from Tannen (1990a).

CHAPTER 10

The role of gender differences in linguistic change

10.1 Introduction

One of the linguistic consequences of gender differentiation in language seems to be linguistic change. Certainly, differences in women's and men's language are regularly associated with changes in language.

Linguistic change occurs in the context of linguistic variation. Linguistic variation exists in all known societies: it distinguishes the speech of different social groups (**social variation**), and it distinguishes the speech of a given individual in different contexts (**stylistic variation**). Linguistic change can be said to have taken place when a new linguistic form, used by some sub-group within a speech community, is adopted by other members of that community and accepted as the norm. Our understanding of the interaction of groups within society is still poor, but we are beginning to see that the linguistic variation which characterises the differentiation of social groups is crucially associated with the rise and fall of linguistic forms.

In this book, I have focused on the linguistic variation associated with speaker's gender. Sociolinguistic research is beginning to improve our understanding of linguistic change, and it now seems that gender differentiation in speech plays an important role in the mechanism of linguistic change. More accurately, the gender of the speaker plays a significant part in innovation – sometimes women and sometimes men are said to be the group which typically initiates change. This debate parallels that described earlier in dialectology (section 3.5.1) on whether women or men are more conservative linguistically. I shall return to this issue later. In this chapter I shall look at work demonstrating (or claiming to demonstrate) a link between gender differences in language and linguistic change. I shall look first at earlier (dialectological) work, and then, in greater detail, at some recent sociolinguistic studies. In this latter section I shall refer back to studies already discussed in Chapters 4, 5 and 6.

10.2   Dialectological evidence

Dialectologists discussed linguistic change in the communities they studied, sometimes in terms of changing patterns of bilingualism, sometimes in terms of changes in vocabulary or pronunciation within one language system. Since they were often trying to make a record of rural dialects before they died out, they were very aware that linguistic change was taking place, and their comments on the social background of such changes are of great interest.

Auguste Brun, a specialist in the language known as Provençal, discusses the relative roles of Provençal and French in one particular community (Brun 1946). He observes that older people (over 50) speak mainly Provençal, as do younger men, but *women* under 45 speak mainly French. He claims that younger women do not speak Provençal at all among themselves ('I have never heard a phrase of Provençal being used in a group of girls or young women'[1]), nor do they speak Provençal to their children, but only occasionally to the old people. As a result, children of both sexes speak French: they don't speak Provençal to each other or to adults (Brun, as quoted in Pop 1950: 281). If Brun's observations are accurate, we see that in three generations this community has switched from being bilingual but mainly Provençal-speaking to being bilingual but mainly French-speaking, with the use of Provençal diminishing rapidly. Women are portrayed as having a crucial role, since it is they and not the men who adopt French as their main language, and they who use it when bringing up the next generation. At all events, the difference between male and female usage is clearly a crucial factor in the linguistic change described here. (Note the similarities between this dialectological study from the first half of the twentieth century and the sociolinguistic research (discussed in section 6.4) carried out by Susan Gal (1998) in a village on the German–Hungarian border, where younger women are leading the shift from Hungarian to German.)

Pée's (1946) account of changing linguistic usage in Flanders is interesting because he is able to give the background to the change described. The older generation, according to Pée, speak patois (varieties of Flemish); Pée found the women particularly good as informants because of their lack of mobility – they hardly ever left their village and so had little contact with other linguistic varieties. But the First World War resulted in an improved standard of living for many peasants, some of whom sent their daughters to French boarding schools. These girls became 'francisées' (Frenchified/Francophile) and insisted on speaking French instead of Flemish when they returned home. Only those who then worked on the land reverted to Flemish. Pée reports that the girls back from boarding school asked for the sermon to be in French at Mass on a Sunday. Clearly the girls in this community were initiating change, and the balance between Flemish and French was changing as a result of their influence.

Gilliéron studied a monolingual French community, and he comments on changes taking place in vocabulary there. He quotes the Torgon peasant who told him: 'In the past the room where we are was called *le pailé*, now we call it *la tsābra*, and my wife, who wants to be more refined than us, calls it *kabiné*.[2] This remark by one of Gilliéron's informants reveals three stages in the linguistic evolution of a lexical item: an old form – *pailé*; a current form – *tsabra*; and a new advanced form – *kabiné*. It is women again who are innovating, using the most advanced form (for status reasons, according to the peasant).

Gauchat's (1905) study of the dialect of Charmey, a remote village in Switzerland, shows a great sensitivity to the social context in which linguistic evolution takes place. He observed that the old inhabitants of the village used forms which were phonetically older than those beginning to be used by the young people. He noted that, among people of the same age, the women's pronunciation was more advanced. In other words, there were gender differences as well as age differences in the language of the community (he had chosen Charmey to try to avoid linguistic variation!). He argues that changes have occurred in French because of women's innovativeness ('women welcome every linguistic novelty with open arms')[3] and that these changes are disseminated by women in their role as mothers: 'Once the woman has accepted the innovation, it is from *her* language that this will pass into the language of the young, because children tend to follow their mother's example'.[4] As this extract shows, Gauchat was one of those dialectologists who believed that women were an innovatory rather than a conservative force. It is clearly a logical extension of this position to argue that women, in their role as primary caretakers of children, initiate linguistic change. I shall pursue this argument in section 10.4.

As these four examples from dialectology show, women are frequently portrayed as playing a crucial role in initiating and furthering linguistic change. However, the following sociolinguistic examples will demonstrate that this is an oversimplistic picture – some innovations are clearly associated with male rather than with female speakers.

10.3 Sociolinguistic studies showing change in progress

Linguists used to think that linguistic change was something which could not be observed: 'such observation . . . is inconceivable' (Bloomfield 1933: 347). This misconception was partly the result of de Saussure's division of linguistic study into **synchronic** and **diachronic**: synchronic study took language at one point in time, while diachronic study took language *through* time, comparing language at different points in time to see how it changed. The study of change, then, was firmly linked with **diachronic** linguistics. It is only with the advent of sociolinguistics, specifically with the work of William Labov, that linguists have demonstrated that linguistic change is amenable to analysis. Quantitative studies, analysing synchronic variation in language, have the capacity to reveal change in progress.

The best-known diagram of change in progress is Labov's diagram for postvocalic (r) in New York City which is reproduced in Figure 10.1. I have already

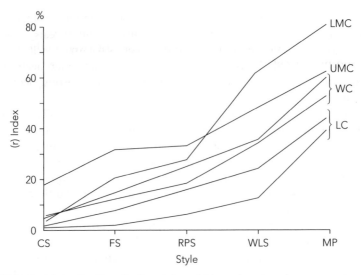

Figure 10.1 Social stratification of a linguistic variable undergoing change – post-vocalic (r) in New York City (Labov 1972a: 114)

discussed this briefly in section 4.2.2. Note again the hypercorrect pattern of the lower middle class, with very low scores for (r) usage in Casual Speech, rising to extremely high scores (higher than the upper middle class) in the two most formal styles. The crossover pattern this produces is said by Labov to be typical of a variable undergoing change. 'The hypercorrect behaviour of the lower middle class is seen as a synchronic indicator of linguistic change in progress' (Labov 1972a: 115).

In his earlier work, Labov reflected the prevailing view that women were innovators. He included a section on 'The Role of Women' in a chapter of his book *Sociolinguistic Patterns* (Labov 1972a: 301–4), where he claimed that women played an important part in linguistic change. However, more recently he has modified his views, and now argues that change is precipitated by linguistic differences between men and women rather than being associated with one particular gender. As we shall see, this latter view accords far better with his own findings.

I shall therefore look first at the work of Labov himself in this field, both his analysis of the variable (a) in New York City and his study of centralised diphthongs on Martha's Vineyard. I shall then re-examine the work of Trudgill in Norwich, Milroy in Belfast and Eckert in Detroit (as discussed in Chapters 4 and 5), paying particular attention this time to the relationship between gender differences in language and linguistic change. Finally, we shall look at two pieces of research from further afield: Nichols' study of linguistic patterns in South Carolina (USA), and Britain's work on changing intonation patterns in New Zealand.

10.3.1 New York City and Martha's Vineyard

Many of the variables studied by Labov in New York City were in the process of change, and he was able to show significant gender differences in their usage. With the variable (a)[5] (the short vowel found in words like *bag, ham, cab*), for example, Labov found that men's pronunciation varied very little between formal and less formal contexts, while women's pronunciation varied a great deal. Style-shifting, then, was typical of female speakers. Moreover, it was women rather than men who were using the new advanced forms [i<:ᵊ] and [e<:ᵊ] in casual speech; women, in other words, are leading in the raising of this vowel and are thus initiating change.

It seems, then, that linguistic change in New York City is crucially associated with women. However, in his work on Martha's Vineyard (an island off the coast of Massachusetts), Labov found a different pattern: men, not women, were initiating change. The two variables investigated by Labov were both diphthongs: (aw) as in *house*, and (ay) as in *white* (diphthongs are glides from one vowel to another vowel). In these two diphthongs, the initial element [a] was becoming centralised to something like [ə] in the speech of many of the people on the island. In other words [au] was shifting towards [əu], and [ai] towards [əi].

Labov conducted interviews with sixty-nine informants; he included only members of the permanent population and excluded the summer visitors. He realised that there was no conscious awareness among the islanders that these sounds were fluctuating, since he found no *stylistic* variation – individuals' pronunciation of the diphthongs was consistent in different styles of speech. He established that the centralised variants were used mostly by *men* (specifically fishermen) aged between 31 and 45 from an area at the western end of the island called Chilmark. It seems that the centralised diphthongs were used by the Chilmark fishermen as a sign of solidarity; use of these variants symbolised their identification with the island and its values, and their rejection of the summer visitors.

These centralised diphthongs are actually very old. They were conservative features of the fishermen's speech which are now spreading to the speech of other islanders. In other words, an older form, which was in the process of dying out, has now become a significant feature of the island phonology; a linguistic change has reversed direction.

What quantitative studies such as this reveal is **change in apparent time**, that is fluctuating usage at one particular point in time. By consulting the Linguistic Atlas of New England and other earlier surveys of pronunciation in this region, Labov was able to confirm that this is actually a **change in real time** (diachronic change). As we shall see, this practice of testing findings against earlier historical records is common in sociolinguistic work charting change in progress.

Linguistic change on Martha's Vineyard, then, has been initiated by a group of *male* speakers, the Chilmark fishermen. Their speech, with its centralised diphthongs, was once seen as old-fashioned, but at some stage, as local feeling grew stronger in the face of the invading 'outsider' (the summer visitors), this type of speech became symbolic of belonging to the island, of being an 'insider'. Note that it is still primarily male speakers who use these centralised diphthongs. Thus the change begins with, and is imitated by, men.

Labov's New York survey shows *women* in the vanguard of linguistic change, while the study of Martha's Vineyard reveals a linguistic change in progress which originated with *male* speakers. As we shall see in the following sections, these two contrasting patterns are found in other studies of linguistic change in progress.

10.3.2 Norwich

Some of the variables investigated by Trudgill in Norwich displayed irregularities of class or style variation which indicated that change was taking place. I shall look at two of these, where gender as well as class and style variation is involved.

The variable (e) displays a very unusual pattern of class differentiation, as can be seen in Figure 10.2. Index scores measure the centralisation of the vowel in words like *tell, well, better*. A score of 200 represents consistent RP pronunciation: [ɛ]; a score of 0 represents consistent non-standard pronunciation: [ʌ].[6] There are two points to notice here. First, in Casual Style the *upper*-working-class group has a *lower* score than the other working-class groups, that is, upper-working-class speakers use more of the non-standard centralised variant. Secondly, in *all* styles the upper- and middle-working-class groups use more of

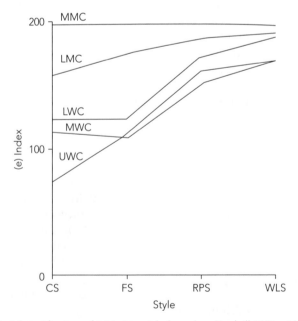

Figure 10.2 Social stratification of (e) in Norwich (based on Trudgill 1974a: 105)

the non-standard variant than the lower working class. So while the stratification of the middle class as a whole and the working class as a whole is as expected, the pattern of groups *within* the working class is upside down, with the upper working class using the highest proportion of non-standard variants.

Trudgill observes that centralisation of (e) is increasing in Norwich, and this change is being innovated by the upper working class. He notes that the use of centralised variants is associated not only with upper-working-class speakers but also with *male* speakers under the age of 30. Younger speakers have much lower scores than older speakers, and male speakers have lower scores than female speakers. In the youngest age group studied by Trudgill (10–19), male and female speakers differed significantly: the average score for the young male speakers was 0, indicating consistent use of the centralised vowel.

We can summarise these findings by saying that the variable (e) in Norwich is undergoing change, this change is manifest in the irregular pattern of class stratification, and the change is being innovated by young *male* upper-working-class speakers in particular.

The variable (o), the vowel occurring in words like *top, fog, lorry*, is also involved in change. Figure 10.3 gives the results for class, gender and style variation: index scores measure the degree of lip-rounding in the pronunciation of the vowel (o). A score of 100 represents consistent RP pronunciation: [ɒ]; a score of 0 represents consistent non-standard pronunciation [ɑ].[6]

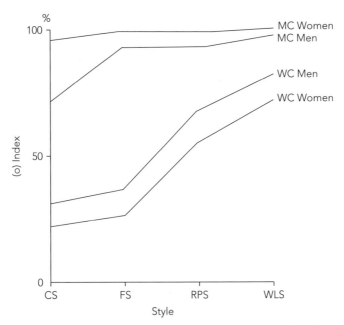

Figure 10.3 Stratification of (o) in Norwich by social class and gender (based on Trudgill 1972: 189)

Figure 10.3 reveals a striking irregularity in the stratification of speakers. Middle-class women use a virtually consistent RP pronunciation of (o); they score higher than middle-class men in all styles. Working-class women, on the other hand, consistently score *lower* than working-class men; in all styles the diagram shows that working-class women used a higher proportion of the non-standard variant [ɑ]. What is the explanation for this unusual pattern? (compare it with the expected pattern shown in Figure 4.5, p. 53). It seems that working-class *men* are innovating with the pronunciation [ɒ], imitating local Suffolk working-class speech (Norfolk speech has traditionally used the unrounded vowel [ɑ]). This change happens to coincide with the standard (RP) form, which is used predominantly by middle-class *women*. Thus, middle-class women are conforming to the prestige norm, while working-class women are conforming to an older vernacular norm. Working-class men, however, are innovating with a new vernacular norm. The coincidence of this Suffolk vernacular form with the prestige form means that working-class men's scores are closer to those of the middle class. With this variable, it is the irregularity in the pattern of gender differentiation which signals change in progress.

10.3.3 Belfast

Several of the variables studied by the Milroys in Belfast are in the process of change. I shall look at two of them – (ɛ) and (a) – since in both cases linguistic change is associated with gender-differentiated usage.

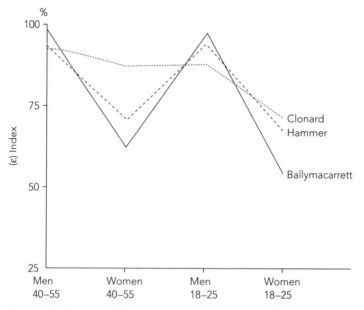

Figure 10.4 The distribution of (ɛ) by age, gender and area in Belfast (Milroy and Milroy 1978: 30)

The variable (ε) occurs in words like *step*, *peck*, *bet*, and variants range from [a] to [ẹ]. The variable is undergoing raising, and the new prestigious raised variants of (ε) are being introduced by women, particularly younger women. Figure 10.4 shows the distribution of (ε) in 'short' phonetic environments, that is, where the vowel is followed by a voiceless stop: [p, t, k]. Note the clear gender-differentiation involved in the use of this variable; this is particularly marked in Ballymacarrett. For many male speakers, the low short variant [a] or [æ] is categorical before voiceless stops. Both older and younger men in Ballymacarrett score 100, that is, use the low short variant consistently. The younger women in all three communities have much lower scores than the men, reflecting their preference for raised variants. Comparison with historical records leads the Milroys to conclude that the raising of (ε) is a change in real time. Change is being initiated by younger female speakers who are introducing a new high-status variant into inner-city Belfast.

The variable (a) is also undergoing change, but here the pattern is different. Backing of (a) is in progress, and backed variants are typical of Ballymacarrett speakers and typical of *male* speakers. In other words, men are more likely than women to pronounce *man* [mɔ.ən]. Figure 10.5 shows the distribution of (a) in the three communities.

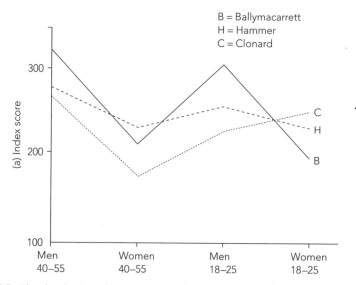

Figure 10.5 The distribution of (a) by age, gender and area in Belfast (Milroy 1980: 124)

The Milroys' data enable us to see how a changing pattern of pronunciation – backing of (a) – is introduced into working-class speech by the Ballymacarrett men (note that Ballymacarrett is a stable and prestigious community.) This new vernacular variant is then adopted by another sub-group, the Clonard young women. As Figure 10.5 shows, young women in the Clonard score higher than the young men of their community and also higher than the Ballymacarrett young women. This produces the crossover pattern typical of a linguistic change in progress. The young Clonard women, then, are introducing into their own community a variant of (a) borrowed from a higher-ranking community. (In Belfast, Protestant ranks higher than Catholic.) Backing of (a) is spreading from East to West Belfast, from a high-ranking to a low-ranking working-class community.

By consulting early records of Belfast pronunciation (Patterson 1860), the Milroys have established that (a) was not normally backed in 1860. Thus we have evidence, in both apparent and real time, that a linguistic change is taking place, and again we find that the variable in question is involved in gender differentiation. It seems that backing of (a) has the status of a vernacular norm and is typical of speakers belonging to close-knit working-class groups; the young Clonard women belong, like the Ballymacarrett men, to dense, multiplex networks. While unemployment in the Hammer has led to a breakdown of networks and a corresponding blurring of gender differences, male unemployment in the Clonard has led to the younger women seeking work, finding work together, and developing a pattern of social interaction similar to the traditional pattern for working-class *men*. This change in social pattern has resulted in a changing *linguistic* pattern for the Clonard community, with the young women acting as innovators. As we can see, changes in network structure can be an important social mechanism of linguistic change.

I have described two variables in the process of change in inner-city Belfast. Prestigious raised variants of (ε) are being introduced into Belfast speech by younger *women*, while backing of (a) has been introduced by Ballymacarrett *men* and this new vernacular norm is now being adopted by the young Clonard women.

10.3.4 Detroit, USA

Eckert's study of phonological variation among high school students in Detroit (discussed in section 4.3.5) revealed sound change in progress. As we saw in that earlier discussion, two of the variables she studied were (uh) and (ay). The vowel in words like *but* is moving back (so *but* can sound more like *bought*), while the first element (the nucleus) [a] of the diphthong in words like *file* is being raised so that *file* may sound more like *foil*. Eckert showed that there is a complex correlation between pronunciation, gender and social category (jock or burnout). The results of Eckert's analysis are reproduced here as Figures 10.6 and 10.7.

In these figures, high numbers indicate that innovative pronunciation is more frequent, while low numbers indicate that innovative pronunciation is less frequent. These variables are not simply gender markers – gender and social category are intertwined. Overall, the burnout girls are the most advanced speakers in terms of new vernacular forms, while the jock girls prefer more conservative variants. In other words, it is the burnout girls who are leading the sound change in this community. We can see the relationship between

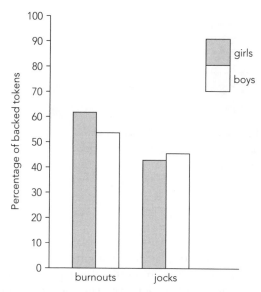

Figure 10.6   Percentage of backed tokens of (uh)

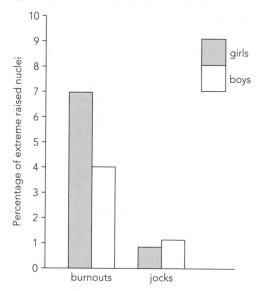

Figure 10.7   Percentage of extreme raised tokens of (ay)

10.6 and 10.7 adapted from Eckert, P. and McConnell-Ginet, S. (1999), pp. 196 and 197. Cambridge University Press.

gender and social class even more clearly if we divide the burnout girls into two groups, depending on the strength of their alignment with burnout norms (see Eckert and McConnell-Ginet 1995). 'Burned-out' burnout girls distinguish themselves from 'regular' – or more 'jocky' – burnout girls. This self-labelling correlates with distinct patterns of pronunciation, as Figure 10.8 shows.[7]

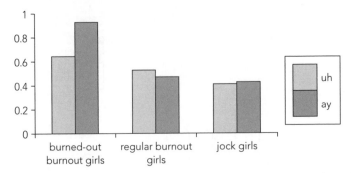

Figure 10.8 Correlation of two phonological variables with social category for Belten High girls

Adapted from Eckert, P. and McConnell-Ginet, S. (1995), eds. K. Hall and M. Bucholtz, pp. 502–3. Routledge/Taylor & Francis Books., Inc.

As Figure 10.8 shows, the 'regular' burnout girls choose variants of (uh) and (ay) which are more innovative than those of the jock girls, but less innovative than those of the burned-out burnout girls. The backing of (uh) in the speech of the burned-out burnout girls is far more extreme than that of the 'regular' burnouts, and the burned-out burnouts are overwhelmingly in the lead when it comes to the raising of the nucleus in (ay).

As Eckert and McConnell-Ginet (1995) emphasise, this linguistic behaviour creates social meaning. In other words, when a girl interviewed by Eckert pronounces the word *all-nighter* so that it sounds like *all-noiter*, she is constructing burned-out burnouthood. She chooses this advanced variant even when she might be expected to converge with the interviewer's more standard accent, as a way of expressing her identity as 'cool', as not aligned with school (and mainstream) norms.

10.3.5 South Carolina, USA

In her work on the changing speech of South Carolina, Patricia Nichols (1983, 1998) draws attention to the importance of another factor in linguistic change: the differing economic opportunities open to women and men in specific speech communities. She carried out fieldwork in two black communities in South Carolina, one on the mainland and one on a nearby island, in order to investigate the shift from an English creole known as Gullah to a more standard variety of English. The variables she investigated were:

1. The *for-to* complementiser
   e.g. *I come for get my coat*

2. The static-locative preposition *to*
   e.g. *Can we stay to the table?*

3. Third person singular pronouns *ee* and *um*
   e.g. *and ee was foggy and they couldn't see but I ain't see she fuh tell um nothing*

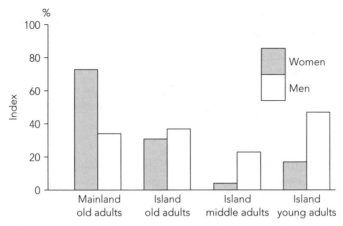

Figure 10.9 The distribution of creole and non-standard grammatical variants by age, gender and area in South Carolina (based on Nichols 1983: 60)

Nichols found that the women in her sample did not behave uniformly. As Figure 10.9 shows, older mainland women were the heaviest users of Gullah variants, scoring higher on these than their male contemporaries, but young and middle-aged island women, in complete contrast, were the most advanced in the shift to standard English. Nichols explains this finding in terms of local job opportunities. Men of all ages in the area she studied work in the construction industry, while older women work in the domestic and agricultural jobs to which black women have until recently been confined. None of these groups has much incentive to speak Standard English, and the older women have little opportunity even to encounter Standard English speakers. Given the circumstances of their lives, these women have no reason not to maintain their vernacular. The younger island women, on the other hand, have different work opportunities in white-collar and service jobs. These jobs require Standard English and bring the younger women into contact with Standard English speakers. Thus the younger black women have both the incentive and the opportunity to acquire the standard variety.

10.3.6 Porirua, New Zealand

The final study we shall look at focuses not on phonology or grammar, but on intonation. David Britain (1998) carried out research on an intonation contour in New Zealand speech known as the high rising terminal contour (or HRT). This intonation contour is a growing phenomenon, especially in the speech of the young, and has been identified in Australia, Canada, the USA and Britain.

Britain's study of HRTs draws on recorded data collected for a large social dialect survey, the Porirua Project, carried out in Porirua, a small city about 12 miles north of Wellington. The following is an example from the data: the clauses in italics end with a high rising terminal, marked with an upwards pointing arrow; pauses are marked with +.

> Pam: and um he just stood there + *and I I've got a real phobia for big moths ↑ I hate them flying around me and that ↑ and I as I was sort of nodding off to sleep I could hear a um + like what I thought was a moth ↑ banging on the window ↑* and I just remember thinking ooh yuck you know . . .

(Britain 1998: 214)

The HRT seems to function in conversation in the same way as tag questions and pragmatic tags like *you know* and *right?* All these forms can in certain contexts – as when someone is telling a story like Pam in the example above – signal that the speaker wants to continue talking and simultaneously check that the addressee is 'in tune with' the speaker. Britain argues that HRTs are used for 'the establishment of solidary common ground between the speaker and the hearer' (1998: 215).

The informant sample consisted of sixty working-class speakers, classified according to age, gender and ethnicity (Maori or Pakeha/white). Fifteen middle-class women were also recruited as a control group, five for each of the three age groups studied. The data were transcribed and each informant's speech was divided into tone groups. (A tone group is a chunk of talk defined in terms of intonation and is often co-terminous with a clause: speakers use tone goups to organise talk into meaningful units of information.) Certain tone groups were excluded from analysis (roughly speaking, questions and imperatives). The remaining tone groups were coded according to presence or absence of HRT.

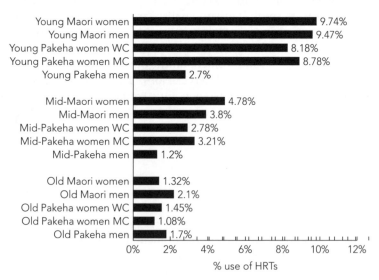

Figure 10.10 Percentage use of HRTs in Porirua according to gender, age, ethnicity and class

From Britain, D. (1998), eds. P. Trudgill and J. Cheshire, p. 225. Reproduced by permission of Hodder Arnold.

Figure 10.10 shows the social stratification of HRT usage. Each bar indicates the percentage of HRT use for that particular group, with the youngest group at the top of the diagram, and the oldest at the bottom. The New Zealand stereotype is that HRTs are mainly used by young women. As Figure 10.10 shows, this stereotype is pretty accurate: the young in this survey use HRTs over five times more than the oldest age group. And among younger Pakeha speakers, female speakers use HRTs three times more than male speakers. But this gender differentiation is not found in the Maori informants: Maori men and Maori women used HRTs with similar frequency. Britain argues that a linguistic change is in progress in New Zealand favouring the use of HRTs, and that Maori speakers and young Pakeha women are leading the change.

10.4 Gender differentiation and linguistic change

The dialectological evidence given in section 10.2 shows women as innovators; the sociolinguistic evidence given in section 10.3 shows both women and men initiating linguistic change. How do we make sense of this?

One way is to distinguish between **conscious** and **unconscious** change, or 'change from above' and 'change from below' as Labov calls them (Labov 1972a). Women seem to initiate changes above the level of social awareness: such changes tend to be in the direction of the prestige norms. Men, on the other hand, seem to initiate changes below the level of social awareness: such changes tend to be *away from* the accepted norms.

The shift to centralised diphthongs on Martha's Vineyard is a good example of change taking place *below* the level of social awareness. According to Labov, the native Vineyarders are not aware of this feature in their language. As a result, he found no style-shifting associated with the diphthongs; speakers have no control over this feature in their speech and their pronunciation is therefore the same whatever the context. As we have seen, it is *men* who are (unconsciously) initiating and furthering this change in the local language.

Labov's work in New York City revealed several variables where change was taking place *above* the level of consciousness. Figure 10.1 – postvocalic (r) – is a very good example of this. Note the steep slope for all groups: (r) is clearly subject to a great deal of style-shifting, with the lower middle class in particular shifting from low usage of (r) in casual speech to very high usage of (r) in Word List Style. The variable (a) – see section 10.3.1 – is another typical example of change taking place from above the level of consciousness. Here it is women who are revealed as being particularly conscious of the variant, as is shown by the extent of their style-shifting.

In Belfast, female speakers are innovating towards a *prestige* norm with raised variants of (ɛ), while male speakers are responsible for the introduction of a new *vernacular* norm to the inner city (backing of (a)). In Norwich change is taking place in two directions at once, with female speakers innovating towards a prestige norm and male speakers innovating away from the prestige norm.

The rural Suffolk vernacular norm which working-class men are taking as their model happens to coincide with the RP norm which female speakers are imitating. This fortuitous coincidence of change from below with change from above means that the shift to the rounded vowel (that is, [ɒ] in place of traditional Norwich [ɑ]) has a good chance of success. In the South Carolina communities studied by Nichols, the younger women are shifting their linguistic usage in the direction of Standard English, away from the local (creole) norms. These women are spearheading a change in the community, and the change is towards more prestigious forms.

So far, so good. But what about the two other studies of linguistic change we have looked at – high school students in Detroit and Maori and Pakeha speakers in Porirua, New Zealand? In both these, we find younger women in the vanguard of change, but the overall picture is more complex than in the other examples of linguistic change we have discussed. Let's look at each of them in turn.

First, the phonological variation found among school students at Belten High in Detroit arises from both gender and class allegiance. As we would expect, more middle-class students – jocks – use a higher proportion of conservative variants, while more working-class students – burnouts – use a higher proportion of innovative variants. But it is difficult to say whether the shift to innovative forms is associated with burnout-ness or with female-ness. However, the burned-out burnout girls are the undisputed leaders in the sound change under way in this community. This sound change is starting in a locally based working-class community and is spreading upwards through the community. In this case, the innovatory behaviour of female speakers is clearly not in the direction of prestige forms.

In the case of the use of the high rising terminal in Porirua, New Zealand, it is again younger women who are leading the change, but this time both working- and middle-class women are involved. Moreover, this change is also being led by younger Maori speakers, and in the Maori community there is no gender distinction in terms of this feature. This pattern of innovation – with younger Pakeha women and young Maoris (both male and female) using a high proportion of HRTs – can be explained by the HRTs' function in talk as a positive politeness marker. As we saw in Chapter 6 (section 6.6), female speakers tend to be more oriented to affective, interpersonal meanings, while male speakers are more oriented to the referential functions of talk. Britain argues that this orientation explains the Pakeha women's use of the HRT, and Pakeha males' avoidance of it. And Britain explains Maori usage of HRTs in similar terms, since, in non-western cultures like those of the Maori and other Pacific groups, 'greater emphasis is placed on interpersonal rather than individualistic constructions of personality and identity' (Britain 1998: 229). Young Maoris of both sexes use high levels of HRTs to achieve conversational solidarity.

These examples demonstrate how complex the sociolinguistic picture is. It is not possible to claim that linguistic change is associated with one gender or the other. Women, for example, are sometimes linguistically innovative, sometimes linguistically conservative. Women, like men, respond to local circumstances: they make linguistic choices in the context of particular speech communities.

Two factors frequently put forward in the past to 'explain' women's linguistic behaviour were sensitivity and conservatism. (Note that men's language was taken as given and so did not need explaining.) As we have seen, both women and men are linguistically sensitive, but to different models. Women's conservatism is merely the converse of male innovation: when male speakers initiate change, then women speakers can be described as conservative – they conserve older forms. Conversely, when female speakers initiate change, then male speakers can be described as conservative (though conservatism is not often ascribed to men, except in the work of traditional dialectologists). Conservatism and sensitivity are two sides of the same coin, and neither sex has the monopoly of either of them.

The idea that only *middle-class* women are innovative seems no longer tenable when we observe the Clonard young women in Belfast who are leading the change to a more backed (a) in their community, or the young black women in South Carolina who are shifting towards Standard English, or the burned-out burnout girls who are leading the change to new vernacular pronunciation in Detroit. This may be because of changing structures in society and the new roles being taken on by women. In Belfast, for example, where male unemployment is now very high in some parts of the city, young women are going out to work and are participating in dense, multiplex social networks similar to those which used to be typical of *men* in the community. In the communities studied by Nichols in South Carolina, younger women have opportunities which older women did not have: they work in service industries or white-collar jobs, and have escaped the domestic and agricultural labour of their mothers' generation. These choices, these changes in lifestyle, have significant linguistic reflexes.

As I have said, linguistic change can take place only in the context of linguistic variation, and linguistic variation reflects and maintains social variation. Societies vary in all kinds of ways, but male and female roles are distinguished in some way in all known societies. It is not surprising, then, that the linguistic variation arising from socially constructed differences between women and men turns out to have a significant role in facilitating linguistic evolution.

In conclusion, it is not true to say that either women or men are linguistically the innovative sex. As we have seen, some linguistic change is initiated by female speakers and some by male speakers. However, it is true to say that male/female differences in language seem to be intimately involved in the mechanism of linguistic change. This being the case, the study of linguistic change can only benefit from the growing interest in the sociolinguistic analysis of gender differentiation in speech.

Notes

1 'Je n'ai jamais entendu une phrase de provençal dans une groupe de jeunes filles ou de jeunes femmes' (Brun 1946, as quoted in Pop 1950: 281).

2 'Autrefois la chambre où nous sommes, on la nommait le *pailé*, maintenant nous l'appelons la *tsābra*, et ma femme, qui veut être plus fine que nous, la nomme *kabiné*' (Gilliéron 1880: iv, as quoted in Pop 1950: 180).

3 'les femmes accueillaient . . . avec empressement toute nouveauté linguistique'.

4 'Une fois que la femme a accepté l'innovation, c'est de son langage que celle-ci passera dans le langage de la jeunesse, parce que les enfants suivent plutot l'exemple des femmes' (Gauchat 1905: 218, quoted in Pop 1950: 194).

5 Labov labels this variable (eh).

6 Trudgill actually scores these variables the other way round, with the highest score representing consistent *non*-standard pronunciation, and 0 representing the prestige form. For consistency in this book (see Chapter 4), all figures showing social stratification have been presented in the same way.

7 In this figure, a probability value is given for each group of speakers. High numbers indicate that innovative pronunciation is more frequent; low numbers indicate that innovative pronunciation is less frequent.

CHAPTER 11

The social consequences of gender differences in language

11.1 Introduction

This chapter will examine the social, as opposed to linguistic, consequences of linguistic differentiation based on gender. I shall focus on two areas: the classroom and the workplace. I shall argue that, in both, there is evidence that female speakers are disadvantaged and this results, in part, from the linguistic practices associated with these two contexts. I shall also examine the fashionable claim that masculinity is in crisis and that, especially in school, it is boys rather than girls who are failing to fulfil their potential.

11.2 Gender in the classroom

Chapters 6, 7 and 8 analysed in detail certain aspects of communicative competence where male and female speakers differ. In this section I shall focus on the school – on the classroom in particular – to look at the differentiated competence of girls and boys and the way this affects their education. In the school context, gender is hugely salient. It becomes 'a highly visible source of individual and social identity, clearly marked by dress *and by language*; everyone is either a female or a male' (Thorne 1993: 34, my italics).

Let's start by looking at an example of classroom talk, to begin to explore how language is implicated in gender construction. This example comes from a class of 10 year olds in the USA (Sadker and Sadker 1994, quoted in Kimmell 2000: 154–5). The class was discussing who was the best president in American history, but discussion became rather noisy, so the teacher intervened:

(1) *Teacher*:   There are too many of us here to all shout out at once. I want you to raise your hands, and then I'll call on you. If you shout out, I'll pick somebody else.

    [. . .]

Stephen: [*calls out*] I think Lincoln was the best president. He held the country together during the war.

Teacher: A lot of historians would agree with you

Mike: [*seeing that nothing happened to Stephen, calls out*] I don't. Lincoln was OK, but my Dad liked Reagan. He always said Reagan was a great president.

David: [*calls out*] Reagan? Are you kidding?

Teacher: Who do you think our best president was, Dave?

David: FDR. He saved us from the Depression.

Max: [*calls out*] I don't think it's right to pick one best president. There were a lot of good ones.

Teacher: That's interesting.

Kimberley: [*calls out*] I don't think that presidents today are as good as the ones we used to have.

Teacher: OK Kimberley, but you forgot the rule. You're supposed to raise your hand.

Not only are the boys doing nearly all the talking in this extract, they are also calling out, something the teacher has explicitly said he will not allow. But it is only when a girl calls out that the rule is invoked. This example shows how boys can dominate in the classroom and how girls learn that their contributions are not treated in the same way as those of the boys. It also shows how the boys' dominance is co-constructed by all participants – including the teacher.

As we saw in Chapter 9, young children acquire gender-appropriate language, and this includes differentiated communicative competence. In the school setting, this differing understanding of when to speak, when to remain silent, how to mark speech for politeness, when it is permissible to interrupt, etc. helps to contribute to different outcomes for girls and boys. In particular, boys' communicative competence enables them to dominate in the classroom.

Dominance is achieved in a variety of ways, as we saw in Chapter 7. By analysing what goes on in the microcosm of the school, I shall test the claim that the classroom setting reproduces gender inequality, that girls are at a disadvantage in the classroom, and that the *language* used by girls and boys is in some way tied up with this disadvantage. I shall then look very briefly at research exploring language use in university classrooms, to show that, even in such privileged environments, the voices of intelligent, articulate young women are undermined.

11.2.1 Classroom talk

As we have seen for adult speakers, there is a great deal of evidence that male speakers prefer a competitive style of talk while female speakers prefer a more cooperative style. David Corson (1997: 152) argues that, 'classroom practices . . . reinforce and reward the competitive discursive tendencies of children while marginalising cooperative tendencies'. If this is true, then we can see that the classroom will feel a comfortable place for many boys but a less comfortable place for many girls.

One way that boys 'do' masculinity in the classroom is by fooling around. As boys get older, 'having a laugh' begins to be a crucial aspect of masculinity. Boys try to be cool and to avoid the label of 'nerd' or 'boffin'. At the same time they brag about how good they are: after a school test, for example, they will say it was 'easy', 'simple', while the girls tend to express anxiety about their performance (their comments are of course unrelated to their results).[1] Boys also respond to questions differently: they participate actively, call out answers, make lots of guesses, while girls listen more passively (Stanworth 1983, 1987; Kelly et al. 1984; Whyte 1986; Kelly 1987; Spender 1990; Swann 1992; Kimmell 2000). Pupils themselves are aware of this discrepancy: 'They all make a lot of noise, all those boys. That's why I think they're more intelligent than us' (female pupil reported in Stanworth 1983: 48). Another piece of evidence showing boys' more active participation in class comes from a boy interviewed in Frosh et al. (2002: 137):

> In class by – like if the teacher asks a question, all the boys will put up their hands of [*yeah*] even if they don't know the answer, they'll still put their hands up just to try, just to try, they will not be sure of the answer but they'll still put their hands up just to try, and NO girls put their hands up . . .

Whether or not this account is accurate, it presents boys as active and girls as passive, and shows how boys despise girls' silence in class – and their timidity in terms of putting their hands up. Boys' contempt for girls' silence is supported by the girls, who are hostile towards girls who adopt a more assertive role. Girls are explicitly taught that loudness is 'unfeminine' (Payne 1980) and it seems that girls' sense of their own identity as female makes them feel that the speech acts of arguing, challenging and shouting are inappropriate behaviour for them. As one 16-year-old girl said: 'Sometimes I feel like saying that I disagree, that there are other ways of looking at it, but where would that get me? My teacher thinks I'm showing off, and the boys jeer . . . there's nothing but aggro if you give any signs of showing THEM how it is done' (Spender 1980b: 150).

The language that pupils use to each other reflects and reinforces their unequal status. Boys in secondary school often ridicule girls: they groan when girls ask questions and make rude comments. The observers in the GIST project (Girls Into Science and Technology, see Kelly et al. 1984; Whyte 1986) give examples of boys' ridicule of girls, and comment that they observed *no* examples of girls ridiculing or putting down boys.

The unequal roles assigned to girls and boys are well illustrated in a Dutch experiment (described in Millman 1983: 7) which set out to investigate male/female interaction. Dutch children were divided into same-sex and mixed-sex pairs for a science experiment. The analysis of the resulting videos revealed that same-sex pairs worked cooperatively, but in the mixed-sex pairs the boys adopted a dominant role which the girls accepted: the boys set up the experiment and reported the results to the teacher while the girls helped and then cleared up afterwards. The dominance of boys in small group work was also the main finding of Fisher (1994).

Sociolinguistic researchers have found that boys in secondary school interrupt others more than girls do, and in particular that boys interrupt each other (Gilbert 1990, cited in Holmes 1995: 53). Moreover, while girls use minimal responses (*mhm* or *yeah*) in a supportive way, boys often use them 'as a subtle form of interruption . . . to gain a foothold in the conversation rather than as a support for the current speaker' (Jenkins and Cheshire 1990: 269). Boys are also far more likely to contradict others or to disagree baldly, that is, without any attempt to protect their addressee's face (Stubbe 1991, cited in Holmes 1995: 62).

11.2.2 Amount of talk

As far as quantity of talk is concerned, it seems that boys take up more 'verbal space' than girls (Swann 1992: 68). The results of research on classroom interaction parallel those for adult interaction in public contexts: boys talk far more than girls (Arnot and Weiner 1987; Stanworth 1987; Spender 1990; Madhok 1992; Fisher 1994; Holmes 1995; Swann 1998). As we shall see, this is ingrained in classroom practice and teachers find it hard to recognise. One consequence of boys' more noisy, undisciplined behaviour in the classroom is that they get more attention (as the example at the beginning demonstrated). Recent research carried out in the USA, Britain and Sweden, analysing teacher–pupil interaction patterns, has arrived at the same result: boys get more of the teacher's attention than girls (Sears and Feldman 1974; Wernersson 1982; Sadker and Sadker 1985; Spender 1990). Spender (1990) estimates that teachers normally give two-thirds of their attention to boys.

This is confirmed by Joan Swann's (1998) research on classroom interaction. Swann and her colleagues made video-recordings of two twenty-minute sequences of small group teaching in two English primary schools. On average, boys contributed more to the sessions, both in terms of the number of turns taken and the number of words uttered, though in both schools there were examples of quieter boys and more talkative girls. Table 11.1 gives a detailed breakdown of results.

In the first group, where spontaneous contributions were welcomed, boys took advantage of this mode to chip in forty-one times to the girls' thirteen. The boys' behaviour seems to have been directly related to the teacher's *gaze* behaviour: analysis of the tape where the teacher's gaze can be seen reveals that

Table 11.1: Contribution to classroom talk from girl and boy pupils in two classes (based on Swann 1998: 188)

Pupils	Amount spoken		
	Total words spoken	Total spoken turns	Average words per turn
Class One			
Sarah	79	17	4.6
Laura	20	5	4.0
Donna	37	5	7.4
Unidentified girls	18	9	2.0
Total girls	154	36	4.3
Matthew	133	23	5.8
Trevor	83	20	4.1
Peter	55	10	5.5
Unidentified boys	48	20	2.5
Total boys	319	73	4.4
Class Two			
Kate	127	9	14.1
Lorraine	13	7	1.8
Anne	23	8	2.9
Emma	8	4	2.0
Unidentified girls	–	–	–
Total girls	171	28	6.1
Mark	47	9	5.2
Ian	80	23	3.5
John	35	5	7.0
Darren	101	15	6.7
Unidentified boys	3	2	1.5
Total boys	266	54	4.9

she looked towards the boys for 61.3 per cent of the time. Moreover, the teacher looks at the boys *at critical points* – when a question requires an answer.

In the second group, calling out was not encouraged, yet the boys still dominated. The teacher selected the child whose hand went up first. This favoured more confident pupils (usually boys), as did the teacher's gaze behaviour (she looked towards the boys 65 per cent of the time and maintained her gaze towards them when she began a question). Girl pupils, on the other hand, themselves contributed to their low level of participation by raising their hands *after* the teacher had directed her gaze to the pupil she intended to select.

Swann argues that these findings confirm that differences between girls and boys are not categorical, since some boys are quieter and some girls are more talkative. However, the boys do succeed in dominating classroom talk, though by different means in the two classrooms surveyed. In other words, to be dominant, a speaker has to use the resources available *in a given context*. Swann also makes the point that boys' domination of classroom talk is achieved in part at least through the behaviour of the girls and of the teacher: in other words, she sees girls and teachers as *colluding* in boys' dominance.

The claim that teachers pay boys more attention and encourage them to talk more has led to calls for intervention in the process. After all, it is now accepted that children learn through talking and that every child has a right to an equal voice in classroom activities. The team who undertook the GIST project (Girls Into Science and Technology) believed that teachers *can* change the balance of pupil–teacher interaction towards greater equality (Kelly et al. 1984; Whyte 1986). In this project, a cohort of 2,000 children in ten co-educational comprehensives in Greater Manchester were followed through from the time they entered secondary school (11 years old) until they made their option choices at the end of Year Nine (13–14 year olds). The GIST team observed thirty-four lessons: all the teachers involved had been briefed on the aims of the project and all knew that girls tend to receive less attention in class. In twenty of the lessons, the teachers involved managed to give the girls as much attention as the boys or more. It should be noted that this measure was crude since it ignored the amount of talk involved (every interaction scored 1 regardless of length) and also ignored the context in which teachers addressed girls or boys. However, the GIST project does at least suggest that Spender (1990) is over-pessimistic in her view that teachers cannot achieve equality in their interaction with girls and boys. On the other hand, it emerged that women teachers were far more successful than men at giving girls a fair share of their attention: 75 per cent of the female teachers observed achieved an interaction ratio which was equal for girls and boys or which favoured girls, while only 50 per cent of male teachers achieved this.

The GIST team found that teachers' perceptions of how they interacted with pupils were at odds with quantitative observations. Most were surprised to find how much attention they gave to boys. A male head of science who successfully achieved a balance in his class remarked afterwards that 'he had *felt* as if ninety per cent of his attention was being devoted to the girls' (Whyte 1986: 196).

11.2.3 Choice of topic

Teachers' awareness of the different communicative competence of girls and boys also affects the choice of topics to be discussed in school. Lessons are organised to reflect boys' interests, because teachers have learned that boys will object – loudly – to topics they see as effeminate, while girls will accept 'boys' topics' (Clarricoates 1987). An exercise observed by Sara Delamont (1990) in a Middle School in England involved using a trio of words in a sentence. These were the trios of words listed on the board:

boy   football   window
gorilla   cage   keeper
monkeys   coconuts   hunters
soldier   army   tank

The teacher read these trios of words out to the class and commented on the last (soldier army tank) 'That's one for the boys really, I suppose'. It is hard to see which of these trios of words might be described as 'one for the girls'.

Teachers have varying success in their efforts to include girls. Elizabeth Sarah (1980) involved girls in a discussion of Space Travel by using passages with the pronoun *he* changed to *she*. The boys in her class hotly disputed the idea of spacewomen, and all wrote about space*men* in the follow-up work; the girls, however, wrote about spacewomen. Sarah claims that they obviously felt actively involved in the class project. Elliot, on the other hand, tried to facilitate girls' participation in his lesson on the topic of war, only to find that the boys ridiculed the girls' contributions, and the girls felt very uncomfortable at being forced to assert themselves in a mixed class (Elliot, cited in Spender 1980b: 150). Both these teachers have grasped the nettle of girls' non-participation in classroom discussions, but even so they have chosen as class topics subjects which are conventionally associated more with boys' interests.

11.2.4 Assessment

Even in a situation where girls should have the advantage, it seems that various forces conspire to minimise or overturn this 'abnormal' pattern. British public examinations in English now involve a compulsory oral communication component. This means that students are tested on both individual and group talk. One aspect of group talk which is assessed is **interpersonal skill**. Since interpersonal sensitivity is at the heart of girls' communicative competence, we would expect girls to do well in this aspect of the new examination. A study which tests this hypothesis (Jenkins and Cheshire 1990; Cheshire and Jenkins 1991) analysed three groups of 14-year-old girls and boys taking part in group discussion as part of the GCSE oral test, as well as examining teachers' assessment of these discussions. This study confirms that girls achieve scores as good as or better than their male counterparts.

However, Cheshire and Jenkins make some worrying observations. First, the conversational work done by the girls helped the entire group; boys were enabled to play a constructive role in discussion through the girls' contributions, but the girls did *not* receive support from the boys in return. In other words, on the evidence of this study, girls are carrying out their traditional role in conversation – doing the 'interactional shitwork' (Fishman 1980b) – and boys are benefiting from it. Secondly, the researchers discovered that teachers used different criteria to assess girls' and boys' contributions: they were very generous in their comments on boys' efforts to be cooperative, but judged the girls more harshly. Thirdly, there was evidence that male and female assessors perceive and evaluate boys' and girls' conversational skills differently.

This last finding also emerges from research done by Shan Wareing (1993) on the oral communication component of the Scottish equivalent of GCSE English. Her analysis of the responses of teachers in six different schools to video-tapes of girls and boys engaged in group discussion revealed that male teachers generally gave higher marks to students displaying *competitive* skills (challenging, refuting, holding the floor for extended turns), while female teachers generally gave higher marks to students displaying *cooperative* skills (supporting other speakers, linking contributions carefully to the previous speaker's, asking questions to draw other participants into the conversation).

11.2.5 The university context

Even at university, there is evidence that competitive tendencies are rewarded and that women's and men's classroom participation is not equal. Brit-Louise Gunnarsson (1997) analysed gender participation in fifteen postgraduate seminars in a Swedish university. She looked at five seminars in each of three different departments – one in the humanities, one in the social sciences and one in the natural sciences. Her analysis showed that, while only about 50 per cent of female students played an active role in seminar discussion, a much higher proportion of male students did so: 84 per cent in the humanities department, 83 per cent in the natural sciences department and 68 per cent in the social science department. She also showed how the pattern of interruptions in the seminars testified to a male-centred culture and allowed men to 'play the central role in the seminar discourse' (Gunnarsson 1997: 232).[2]

At Cambridge University there was concern about gender discrepancies in terms of first-class degrees (Hunt 2003). While all students accepted at Cambridge have an outstanding academic record, more male students go on to get a first-class degree (26.2 per cent compared with only 16.6 per cent of female students in 2002). A study to investigate this pattern found that female students asked more questions than men in tutorials and seminars, and advanced more tentatively, whereas male students made more suggestions, moved forward more rapidly and were more challenging with staff and other students. This masculine 'intellectual muscle-flexing' was more likely to be seen as an indicator of excellence by the predominantly male teaching staff. Maths, for example, was actually described by one member of staff as 'a kind of competition you train for'. Female students, many of whom demonstrated a readiness to listen, absorb and synthesise, were much less comfortable in this competitive ethos. Their confidence is slowly undermined over three years of intimidating tutorials, and when it comes to the final 'sudden-death' examinations the system does not reward their strengths.

11.2.6 Conclusions

Overall, research into classroom life has discovered many ways, both linguistic and non-linguistic, in which female and male students are treated differently.

The differential usage of interactional resources by teachers, girls and boys inside the classroom is a key element in sustaining male dominance. All participants in the classroom collude in this. Moreover, the cooperative conversational skills which female students bring to the classroom are not valued. Schools – and universities – tend to view favourably the adversarial style of debate more typical of male peer groups. On the other hand, in situations where students are expected to work collaboratively, boys benefit from girls' interactive skills. Some schools are making brave efforts to combat these social pressures, for example, by encouraging teachers to make sure they talk to and listen to girls as much as boys. But these interventions have themselves led to controversy, with some educationalists convinced that the pendulum has swung too far and that boys are now at a disadvantage. This will be pursued in section 11.4 below.

11.3 Gender in the workplace

I shall now turn to language use in the public domain. The public domain is a male-dominated domain, and the discourse patterns of male speakers have become the established norm in public life. Historically, the split between public and private is associated with industrialisation. In Britain, for example, the split was established in the early nineteenth century, and involved a new demarcation of gender roles: 'men were firmly placed in the newly defined public world of business, commerce and politics; women were placed in the private world of home and family' (Hall 1985: 12).

Over the last twenty years or so, there has been a significant change in the gender composition of the workforce. Women have entered workplaces of many different kinds, and having a job or a career is taken for granted by women. Yet according to many commentators, the workplace remains a decidedly unequal arena. What role does language play in this? And have the growing numbers of women workers had any impact on workplace talk? I shall look first at the androcentric norms of the workplace, then at the dilemma women face in having to adjust to these androcentric norms while maintaining their own (feminine) identity. Finally, I shall look at women's ways of talking and enquire whether these ways of talking might be valuable in the workplace.

11.3.1 Competitive talk in the workplace

Given that men's ways of talking are the norm in the public domain, is it true to say that workplace talk is competitive? Certainly, the findings of a range of studies suggest that women and men bring different conversational strategies to the workplace. Janet Holmes and Maria Stubbe's (2003) summary of these findings is given in Table 11.2. Holmes (2000) argues that the features listed in the right-hand column of Table 11.2 are often regarded by career consultants as the characteristics needed to be a successful manager. To see how well this

Table 11.2: Widely cited features of 'feminine' and 'masculine' interactional style

Feminine	Masculine
indirect	direct
conciliatory	confrontational
facilitative	competitive
collaborative	autonomous
minor contribution (in public)	dominates (public) talking time
supportive feedback	aggressive interruptions
person/process-oriented	task/outcome-oriented
affectively oriented	referentially oriented

Adapted from Holmes, J. and Stubbe, M. (2003), eds. J. Holmes and M. Meyerhoff. Blackwell Publishers.

picture matches research findings on workplace interactive practices, I shall look briefly at four examples before discussing one case study in more detail.

Jane Pilkington (1998) studied the interactive patterns of male and female workers at a bakery in Wellington, New Zealand (discussed in section 8.2.3). She showed how different the women's and men's talk was when they talked with members of their own sex. The female workers used overlapping turns, co-constructed talk and positive feedback in their talk with each other, while the men's talk exhibited playful conflict and competition (see example (18), p. 135). Susan Schick Case (1988) carried out detailed analysis of a group of male and female business managers. She comments that 'the masculine style was an assertively aggressive one that proposed, opposed, competed' (Schick Case 1988: 52). Nicola Woods (1989) demonstrated that, even where a woman has a high-status position in the workplace, she is more likely to be interrupted by a male subordinate than to interrupt him. And, as the following example from a meeting of colleagues in a government department shows (Holmes 1995: 51, first discussed in section 7.3), men's use of interruption can make it difficult for women to get their points across in public arenas:

(2) *Peter:*   what has your section done in this area for instance?

   Judith: well we have begun thinking about it/ we've been holding regular

   Judith: review ⌈sessions on-

   Peter: ⌊it'll take a lot more than that I can tell you/ this is

   Peter: a serious matter/
   [from Holmes 1995: 51]

These four examples suggest that there is some truth in the idea of the workplace as a competitive arena where the prevailing norms are those typically associated with male speakers. I shall now look in more detail at a piece of recent sociolinguistic research which analyses the linguistic practices of two businesses situated in Nottingham. Louise Mullany (2003) recorded the talk at six business meetings (three in each company) as a participant observer. She also carried out interviews with many of the participants and shadowed some of them as they worked.

In the following example, four members of the technical department of a large retail firm are taking part in their weekly meeting. The participants are Steve (the Chair), Sue (a middle manager, Steve's deputy), and Mike and Matt (both lower-level managers).

(3)   [*Steve is informing his subordinates of a technical conference that he will attend*]

1	*Steve:*	Simon Jones will be there so that's something to
2		look forward to
3	*Mike:*	so much better to know they'll be there
4	*Steve:*	\<LAUGHS\> they'd not tell you that they're coming
5	*Matt:*	⌈no they didn't did they?⌉
6	*Steve:*	⌊no no no ⌋ no
7	*Matt:*	we got stitched up for the evening (.) and I
8		don't know what they've done to you yet
9	*Steve:*	\<LAUGHING\> oh well I'm waiting to find out actually
10	*Sue:*	\<LAUGHS\>

Here, Mike (in line 3) refers to an incident when he and Matt had not realised they were supposed to look after senior members of the company for an evening. Steve's laughter in line 4 indicates that he is amused by Mike's remark. Steve and Matt then continue the joke simultaneously (lines 5 and 6) and Matt extends the humorous sequence by teasing Steve. The topic ends with Steve joking that he is *waiting to find out* whether he has been 'stitched up' too. At this point Sue signals her amusement by laughing (line 10). Although superficially this is a bit of light-hearted talk from a meeting, what this talk does (among other things) is create solidarity among the three men, even though one is the boss and the other two are quite junior. Sue does not contribute to this jokey talk and is left to do the 'interactional shitwork' (see section 6.3), supporting the all-male chat with her laughter. During this forty-five-minute meeting, there are five instances of humour, all initiated by the men. Sue does not initiate any humorous episodes, but she contributes supportive laughter in all five examples.

But more often what Mullany found was that participants' strategies did *not* conform to the stereotype. For example, if we look at the use of directives, we find managers using both aggravated and mitigated directives, regardless of the gender of the speaker or of the addressee. For instance, in the following example, Phyllis is telling the female Chair, Carrie, about a problem she has with the local media:

(4)	*Phyllis:*	I'm still getting a lot of er external like students (.) press getting through
	Carrie:	tell the board

Carrie uses a bald imperative to tell her subordinate, Phyllis, what to do. The evidence of subsequent talk is that this is seen as perfectly appropriate in this setting. By contrast, in the following example, the male Chair, Steve, uses mitigated directives as part of his strategy to get his team to run an induction day on a Sunday:

(5)	*Steve:*	if we let let's look at some dates er (-) did we think Sunday
	Steve:	was a good idea to do it?
	Sue:	Sunday's a good idea yeah Sundays would definitely ⌈work⌉
	Steve:	⌊yeah⌋ (-) cos
	Sue:	⌈yeah ⌉ ⌈in the evening⌉
	Steve:	we close at five don't we so ⌊we co⌋uld say (-) ⌊six ⌋
	Steve:	six o'clock Sunday?

Steve's judicious use of the first person inclusive pronoun *we* combined with interrogative forms rather than statements or commands functions to reduce the status distance between himself and his subordinates.

What this in-depth study of two workplaces demonstrates is that, in the twenty-first century in Britain, chairing a meeting, or being more senior than others, is often the motivating factor behind particular linguistic practice, rather than gender. Mullany establishes that male and female managers draw on a range of similar strategies to carry out their role as Chair in the six meetings under scrutiny.

However, Mullany looked not only at micro-level linguistic practices in these two workplaces, but also at the discourses current there. She shows that hegemonic discourses of masculinity and femininity are entrenched in these workplaces, and that both women and men align themselves with these discourses. These dominant discourses expect women to be caring and nurturing, yet view women as uncommitted to work if they take time off to have children. Women are also expected to make an effort with their appearance and to be attractive to men, while at the same time being perceived as exploiting their gender to manipulate men. Finally, both women and men in this study described women as emotional and irrational, and so, by extension, unfit for positions of authority.

The problems this creates for female managers are illustrated by the reactions Mullany uncovered to different styles of management. First, a more assertive female manager, Amy, was described by her co-workers as 'bossy', 'bombastic' and 'dragon-like'. From the evidence of Mullany's transcripts, we can see that Amy adopts a speech style not unlike that of her male counterparts. This assertive management stye is negatively evaluated by her peers and by her subordinates. So, although she is regarded as an effective manager by the company, her deviation from the hegemonic norms of feminine behaviour mean that she attracts criticism in the workplace.

But a female manager who aligns herself more with hegemonic feminine norms also attracts criticism from colleagues. Carrie has recently had time off to have a baby: one of her female colleagues criticised as unprofessional her decision to go on maternity leave at the busiest time in the company's year. Carrie herself told Mullany about a male subordinate who had acted in a 'hostile' manner towards her, accusing her of making her department too feminine:

> He said to me 'there are too many women in your department, you ought to take on more men' and I said 'have you any idea how sexist that is?' 'That's not sexist, that's just equaling the balance a bit' he said, 'there just aren't enough men' and I could understand that kind of atmosphere could become too female . . . he finds it threatening and I find it shockingly stupid to be honest but it made me stop and think . . . is it too female? Has everything gone pink and fluffy? And it hadn't.
> (Mullany 2003: 228)

Here we see evidence of male resistance to the growing number of women in the workplace and to their rise to managerial positions. Mullany's informant complains that there are 'too many women' and implies the atmosphere is 'too female'. At no point during Mullany's study did anyone complain that teams they worked on were 'too male' – the male-dominated workplace is regarded as normal. It is only when women are in a majority or when women become committee chairs that there is evidence of resistance. Overall, then, the overarching ideology in these workplaces is one that supports stereotypical views of women and men, and which therefore does not support women in positions of power and seniority.

11.3.2 Catch 22 for women in the public domain

As the case studies of Amy and Carrie above have shown, women in the workplace are linguistically in a Catch 22 situation. They are expected to adopt the more adversarial, information-focused style characteristic of all-male talk, and typical of talk in the public domain, but if they do (like Amy), they run the risk of being perceived as aggressive and confrontational, as un-feminine. In other words, there is a clash between what is expected of a woman and what is expected of a person with high status in the public sphere.

So women are criticised if they do not adapt to the norms of the public domain – but then criticised when they do. A rare high-achieving woman, Mary Warnock (who was Mistress of Girton College Cambridge and Chair of the Warnock Committee), wrote a forceful article for the *Daily Telegraph* entitled 'Why women are their own worst enemies'. This title presages the critical tone of the piece, which looks at women's behaviour on committees: 'I wonder whether women themselves realise quite how bad they can be as members of boards' (Warnock 1987). She includes among women's 'shortcomings' their proneness 'to think they are entitled to make fey, irrelevant, "concerned" interventions' and 'to disregard economic considerations for "human" ones'. She urges women to 'adapt to what is required' and to adopt a 'disciplined professionalism', implicitly accepting the male-dominated discourse patterns of conventional committee meetings.

However, women who succeed in adopting a more competitive discourse style in public meet other problems. Jeanne Kirkpatrick, former US ambassador to the United Nations, describes the dilemma faced by women in high positions, where there is a clash between gender and work identities.

> There is a certain level of office the very occupancy of which constitutes a confrontation with conventional expectations. . . . Terms like 'tough' and 'confrontational' express a certain general surprise and disapproval at the presence of a woman in arenas in which it is necessary to be – what for males would be considered – normally assertive.
>
> (Kirkpatrick, quoted in Campbell and Jerry 1988)

In other words, women are in a double-bind: they are urged to adopt more assertive, more masculine styles of discourse in the public sphere, but when they do so, they are perceived as aggressive and confrontational.

The election of a Labour Government in Britain in May 1997 resulted in a large increase in the number of women MPs. This has led to women being available to take on senior positions in an unprecedented way. Some of these women, for example, Margaret Becket (Secretary of State for the Environment, Food and Rural Affairs) and Tessa Jowell (Secretary of State for Culture, Media and Sport), seem to have achieved a balance between doing their job efficiently and yet maintaining their gender role. Such women, however, do not seem to have endeared themselves to the general public.

By contrast, two high-flying women who have fallen from grace – Mo Mowlam, who was Secretary of State for Northern Ireland, and Estelle Morris, who was Secretary of State for Education – *did* endear themselves to the public. Their resistance to political norms attracted a great deal of media attention. There is evidence that the public warmed to them precisely because they disobeyed Mary Warnock's stricture: they chose to be human rather than adopt the masculine discourse of 'disciplined professionalism'. Estelle Morris, for example, talked about not being good enough in her letter of resignation to the Prime Minister. Her actual words were:

> I've learned what I'm good at and also what I'm less good at. I'm good at dealing with the issues and in communicating to the teaching profession. I am less good at strategic management of a huge department and I am not good at dealing with the modern media. All this has meant that with some of the recent situations I have been involved in, I have not felt I have been as effective as I should be, or as effective as you need me to be.[3]

This kind of honesty is very rare in the current political climate, yet the public, who are becoming more and more critical of politicians' 'spin', found it refreshing. Unfortunately, while such women may be admired, they tend to be demoted because they fail to play the game in the expected way.

As women win the right to enter occupations previously reserved for men, they are confronted with this clash of expectations: the clash between doing what is expected of a woman and doing what is expected of a person with high status in the public sphere. This problem is certainly not reserved for women in the west. For example, there is conflict in Japan between the contemporary ideology that women and men are equal, and the pressure on women to speak in a way that is *onna-rasiku* (Reynolds 1998). *Onna-rasiku* language expresses an older female identity, one which is more in line with the Confucian doctrine of 'men superior, women inferior'. Overall, in Japanese, women have a much more restricted stylistic range available to them than men have. 'In order to be accepted as a "good" woman, a female speaker of Japanese must choose to talk non-assertively, indirectly, politely, deferentially: but in order to function as a supervisor, administrator, teacher, lawyer, doctor, etc. or as a colleague or associate, she must be able to talk with assurance' (Reynolds 1998: 302). This sort of conflict exists world-wide, but the Japanese situation is more extreme than most. Reynolds reports on current perceptions of women in public life and describes the linguistic strategies they are (often unconsciously) adopting to resolve the conflicting demands on them. These strategies seem to consist predominantly of 'defeminising' their language, that is, choosing variants towards the middle of an imaginary masculine–feminine spectrum, and avoiding variants associated with the feminine end of the spectrum.

The defeminisation of interactional patterns is also found in specific workplaces, such as the police. Bonnie McElhinny (1998) analyses the linguistic behaviour of women police officers in the Pittsburgh police. The police force is a workplace which has traditionally been defined as all-male and masculine, and McElhinny argues that such a workplace is itself gendered and that this affects how people are able to behave. She shows how women police officers have learned to adopt the strategies typically employed by male police officers, which damp down the personal and the emotional. Her telling analysis of two specific incidents of domestic violence where the police were called in, one involving a male police officer and one a female police officer, illustrates the way in which police officers stick to a prescribed agenda of questions and fail to respond to the emotion of the woman who has asked for police help. She argues that gender differences in language are not found when both women and men work in a workplace with established masculine practices.

Wodak (1997) arrives at a similar conclusion in her analysis of the linguistic strategies adopted by three female head teachers in Austria. She argues that the hierarchies and power networks present in the institution of the school make it impossible for these women to adopt the cooperative style typically associated with women. Instead, they achieve their aims through using controlling and authoritarian strategies, deriving from 'the mother's repertoire of rules' (Wodak 1997: 367). While this 'maternal' strategy was accepted by all involved, it means that women's ability to alter the norms of public discourse are restricted.

It remains to be seen whether this conflict between gender and status is a temporary phenomenon, arising during a period of social transition from an all-male to a mixed workforce, or whether it will prove to be an enduring problem for women in the public sphere.

11.3.3 Women's cooperative style in the public domain

There is, however, evidence to suggest that in some workplaces women are resisting the androcentric discourse norms of the public sphere and are employing their own more cooperative speech style in the working environment. Candace West's (1998a) research on doctor–patient talk was discussed in Chapter 6 (section 6.3). She analysed directive–response speech sequences between doctor and patient, and discovered that women and men doctors issue directives in very different ways. While male doctors preferred to use imperative forms, or statements in which they told patients what they 'needed' to do, or what they 'had to' do, female doctors preferred to use more mitigated forms. Moreover, women doctors are more likely than men to use directive forms which elicit a compliant response from the patient. West shows how women doctors' use of more mitigated directive forms had the effect of minimising status distinctions between themselves and their patients. The more egalitarian relationships they established with their patients emphasised doctors' obligations as well as patients' rights. The evidence from this study is that such an approach has better outcomes for patients than more traditional approaches which emphasise asymmetry in doctor–patient relationships.

Another piece of work which focuses on the successful use of collaborative interactive strategies by women professionals is Marie Wilson Nelson's (1998) study of female-dominated research teams (first discussed in section 8.2.1). Nelson observed and recorded the interactive patterns of five successive teacher-research teams, working in a university writing centre in Washington, DC. These teams were made up of graduate Teaching Assistants (TAs), who were mostly female. Nelson's research shows how the women successfully used the interactive patterns familiar to them, while the occasional male TAs adapted to these interactive patterns and were positive about the experience. Transcripts of team discussion sessions confirm the claim that the interactions are based on an ethic of reciprocity, and are cooperative rather than competitive. They show what Miller (1978) calls 'productive conflict', that is, conflict which is beneficial to all participants, as opposed to conflict which results in one winner and many losers. Nelson discusses the problems women face in trying to maintain their collaborative style in more competitive environments, but argues that we must try to overcome these problems since the interactive patterns into which women are socialised 'offer substantial benefits to academic and professional teams' (Nelson 1998: 357).

A major study of workplace interaction in New Zealand (Holmes 2000, Stubbe et al. 2000; Holmes et al. 2001; Holmes and Stubbe 2003) has analysed among other things the role of humour in the workplace, with female managers using humour to establish solidarity and collegiality. Female managers encouraged what Holmes calls collaborative humour, where several participants co-constructed a humorous sequence, an activity which clearly promotes solidarity. In a quantitative analysis of twenty-two meetings, Holmes and her colleagues observed the following patterns:

- there was more humour in meetings in which women were participants
- there was more collaborative or extended humour in meetings in which women were participants
- there was both more overall humour and more collaborative humour in meetings with a female chair than in meetings with a male chair
- women were more likely than men to instigate or 'seed' collaborative humour sequences in mixed gender settings
- female chairs instigated collaborative humour sequences more often than male chairs.

(Holmes et al. 2001: 104)

Holmes's findings were supported by Mullany's (2003) study: Mullany found that humour was more likely to occur in meetings where there were more women present. Male-dominated meetings produced fewer instances of humour. The following example is a brief extract from the weekly meeting of the product department of a retail company in Nottingham. The meeting is chaired by a senior manager (Amy) and involves six participants: four women and two men.

(6)   [Amy has asked the group to bring in photos of themselves as babies because the company are having a spot the baby competition]

1 Karen: <LAUGHS> Stuart] made my rin- made me ring my mum from the
  Mary: mhm

2 Karen: office on <LAUGHING> Mon┌day to stop by cos he knew I was
  Mary: └<LAUGHS>

3 Karen: seeing on ┌Tuesday
  Mary: └he did yeah ┌<LAUGHS----------------->]
  Amy: └we did this as a business managers]

4 Karen: ┌<LAUGHTER>
  Mary: <LAUGHTER>
  Amy: team and everybody guessed me straight│ away so I thought
  Others: └<LAUGHTER>

5 Karen: ┌<LAUGHTER>
  Mary: <LAUGHTER>
  Amy: well you know I've obviously retained my youth│ ful looks
  Others: └<LAUGHTER>

6 Karen: ┌there were] a whole stack as well yester┌day she just] like
  Amy: └yeah   └did she?

7 Karen: like reminiscing for ┌((xxx))
  others: └<LAUGHTER>

Karen introduces a personal note to the meeting by telling the others how Stuart (the manager who is running the baby competition) made her ring her mother to get a photograph of herself as a baby. Instead of steering the talk back to the agenda, Amy (in stave 3) overlaps with Karen to tell a personal anecdote of her own. The humour of this short extract is shared by all participants and is instigated by two of the women present. It clearly functions to build group solidarity and to reduce power differentials. The findings of both Mullany and Holmes and her colleagues (Holmes et al. 2001) challenge the stereotype that women do not have a sense of humour. On the contrary, it seems that women have a well-developed sense of humour and are able to draw on humour as a resource in meetings.

These studies suggest that, in certain contexts, women's interactional patterns can be used to good effect. In these contexts, it appears that gender and status don't come into conflict. But it remains to be seen whether women's ways of talking will be welcomed overall in the public sphere as a new resource, or whether in many contexts women will be expected to adapt to androcentric norms. The androcentric norms of public discourse are alien to many women. This discourse is extremely powerful in promoting and maintaining the competitive ethos of the world of work. If women are forced to acquire a public 'voice', then society as a whole will lose out.

11.4 Masculinity in crisis?

Given the evidence we have looked at so far in this chapter, the idea that we are witnessing some kind of crisis of masculinity may seem implausible. But the phrase 'masculinity in crisis' turns up frequently in media commentary and some have labelled this a 'globalised moral panic' (Epstein et al. 1998, quoted in Swann 2003: 632). For example, Anthony Clare, well-known for the radio series *In the Psychiatrist's Chair*, recently published a book entitled *On Men* which has the phrase *Masculinity in Crisis* as its sub-title (Clare 2001). In the book he argues that 'the roles that make men secure in their maleness – provider, protector, controller, father – are all under assault'. He points out that male suicide rates are growing and that 'when it comes to aggression, delinquent behaviour, risk taking and social mayhem, men win gold' (Clare 2001: 3). Michael Kimmel (2000: 8), in a recent summary of work on gender, asks the following question: 'What gender comes to mind when I invoke the following current American problems: "teen violence", "gang violence", "suburban violence", "drug violence", "violence in the schools"?'. Certainly, daily news items about conflict around the globe, about race riots in British cities, or about football hooliganism, underline the fact that men, in particular young men, seem to be angry and out of control.

At the heart of the problem seems to be the fact that the old certainties about the male role are disappearing and that traditional assumptions about gender identity are being challenged. Much of this challenge has come from feminism and from the social changes resulting from women's struggle for equal rights. Although popular commentators use the phrase 'crisis of masculinity', this is short-hand for a phenomenon that involves women as well as men, femininity as well as masculinity. The sociologist Bob Connell argues that it is more accurate to talk about a crisis in 'the modern gender order', because what is under threat is the entire system of gender relations (Connell 1995: 84). This is a better way of thinking about the changes that are going on in women's and men's lives, and the impact these changes are having on cultural notions of masculinity and femininity.

11.4.1 Boys at a disadvantage?

So can it be claimed that it is boys whom we need to worry about in school? And that it is boys, not girls, who are under-achieving? Some commentators argue that the classroom has been 'feminised' (Graddol and Swann 1995) and that this has had a major impact on boys and on their (increasingly negative) attitude to school.

One very obvious change that has occurred in the last ten or twenty years is the growing success of girls in public examinations. Boys are gradually slipping behind girls in terms of the educational qualifications they achieve. In the past, girls did better than boys in primary school, but once they hit adolescence they began to fall behind.[4] This is no longer true: girls now do better than boys at both GCSE and A level. This success comes not just in subjects traditionally associated with girls (English, art, drama, modern languages, domestic science), but also in subjects which used to be seen as 'masculine' (physics, chemistry, political studies, law).

However, subject choice is still highly gendered. Far more boys than girls enter subjects like maths, physics, chemistry, computing. For example, in summer 2003, 77 per cent of candidates for A level physics were male, as were 74 per cent of candidates for A level computing and 67 per cent of candidates for A level economics. So even though a higher percentage of female students achieved the top grade of 'A' in physics, for example (32 per cent compared with 26 per cent of the male students), that still only means 2,236 female students compared with 6,064 male students.

The central problem seems to be that boys nowadays view resistance to school and schooling as 'a marker of ideal masculinity' (Frosh et al. 2002: 20). In other words, boys align themselves with an 'anti-swot' culture in which working hard academically is seen as seriously uncool. For young males aged 11–14, popular masculinity is characterised by toughness, by being good at football, and by resistance to teachers and education.

This means that boys who align themselves with the hegemonic ideal are expected to fool around in the classroom, to confront the teacher, and to do very little academic work. Stephen Frosh, Ann Phoenix and Rob Pattman (2002) carried out an ethnographic study of boys in twelve London secondary schools. They interviewed the boys both in groups and individually. One of the things that emerged from these interviews was that boys create a hierarchy of popularity in school, with those who are seen as swots being the most unpopular. Here is an extract from one of the interviewers (the interviewer is Rob Pattman – RP).

(7) *Sadeem*: We are a less popular group of people. We're not the least popular group of people.

    RP: So the least popular group of people, could you describe them?

    Sadeem: Um (3) I would say it's people who, who do lots of work and things like that and (4) um (7) um, that's mainly it actually, just people who are sort of boffins. . . . We just all play basketball together – and most of the ones, the ones at the top they play football (1) and (1), the bottom ones just stay [laughter] stay in the classroom and do homework (2), and play cards or something.

(Frosh et al. 2002: 198)

Sadeem's comments here suggest there is a hierarchy based on sport (with football players at the top), and this hierachy correlates with **not** 'doing lots of work'. Boys police these norms – boys who work hard are often bullied by other boys, as the next extract shows:

(8) *Thomas*: There's a boy in our year called James and he's really clever, and *he's basically got no friends* and that's really sad because he's such a clever boy and he gets top marks in every test and *everyone hates him*.

(Frosh et al. 2002: 199, italics added)

But boys' attitudes to school are seen as only part of the problem. The problem may also lie in the curriculum. English, for example, is increasingly seen as a 'girls' subject' and so, it is argued, teachers need to work harder at appealing to boys. The Qualifications and Curriculum Authority published a document in 1998 entitled 'Can Do Better: Raising Boys' Achievements in English', which recommends among other things setting well-defined tasks in class (boys have limited tolerance of ambiguity), short sharp bursts of activity, a focus on stories featuring sport and computers, and recognition of boys' preference for non-fiction and action and fantasy. According to an article about A level English in the *Observer* newspaper (19 October 2003): 'There is a real question of feminisation with the subject. Boys prefer writing styles similar to comics, a stop-start style and manuals rather than a long discursive narrative'.

But does this mean that boys should be encouraged to write about Shakespeare using 'writing styles similar to comics'? As Joan Swann (2003) comments, this approach means that boys' habitual patterns are not being challenged. The moral panic about masculinity in crisis seems to be triggering a return to the androcentric patterns of the past. Boys' ways of talking, boys' preference for action-packed fiction, boys' need to work in short bursts, are being reinstated at the heart of classroom practice. In the last twenty years, teachers have worked hard to recognise what girls bring into the classroom; now, it seems, there is a danger that girls' ways of reading, writing and speaking will again be marginalised as teachers are exhorted to make their class-rooms more boy-friendly.

There is no doubt cause for concern in some of these findings. But is the situation being exaggerated? Despite all the media uproar about a current 'crisis', there have always been boys who have not done well at school (in par-ticular, working class boys and boys from some ethnic minority backgrounds), just as there continue to be boys who do well at school (those boys who go on to out-perform their female peers at university). Moreover, there is a real danger that some of the gains of equal opportunities initiatives of the last twenty years will be lost, as girls' needs are once again relegated to the margins.

11.4.2 Male disadvantage in the workplace?

Whether or not boys are under-achieving in school, the evidence from the public world of work is that men still dominate. Depressingly, the gap between women's and men's earnings widened in 2002: despite the Equal Pay Act, women in full-time employment still earn only 78 per cent of what men earn.[5] The pay gap is even more apparent higher up the management chain: in 2002 male financial managers and treasurers were found to be earning 40 per cent more than women in the same role.

The 2002 statistical survey, *Social Trends*, shows that there are now more women than men in higher education. But as employees, women are concen-trated in poorly paid, low prestige jobs: they constitute less than 10 per cent of those at the top of prestigious professions (architects, barristers, accountants, university professors, top civil servants, and so on).[6] A 1996 survey of 300 enterprises in the UK found that 3 per cent of board members were women. In 2001, there were only ten women among the 639 executive directors around the boardroom tables of Britain's top 100 companies, four of whom left their jobs during the course of the year. The judiciary is still very male-dominated, with few women judges. It was only in October 2003 that the first woman law lord was appointed (the title 'law lord' in itself signals the masculine exclusiv-ity of this role).

So, for complex reasons, girls' academic achievement is not rewarded in the job marketplace. At the same time, that marketplace is changing. The loss of heavy industries in Britain and the growth of the service sector have meant the end of traditional working patterns for many working-class communities – and the development of new opportunities which favour skills associated with women. The more significant changes are not in the daily patterns of women's and men's lives but in the values we attach to those patterns. In the past, the following traits were associated with men and seen as good: *logical, disciplined, controlled, rational, aggressive*. By contrast, women were associated with the following traits, which were seen as weak: *emotional, spontaneous, intuitive, expressive, compassionate, empathic*. Today, however, these values are being reversed: the traits associated with women are now seen as markers of maturity and health (Clare 2001: 68).[7] So although there is still glaring inequality in the workplace, the sense of masculinity in crisis comes from the perception that things have begun to change and that the exclusion of women from senior positions in society cannot last.

11.5 Conclusions

Studies of classroom talk show that boys tend to monopolise both physical and verbal space, and that teachers tend to give more time and attention to boys. Attempts have been made to counteract this tendency. Teachers have tried to pay more attention to girls' interests in terms of what stories are read and what writing tasks are set. They have also introduced more collaborative styles of teaching and learning into the classroom. This, however, has led to anxiety that the classroom has been 'feminised'. So we see a cycle where the perception that girls are disadvantaged has led to changes in the classroom which have in their turn provoked concern that boys are now disadvantaged.

In the world of work, there is a growing body of research showing that the interpersonal skills that women bring into the workplace are beginning to be valued. Modern workplaces need to draw on a range of interactive styles, including both those traditionally associated with male speakers and those traditionally associated with female speakers.

Overall, then, there are no clear-cut conclusions to draw from the research evidence. The main point to emerge is that gender relations are changing. We are living through a period of transition, with changes going on in the every-day worlds of school and work, accompanied by changes in the theoretical frameworks which help us to understand gender and the way gender is expressed through language.

Notes

1   A report by the inspection service Ofsted concluded: 'Boys are good at fancy footwork but often wildly over-estimate their ability and believe they will succeed without expending any energy' (*The Observer*, 19 October 2003).
2   See also Bergvall and Remlinger (1996). They observed that the contributions of female students were not supported by other students in the college classroom.
3   Estelle Morris' resignation letter, 25 October 2002.
4   Girls always did better in the eleven-plus examination in Britain (this exam is now largely obsolete), and so the results were separated by gender to make sure grammar schools did not receive a 'disproportionate' number of girls – in other words, to make sure an equal number of boys obtained grammar school places. Even earlier, in the 1920s, when IQ tests were first invented, women scored higher than men. As a result the questions were changed (Kimmell 2000: 31).

5 'Individual incomes of women and men, 1996/7 to 2001/2: a summary', Women and Equality Unit, 2002.

6 In 2004, the Equal Opportunities Commission published a report, 'Sex and Power: Who Runs Britain?', which shows that the pattern continues: 10 per cent of the most senior jobs in public life are held by women.

7 However, as Deborah Cameron (2003) points out, while women's supposed linguistic skills are now praised, this praise serves to conceal the fact that women are segregated in low-paid repetitive work, for example, in call-centres. Moreover, the new 'ideal' speaker, according to Cameron, is still a man. Examples are the former US president, Bill Clinton, or the British Prime Minister, Tony Blair: these men combine 'masculine' qualities of authority and leadership with emotional expressiveness.

PART FOUR

Looking to the future

CHAPTER 12

New developments in language and gender research

12.1 Introduction

Over the last twenty years, language and gender has established itself as a key research area in sociolinguistics. It is very difficult to believe that thirty years ago the field did not exist: it is now a thriving industry. Countless books and articles and conference papers are written every year on the topic. But inevitably there have been changes. Since Robin Lakoff's seminal work *Language and Woman's Place* appeared in 1975, research topics have multiplied and theoretical approaches have come into fashion and gone out of fashion again. In particular, ideas about gender have changed radically.

In this chapter I shall provide an overview of some of the key changes that have taken place, and some of the new ideas that currently hold sway in the academic community. Inevitably this overview will be limited, both by space and by my own filtering of the literature: what I include in this chapter is what I judge to be significant, but time may well prove me wrong.

The chapter will be divided into four main sections. The first two will deal, not surprisingly, with key developments in the conceptualisation of *language* and in the conceptualisation of *gender*. The two final sections will look briefly at the concept of Communities of Practice, and at the new field of queer linguistics and work on language and sexuality.

12.2 Language as discourse

Since this book was first written, ideas about language and its role in society have become more sophisticated. These more sophisticated ideas about language have led, among other things, to an awareness that 'language' is not always the best term to use. The whole idea of 'language', from this new perspective, is something of a fiction. What we normally refer to as 'language' can more realistically be seen as a heterogeneous collection of **discourses**.[1] A discourse can be conceptualised as a 'system of statements which cohere around common meanings and values' (Hollway 1983: 131). So, for example, in contemporary Britain there are discourses which can be labelled 'conservative', that is, discourses which emphasise values and meanings where the status quo is cherished, and there are discourses which could be labelled 'patriarchal', that is, discourses which emphasise meanings and values which assume the superiority of males. Dominant discourses such as these appear 'natural': they are powerful precisely because they are able to make invisible the fact that they are just one among many different discourses.

One of the advantages of talking about 'discourses' rather than about 'language' is that the concept 'discourse' acknowledges the value-laden nature of language. There is no neutral discourse: whenever we speak we have to choose between different systems of meaning, different sets of values. Each of us has access to a range of discourses, and it is these different discourses which give us access to, or enable us to perform, different 'selves'. This is because different discourses position us in different ways in relation to the world.

The phrase 'discourses position us' may give the impression that speakers are passive, that they are at the mercy of different discourses. But language use is *dynamic*: we make choices when we speak; we can resist and subvert. Social and cultural change are possible precisely because we do not use the discourses available to us uncritically, but participate actively in the construction of meaning. We choose between *competing* discourses in our construction and re-construction of ourselves. These choices are particularly significant in our construction and re-construction of ourselves as gendered subjects. Our construction of ourselves as masculine or feminine is profoundly affected by the discourses on gender current at any given time. As we saw in Chapter 8, speakers can choose to align themselves with dominant (or hegemonic) discourses of masculinity or femininity, or can choose to resist those discourses.

12.3 Changing ideas of gender

In Chapter 1, I defined gender as 'the term used to describe socially constructed categories based on sex' (p. 4). The understanding that gender is a social or cultural construction only became widespread in sociolinguistics in the early 1990s, as did the distinction between sex (biology) and gender (culture). In the years since then, notions of gender have been increasingly problematised.

The idea of gender as culturally constructed was extended by the theory of performativity (which has already been discussed in section 8.3). In her influential book *Gender Trouble* (1990), Judith Butler argues that gender is something that is 'done', and that it is something that has to be 'done' over and over again. 'Gender is the repeated stylisation of the body, a set of repeated acts within a rigid regulatory framework which congeal over time to produce the appearance of substance, of a "natural" kind of being' (Butler 1990: 33). Gender is never static but is produced actively and in interaction with others every day of our lives. This view of gender inevitably alters the aims of the language and gender researcher. In the past, researchers aimed to show how gender correlated with the use of particular linguistic features. Now, the aim is to show how speakers use the linguistic resources available to them to *accomplish* gender. Every time we speak, we have to bring off being a woman or being a man.

But this binary distinction – being a woman or being a man – has also been challenged. It is now felt that binary pairs such as *man–woman, male–female, masculine–feminine* distort – and oversimplify – our thinking. Gender is not a matter of two separate and homogeneous social categories, one associated with being female, the other associated with being male: male and female speakers differ in many ways, but there are also many areas of overlap. The preoccupation with difference relies on an essentialist idea of gender, that is, on the idea that male and female can be reduced to unquestioned essences. Sally Johnson (1997: 15) warns: 'an over-celebration of the essentially female always runs the risk of appropriation by the oppressor', because such conceptualisations of gender 'can easily be distorted to uphold the most misogynistic adage of all: *vive la difference*'. In other words, difference can always be interpreted in hierarchical terms.

The overthrow of binary thinking has involved the deconstruction of the notion of a single masculinity or femininity. Instead, gender is conceptualised as plural. At any point in time, there will be a range of femininities and masculinities extant in a culture, which differ in terms of class, sexual orientation, ethnicity and age, as well as intersecting in complex ways. Moreover, neither femininity nor masculinity can be understood on its own: the concepts are essentially relational. In other words, masculinity is only meaningful when it is understood in relation to femininity and to the totality of gender relations (Connell 1995: 68).

The 1990s saw seismic shifts in academic understandings of gender. As Deborah Cameron puts it: 'gender . . . has turned out to be an extraordinarily intricate and multi-layered phenomenon – unstable, contested, intimately bound up with other social divisions' (Cameron 1996: 34). Acknowledgement of these 'other social divisions' and the way they intersect with gender is the subject of the next section.

12.4 Communities of practice

As notions of gender have become more fluid, sociolinguistic researchers have been urged to pay attention to the particularities of social context. Researchers have been especially urged to work in terms of *communities of practice*. The notion of 'community of practice' (or CofP) originates with Etienne Wenger (1998) and was introduced into sociolinguistic analysis by Penny Eckert and Sally McConnell-Ginet (1992, 1995, 1998). They define a CofP as follows:

An aggregate of people who come together around mutual engagement in an endeavour. Ways of doing things, ways of talking, beliefs, values, power relations – in short,
practices – emerge in the course of this mutual endeavour.
(Eckert and McConnell-Ginet 1992: 95)

Eckert and McConnell-Ginet argue that language and gender research needs to
be grounded in 'detailed investigations of the social and linguistic practice of
specific communities of practice' (Eckert and McConnell-Ginet 1995: 469).

How we talk functions to display our membership of certain CofPs, and our
rejection of others. But these ways of talking are not immutable – within a
CofP, ways of talking are constantly being modified. The CofP is a resource for
members: it enables a speaker to establish who they are and who they are not
and how they stand in relation to significant others.

A single individual participates in a variety of communities of practice at any given
time, and over time: the family, a friendship group, an athletic team, a church group.
These communities may be all-female or all-male; they may be dominated by women
or men; they may offer different forms of participation to women or men; they may
be organised on the presumption that all members want (or will want) heterosexual
love relations. Whatever the nature of one's participation in communities of practice,
one's experience of gender emerges in participation as a gendered community member with others in a variety of communities of practice.
(Eckert and McConnell-Ginet 1995: 469)

Research taking a CofP approach emphasises the importance of 'looking locally'. This bottom-up approach starts with the individual speaker in his or her
communities of practice and views gender as a local performance.

The early years of language and gender research revolved around English-
speaking cultures and around white, middle-class speakers. The CofP approach
has encouraged researchers to study the speech patterns of women and men
in a variety of cultures. It has emphasised that gender is constructed locally
and that it interacts with race, class, sexuality and age. It has thus enabled
researchers to 'diversify the canon' (Hall 2003: 354) and to move away from
white, middle-class and anglocentric norms.

12.5 Queer linguistics

Another stimulus to fresh thinking about gender is the new field of **queer
linguistics**. This new field 'has the sexual and gender deviance of previous
generations at its centre' (Hall 2003: 354). So research on the language of
gay, lesbian, bisexual and transsexual communities is at the heart of queer
linguistics. Recent examples include a study of British gay slang, known as
Polari (Lucas 1997), of lesbian coming-out stories in the USA (Wood 1999), of
the use of sexual insults by *hijras*, a class of transgendered individuals in India
(Hall 1997), of the 'polyphonous' speech of African American drag queens
(Barrett 1999). The notion of gender as fluid and multiple is intrinsic to queer

linguistics, since binary categories like *man/woman* are unhelpful when study-ing communities like these. For example, the point Barrett is making in his paper is that drag queens are *not* men who are acting like women, but men who are acting like drag queens.

Language in queer linguistics is studied from the twin perspectives of gender and **sexuality**. For a long time, sexuality has been confused with gender – in other words, we have tended to understand sexuality in terms of gender. For example, gay men are often conceptualised as 'effeminate' men, as men who are not 'proper' men, while lesbians are seen as a masculine kind of woman. The *separation* of gender and sexuality is one of the goals of queer theory, but this may prove difficult. It has become clear, for example, that heterosexuality is a central component of hegemonic masculinity (see Cameron 1997; Coates 2005) and that, as Lynne Segal has argued, the stability of contemporary heterosexual masculinity depends on the obsessive denunciation of homo-sexuality (Segal 1990: 137).

Sexual behaviour is stereotypically gendered. Kimmell (2000: 221) argues that we are witnessing what he calls 'the masculinisation of sex', by which he means 'the pursuit of pleasure for its own sake, the increase of attention to orgasm, the multiplication of sexual partners, the universal interest in sexual experimentation, and the separation of sexual behaviour from love'. He con-trasts this phenomenon with the 'feminisation' of love and friendship. In recent years, women's and men's sexual behaviour has become more similar – but that is because women have adopted a more active, less passive role in sexual relations, not because men have increased their capacity for emotional connectedness. So the evidence is that gender and sexuality are closely inter-twined and that studies of language associated with sexuality will inevitably have many links with studies of language and gender.

Not only do sexuality and gender get blurred, the term 'sexuality' itself is not used consistently (as this section will have demonstrated). Some writers use it to refer to 'sexual identity' or 'sexual orientation' (i.e. to categories like 'gay', 'lesbian', 'bisexual'), others to refer to sexual behaviour (i.e. to what people *do* in sexual encounters), while often it is used in a broad way to refer to anything that could be called sexual. The first book devoted to the subject of language and sexuality appeared in 2003 (Cameron and Kulick 2003).[2] We can anticipate growing interest in this area, with a preoccupation with gay and lesbian lan-guage being overtaken by wider concerns, such as the linguistic representation of erotic desire, the politics of sexual consent and the language of sexual prejudice.

Perhaps most importantly, the focus on language and sexuality will serve to problematise heterosexuality, and to make more visible the way language is used to impose **heteronormativity**. Heteronormativity is a term used by queer theorists to refer to a system in which heterosexual identities, relationships and practices are seen as the norm against which all sexuality is judged. Discourses of heteronormativity inevitably 'other' homosexuality and underpin homo-phobia. While homophobia clearly has a huge impact on gay experience, it also structures the experience and identities of heterosexuals, since heterosexual men, for example, live in fear of being 'perceived as unmanly, effeminate or worst of all gay' (Kimmell 2000: 238).

12.6 A note of caution

In any scholarly field, new theories and new methodologies are a sign of health. Language and gender research has benefitted from better understandings of language and better understandings of gender. However, one or two caveats are in order here. First, even though as theorists we now talk in terms of the fluidity and plurality of gender, we need to acknowledge the power of the social ideology of gender as dichotomous. Most people in most cultures align themselves with this ideology. Gender is seen as a simple mapping on to sex, and sex is construed as binary (male/female). And the ideology has force because gender is not just a cultural construct – it is also a physical reality. 'There is an irreducible bodily dimension in experience and practice' (Connell 1995: 51). We speak from our embodied experience, and our bodies are discursively reproduced according to a two-sex model (Laqueur 1990). According to Laqueur, this two-sex model was only adopted about 200 years ago, and with it was introduced a theory of difference. Ideologies of gender and language have varied over the last 200 years, but one thing that is constant is 'the insistence that in any identifiable social group, women and men are *different*' (Cameron 2003: 452, italics in original). These ideologies of gender and language maintain gender distinctions and help to naturalise the idea that there are two 'opposite' sexes. While it is good to widen the scope of language and gender research to include the whole range of speakers and communities and to resist the stranglehold of binary thinking, it is also important to acknowledge the existence of prevailing ideologies of gender (see Cameron 2003; Talbot 2003). When speakers perform gender, they are inevitably influenced by the prevailing norms, even if they choose to resist them.

A second caveat relates to the links between feminism and language and gender research. Feminists in the past carried out research on language and gender with the aim of exposing inequalities between women and men. There is a danger that, in developing new ideas, we are losing sight of the feminist goals which underpinned this early work in the field. In the language and education field, for example, researchers refer to a 'cold climate', by which they mean that 'feminist interests and insights have been marginalised' (Swann 2003: 631). In their seminal papers on communities of practice, Eckert and McConnell-Ginet (1992, 1995, 1998) urge researchers to avoid generalising, to avoid abstractions, and to 'think practically and look locally'. But if researchers cannot appeal to the notion of 'man' or 'male' without being accused of generalising or 'essentialising', how can the continuing practical problems with men and male behaviour be challenged (Segal 1990)? The last chapter, for example, asked the question: 'What gender comes to mind when I invoke the following current American problems: "teen violence", "gang violence", "suburban violence", "drug violence", "violence in the schools"?' (Kimmell 2000: 8). If we are to encourage work which looks at 'the modern gender order' (Connell 1995: 84) as a whole and at the entire system of gender relations, then we have to be careful that terms like 'essentialist' are not used to stifle discussion. So one point to bear in mind at the end of this book is that the exponential growth of this field of research may have led to a loss of political vision. As researchers have described and analysed more and more trees, so the picture of the wood has lost some of its clarity.

12.7 Women, men and language: conclusions

At the beginning of the twenty-first century, sociolinguistic research has moved on from the simple correlation of linguistic form with social category. Researchers now analyse spoken and written data with the aim of understanding how gender is constructed in everyday life and of assessing the role of language in the creation and maintenance of contemporary masculinities and femininities. There is increasing emphasis on the need to be aware of similarities as well as differences between male and female speakers, as well as to assert the plurality of masculinities and femininities. The spread of language and gender research to non-English-speaking communities and the adoption of the CofP approach have led to more studies which emphasise the importance of 'looking locally'. This has inevitably improved understanding of the variety of ways gender is manifested linguistically in different communities. It has also brought new communities of practice to general notice. Finally, the study of gay, lesbian, bisexual and transgendered speakers has unsettled the heteronormativity of earlier research and is widening the questions we ask.

It is likely that some of these initiatives will prove in the long run to be more fruitful than others. But what does seem certain is that the field of language and gender will continue to flourish, not least because of our continuing fascination with gender and with sexuality. We understand that women and men are similar in many ways, but it is difference which fascinates us, and so we will continue to be in thrall to research which we can read as telling us about women's ways of talking, men's ways of talking, and differences between them.

Notes

1 The term 'discourse' is particularly associated with the work of Michel Foucault. For further discussion of Foucault's theories of discourse, see Fairclough (1992) and Weedon (1987).
2 Another significant book in this area is Kyratzis and Sauntson (eds) *Language, Sexualities and Desires: Cross-cultural Perspectives* (2005).

Bibliography

Abu-Haidar, Farida (1995) Dominance and communicative incompetence: the speech habits of a group of 8–11 year old boys in a Lebanese rural community, pp. 181–93 in Mills, Sara (ed.) *Language and Gender: Interdisciplinary Perspectives*. Longman, London.

Amis, Kingsley (1984) *Stanley and the Women*. Hutchinson, London.

Andersen, G. (1997) 'They like wanna see like how we talk and all that': the use of *like* as a multifunctional discourse marker in London teenage speech. in Ljung, M. (ed.) *Corpus-based Studies in English: Chapters from the 17th International Conference on English Language Research on Computerised Corpora*. Rodopi, Amsterdam.

Ardener, Shirley (ed.) (1975) *Perceiving Women*, Mallaby Press, London.

Ardener, Shirley (1978) The nature of women in society, pp. 9–48 in Ardener, Shirley (ed.) *Defining Females*, Croom Helm, London.

Argyle, Michael, Lalljee, Mansur and **Cook, Mark** (1968) The effects of visibility on interaction in a dyad, *Human Relations* **21**: 3–17.

Aries, Elizabeth (1976) Interaction patterns and themes of male, female and mixed groups, *Small Group Behaviour* **7** (1): 7–18.

Aries, Elizabeth and **Johnson, Fern** (1983) Close friendship in adulthood: conversational conduct between same-sex friends, *Sex Roles* **9** (12): 1,183–96.

Arnot, Madeleine and **Weiner, Gaby** (eds) (1987) *Gender and the Politics of Schooling*. Hutchinson, London.

Aronsson, Karin and **Thorell, Mia** (1999) Family politics in children's play directives. *Journal of Pragmatics* **31**: 25–47.

Austen, Jane (1972) *Northanger Abbey*. Penguin, Harmondsworth.

Baptiste, Tamsin (1990) A contrastive study of male and female complimenting behaviour in British English. Unpublished BA dissertation, Roehampton Institute.

Barnard, Stephen (2000) *Studying Radio*. Arnold, London.

Barnes, Douglas (1971) Language and learning in the classroom, *Journal of Curriculum Studies* **3** (1).

Barrett, Rusty (1999) Indexing polyphonous identity in the speech of African American drag queens, pp. 313–31 in Bucholtz, M., Liang, A.C. and Sutton, L. (eds) *Reinventing Identities: The Gendered Self in Discourse*. Oxford University Press, Oxford.

Bashiruddin, Ayesha, Edge, Julian and **Hughes-Pelegrin, Elizabeth** (1990) Who speaks in seminars? Status, culture and gender at Durham University, pp. 74–84 in Clark, Romy, Fairclough, Norman, Ivanic, Roz, McLeod, Nicki, Thomas, Jenny and Meara, Paul (eds) *Language and Power*. CILT, London.

Bate, Barbara and **Taylor, Anita** (eds) (1988) *Women Communicating: Studies of Women's Talk*, Ablex, Norwood, NJ.

Bem, Sandra (1974) The measurement of psychological androgyny, *Journal of Consulting and Clinical Psychology* **42**: 155–62.

Bem, Sandra (1975) Sex role adaptability: one consequence of psychological androgyny, *Journal of Personality and Social Psychology* **31** (4): 634–43.

Bergvall, Victoria and Remlinger, Kathryn (1996) Reproduction, resistance and gender in educational discourse: the role of critical discourse analysis, *Discourse and Society* **7** (4): 453–79.

Bernard, Jessie (1972) *The Sex Game*. Atheneum, New York.

Bevan, J. (1990) Compliments and compliment-responses in British English. Unpublished MA project, Birkbeck College, University of London.

Blom, Jan-Petter and Gumperz, John (1972) Social meanings in linguistic structures: code switching in Norway, pp. 407–34 in Gumperz, John and Hymes, Dell (eds) *Directions in Sociolinguistics*. Holt Rinehart & Winston, New York.

Bloom, Lois (1975) *One Word at a Time*. Mouton, The Hague.

Bloomfield, Leonard (1933) *Language*. George Allen & Unwin, London.

Bodine, Ann (1975) Sex differentiation in language, pp. 130–51 in Thorne, Barrie and Henley, Nancy (eds) *Language and Sex: Difference and Dominance*. Newbury House, Rowley, MA.

Bodine, Ann (1998) Androcentrism in prescriptive grammar, pp. 124–38 in Cameron, Deborah (ed.) *The Feminist Critique of Language* (2nd edition). Routledge, London.

Bourdieu, Pierre and Boltanski, Luc (1975) Le fétichisme de la langue, *Actes de la recherche en sciences sociales* **4**: 2–32.

Bridge, Joseph C. (1917) *Cheshire Proverbs and Other Sayings and Rhymes Connected with the City and County Palatine of Chester*. Phillipson and Golder, Chester.

Britain, David (1998) Linguistic change in intonation: the use of high-rising terminals in New Zealand English, pp. 213–39 in Trudgill, Peter and Cheshire, Jenny (eds) *The Sociolinguistics Reader. Vol I: Multilingualism and Variation*. Arnold, London.

Brouwer, Dede, Gerritsen, Marinel and de Haan, Dorian (1979) Speech differences between women and men: on the wrong track?, *Language in Society* **8**: 33–50.

Brown, Penelope (1998) How and why are women more polite: some evidence from a Mayan community, pp. 81–99 in Coates, Jennifer (ed.) *Language and Gender: A Reader*. Blackwell, Oxford.

Brown, Penelope and Levinson, Stephen (1978) Universals in language usage: politeness phenomena, pp. 56–289 in Goody, Esther (ed.) *Questions and Politeness*. Cambridge University Press, Cambridge.

Brown, Penelope and Levinson, Stephen (1987) *Politeness*. Cambridge University Press, Cambridge.

Brown, Roger (1976) *A First Language*. Penguin Books, Harmondsworth.

Brun, A. (1946) *Parlers régionaux, France dialectale et unité française*. Didier, Paris.

Bucholtz, Mary, Liang, A.C. and Sutton, Laurel (eds) (1999) *Reinventing Identities: The Gendered Self in Discourse*. Oxford University Press, Oxford.

Butler, Judith (1990) *Gender Trouble: Feminism and the Subversion of Identity*. Routledge, New York.

Cameron, Deborah (1992) Review of Tannen *You Just Don't Understand. Feminism and Psychology* **2**: 465–8.

Cameron, Deborah (1996) The language–gender interface: challenging co-optation, pp. 31–53 in Bergvall, Victoria, Bing, Janet and Freed, Alice (eds) *Rethinking Language and Gender Research: Theory and Practice*. Longman, London.

Cameron, Deborah (1997) Performing gender identity: young men's talk and the construction of heterosexual masculinity, pp. 47–64 in Johnson, Sally and Meinhof, Ulrike H. (eds) *Language and Masculinity*. Blackwell, Oxford.

Cameron, Deborah (2003) Gender and language ideologies, pp. 447–67 in Holmes, Janet and Meyerhoff, Miriam (eds) *The Handbook of Language and Gender*. Blackwell, Oxford.

Cameron, Deborah and Coates, Jennifer (1989) Some problems in the sociolinguistic explanation of sex differences, pp. 13–26 in Coates, Jennifer and Cameron, Deborah (eds) *Women in their Speech Communities*. Longman, London.

Cameron, Deborah and Kulick, Don (2003) *Language and Sexuality*. Cambridge University Press, Cambridge.

Cameron, Deborah, McAlinden, Fiona and O'Leary, Kathy (1989) Lakoff in context: the social and linguistic functions of tag questions, pp. 74–93 in Coates, Jennifer and Cameron, Deborah (eds) *Women in their Speech Communities*. Longman, London.

Campbell, K. and Jerry, C. (1988) Woman and speaker: a conflict in roles, in Brehm, S.S. (ed.) *Seeing Female: Social Roles and Personal Lives*. Greenwood Press, New York.

Chambers, J.K. and Trudgill, Peter (1980) *Dialectology*. Cambridge University Press, Cambridge.

Cheshire, Jenny (1978) Present tense verbs in Reading English, pp. 52–68 in Trudgill, Peter (ed.) *Sociolinguistic Patterns in British English*. Edward Arnold, London.

Cheshire, Jenny (1982) *Variation in an English Dialect*. Cambridge University Press, Cambridge.

Cheshire, Jenny (1998) Linguistic variation and social function, pp. 29–41 in Coates, Jennifer (ed.) *Language and Gender: A Reader*. Blackwell, Oxford.

Cheshire, Jenny and Jenkins, Nancy (1991) Gender issues in the GCSE oral English examination: Part 2, *Language and Education* 5 (1): 19–40.

Cheshire, Jenny and Trudgill, Peter (eds) (1998) *The Sociolinguistics Reader*. Vol. 2: *Gender and Discourse*. Arnold, London.

Clare, Anthony (2001) *On Men: Masculinity in Crisis*. Arrow Books, London.

Clarke-Stewart, Alison (1973) Interactions between mothers and their young children: characteristics and consequences, *Monographs of the Society for Research in Child Development* 153, 38 (6–7).

Clarricoates, Katherine (1987) 'Dinosaurs in the classroom': the 'hidden' curriculum in primary schools, pp. 155–65 in Arnot, Madeleine and Weiner, Gaby (eds) *Gender and the Politics of Schooling*. Hutchinson, London.

Coates, Jennifer (1989) Gossip revisited: language in all-female groups, pp. 94–121 in Coates, Jennifer and Cameron, Deborah (eds) *Women in their Speech Communities*. Longman, London.

Coates, Jennifer (1991) Women's cooperative talk: a new kind of conversational duet?, pp. 296–311 in Uhlig, Claus and Zimmerman, Rudiger (eds) *Proceedings of the Anglistentag 1990 Marburg*, Max Niemeyer Verlag, Tübingen.

Coates, Jennifer (1994) No gap, lots of overlap: turn-taking patterns in the talk of women friends, pp. 177–92 in Graddol, David, Maybin, Janet and Stierer, Barry (eds) *Researching Language and Literacy in Social Context*. Multilingual Matters, Clevedon.

Coates, Jennifer (1996) *Women Talk: Conversation Between Women Friends*. Blackwell, Oxford.

Coates, Jennifer (1997) One-at-a-time: the organisation of men's talk, pp. 107–29 in Johnson, Sally and Meinhof, Ulrike H. (eds) *Language and Masculinity*. Blackwell, Oxford.

Coates, Jennifer (1998) *Language and Gender: A Reader*. Blackwell, Oxford.

Coates, Jennifer (1999) Changing femininities: the talk of teenage girls, pp. 123–44 in Bucholtz, Mary, Liang, A.C. and Sutton, Laurel (eds) *Reinventing Identities: The Gendered Self in Discourse.* Oxford University Press, Oxford.

Coates, Jennifer (2003) *Men Talk: Stories in the Making of Masculinities.* Blackwell, Oxford.

Coates, Jennifer (2005) 'Everyone was convinced that we were closet fags': the role of heterosexuality in the construction of hegemonic masculinity, to appear in Kyratzis, Sakis and Sauntson, Helen (eds) *Language, Sexualities and Desires: Cross-cultural Perspectives.* Palgrave, London.

Coates, Jennifer and Cameron, Deborah (eds) (1989) *Women in their Speech Communities.* Longman, London.

Coates, Jennifer and Sutton-Spence, Rachel (2001) Turn-taking patterns in Deaf friends' talk, *Journal of Sociolinguistics* 4 (4): 507–29.

Connell, R.W. (1995) *Masculinities.* Polity Press, Cambridge.

Corsaro, William and Rizzo, Thomas (1990) Disputes in the peer culture of American and Italian nursery-school children, pp. 21–66 in Grimshaw, Allen (ed.) *Conflict Talk.* Cambridge University Press, Cambridge.

Corson, David (1997) Gender, discourse and senior education: ligatures for girls, options for boys?, pp. 140–64 in Wodak, Ruth (ed.) *Gender and Discourse.* Sage, London.

Crawford, Mary (1995) *Talking Difference: On Gender and Language.* Sage, London.

Crystal, David and Davy, Derek (1975) *Advanced Conversational English.* Longman, London.

Dale, Philip (1976) *Language Development* (2nd edition). Holt Rinehart & Winston, New York.

Daly, Mary (1988) *Webster's First New Intergalactic Wickedary of the English Language.* Women's Press, London.

Davies, Reginald T. (ed.) (1963) *Medieval English Lyrics.* Faber & Faber, London.

DeFrancisco, Victoria L. (1998) The sounds of silence: how men silence women in marital relations, pp. 176–84 in Coates, Jennifer (ed.) *Language and Gender: A Reader.* Blackwell, Oxford.

De Klerk, Vivian (1992) How taboo are taboo words for girls?, *Language in Society* 21: 277–89.

De Klerk, Vivian (1997) The role of expletives in the construction of masculinity, pp. 144–58 in Johnson, Sally and Meinhof, Ulrike H. (eds) *Language and Masculinity.* Blackwell, Oxford.

Delamont, Sara (1990) *Sex Roles and the School.* Methuen, London.

Delphy, Christine (1981) Women in stratification studies, in Roberts, H. (ed.) *Doing Feminist Research.* Routledge, London.

De Lyon, Hilary (1981) A sociolinguistic study of aspects of the Liverpool accent. Unpublished MPhil. thesis, University of Liverpool.

Dobson, Eric J. (1969) Early modern standard English, in Lass, Roger (ed.) *Approaches to English Historical Linguistics.* Holt Rinehart & Winston, New York.

Donovan, Josephine (1980) The silence is broken, pp. 205–18 in McConnell-Ginet, Sally Borker, Ruth and Furman, Nelly (eds) *Women and Language in Literature and Society.* Praeger, New York.

Dorval, Bruce (1990) *Conversational Organization and its Development,* Ablex, Norwood, NJ.

Dubois, Betty Lou and Crouch, Isabel (1975) The question of tag questions in women's speech: they don't really use more of them, do they?, *Language in Society* 4: 289–94.

Dunbar, Robin (1996) *Gossip, Grooming and the Evolution of Language.* Faber & Faber, London.

Eakins, Barbara W. and Eakins, R. Gene (1978) *Sex Differences in Human Communication.* Houghton Mifflin, Boston, MA.

Eakins, Barbara W. and Eakins, R. Gene (1979) Verbal turn-taking and exchanges in faculty dialogue, pp. 53–62 in Dubois, B.-L. and Crouch, I. (eds) *The Sociology of the Languages of American Women.* Trinity University, San Antonio, TX.

Eckert, Penelope (1990) The whole women: sex and gender differences in variation, *Language Variation and Change* 1: 245–67.

Eckert, Penelope (1998) Gender and sociolinguistic variation, pp. 64–75 in Coates, Jennifer (ed.) *Language and Gender: A Reader.* Blackwell, Oxford.

Eckert, Penelope (1999) *Variation and Social Practice: The Linguistic Construction of Social Meaning in Belten High.* Blackwell, Oxford.

Eckert, Penelope and McConnell-Ginet, Sally (1992) Think practically and look locally: language and gender as community based practice, *Annual Review of Anthropology* 21: 461–90.

Eckert, Penelope and McConnell-Ginet, Sally (1995) Constructing meaning, constructing selves: snapshots of language, gender and class from Belten High, pp. 469–507 in Hall, Kira and Bucholtz, Mary (eds) *Gender Articulated: Language and the Socially Constructed Self.* Routledge, London.

Eckert, Penelope and McConnell-Ginet, Sally (1998) Communities of practice: where language, gender and power all live, pp. 484–94 in Coates, Jennifer (ed.) *Language and Gender: A Reader.* Blackwell, Oxford.

Eckert, Penelope and McConnell-Ginet, Sally (1999) New generalisations and explanations in language and gender research, *Language in Society* 28: 185–201.

Edelsky, Carole (1976) The acquisition of communicative competence: recognition of linguistic correlates of sex roles, *Merril-Palmer Quarterly* 22: 47–59.

Edelsky, Carole (1993) Who's got the floor?, pp. 189–227 in Tannen, Deborah (ed.) *Gender and Conversational Interaction.* Oxford University Press, Oxford.

Edelsky, Carole and Adams, Karen (1990) Creating inequality: breaking the rules in debates, *Journal of Language and Social Psychology* 9 (3): 171–90.

Eder, Donna (1990) Serious and playful disputes: variation in conflict talk among female adolescents, pp. 67–84 in Grimshaw, Allan (ed.) *Conflict Talk.* Cambridge University Press, Cambridge.

Eder, Donna (1993) 'Go get ya a french': romantic and sexual teasing among adolescent girls, pp. 17–31 in Tannen, Deborah (ed.) *Gender and Conversational Interaction.* Oxford University Press, Oxford.

Edwards, John R. (1979a) Social class differences and the identification of sex in children's speech, *Journal of Child Language* 6: 121–7.

Edwards, John R. (1979b) *Language and Disadvantage.* Edward Arnold, London.

Eisikovits, Edina (1987) Sex differences in inter-group and intra-group interaction among adolescents, pp. 45–58 and Pauwels, Anne (ed.) *Women and Language in Australian and New Zealand Society.* Australian Professional Publications, Sydney.

Eisikovits, Edina (1998) Girl-talk/boy-talk: sex differences in adolescent speech, pp. 42–54 in Coates, Jennifer (ed.) *Language and Gender: A Reader.* Blackwell, Oxford.

Ellis, Havelock (1894) *Man and Woman.* Walter Scott Publishing Co.

Elyan, Olwen, Smith, Philip, Giles, Howard and Bourhis, Richard (1978) RP-accented female speech: the voice of perceived androgyny?, pp. 122–31 in Trudgill, Peter (ed.) *Sociolinguistic Patterns in British English.* Edward Arnold, London.

Elyot, Thomas (1531) *The Governour.* Scolar Press, Menston, Yorks, 1970.

Emler, Nicholas (2001) Gossiping, in Giles, H. and Robinson, W.P. (eds) *The New Handbook of Social Psychology and Language* (2nd edition). John Wiley & Sons, Chichester.

Emler, Nicholas (forthcoming) *Secrets, Scandals, Rumours and Reputations: The Gossip Process in Everyday Life*. Harvester Wheatsheaf, Brighton.

Engle, Marianne (1980) Language and play: a comparative analysis of parental initiatives, pp. 29–34 in Giles, Howard, Robinson, W. Peter and Smith, Philip M. (eds) *Language: Social Psychological Perspectives*. Pergamon Press, Oxford.

Equal Opportunities Commission (2004) *Sex and Power: Who Runs Britain?* EOC Press Office, Manchester.

Erickson, Frederick (1990) The social construction of discourse coherence in a family dinner table conversation, pp. 207–38 in Dorval, Bruce (ed.) *Conversational Organization and its Development*. Ablex, Norwood, NJ.

Fairclough, Norman (1992) *Discourse and Social Change*. Polity Press, Cambridge.

Fichtelius, Anna, Johansson, Irene and **Nordin, Kerstin** (1980) Three investigations of sex-associated speech variation in day school, pp. 219–25 in Kramarae, Cheris (ed.) *The Voices and Words of Women and Men*. Pergamon Press, Oxford.

Fischer, John L. (1964) Social influences on the choice of a linguistic variant, pp. 483–8 in Hymes, Dell (ed.) *Language in Culture and Society*. Harper International, New York.

Fisher, Julie (1994) Unequal voices: gender and assessment, pp. 168–76 in Graddol, David, Maybin, Janet and Stierer, Barry (eds) *Researching Language and Literacy in Social Context*. Multilingual Matters, Clevedon.

Fishman, Pamela (1980a) Conversational insecurity, pp. 127–32 in Giles, Howard, Robinson, W.P. and Smith, Philip M. (eds) *Language: Social Psychological Perspectives*. Pergamon Press, Oxford.

Fishman, Pamela (1980b) Interactional shitwork, *Heresies* 2: 99–101.

Flannery, Regina (1946) Men's and women's speech in Gros Ventre, *International Journal of American Linguistics* 12: 133–5.

Fletcher, Paul and **Garman, Michael** (1986) *Language Acquisition* (2nd edition). Cambridge University Press, Cambridge.

Fletcher, Paul and **Ingham, Richard** (1995) Grammatical impairment, pp. 603–22 in Fletcher, Paul and MacWhinney, Brian (eds) *The Handbook of Child Language*. Blackwell, Oxford.

Flexner, Stuart B. (1960) Preface to *Dictionary of American Slang*. Thomas Y. Crowell, New York.

Foster, Susan (1990) *The Communicative Competence of Young Children*. Longman, London.

Francis, W. Nelson (1983) *Dialectology: An Introduction*. Longman, London.

Freed, Alice (1992) We understand perfectly: a critique of Tannen's view of miscommunication, pp. 144–52 in Hall, Kira, Bucholtz, Mary and Moonwomon, Birch (eds) *Locating Power: Proceedings of the Second Berkeley Women & Language Conference*. BWLG group, University of California, Los Angeles.

Frosh, Stephen, Phoenix, Ann and **Pattman, Rob** (2002) *Young Masculinities*. Palgrave, London.

Gal, Susan (1979) *Language Shift*. Academic Press, New York.

Gal, Susan (1998) Peasant men can't get wives: language change and sex roles in a bilingual community, pp. 147–59 in Coates, Jennifer (ed.) *Language and Gender: A Reader*. Blackwell, Oxford.

Gardette, P. (1968) *Atlas linguistique et ethnographique du Lyonnais*. Vol. IV: *Exposé méthodologique et tables*. Centre Nationale de la Recherche Scientifique, Paris.

Gauchat, L. (1905) *L'unité phonetique dans le patois d'une commune*. D.S. Niemeyer, Halle.

Gleason, Jean Berko (1980) The acquisition of social speech routines and politeness formulas, pp. 21–7 in Giles, Howard, Robinson, W.P. and Smith, Philip M. (eds) *Language: Social Psychological Perspectives*. Pergamon Press, Oxford.

Gomm, Isabel (1981) A study of the inferior image of the female use of the English language as compared to that of the male. Unpublished BA dissertation, Edge Hill College, Ormskirk.

Goodwin, Marjorie Harness (1980) Directive-response speech sequences in girls' and boys' task activities, pp. 157–73 in McConnell-Ginet, Sally, Borker, Ruth and Furman, Nelly (eds) *Women and Language in Literature and Society*. Praeger, New York.

Goodwin, Marjorie Harness (1990) *He-said-she-said. Talk as Social Organization among Black Children*. Indiana University Press, Bloomington.

Goodwin, Marjorie Harness (1998) Cooperation and competition across girls' play activities, pp. 121–46 in Coates, Jennifer (ed.) *Language and Gender: A Reader*. Blackwell, Oxford.

Goodwin, Marjorie Harness (2003) The relevance of ethnicity, class, and gender in children's peer negotiations, pp. 229–51 in Holmes, Janet and Meyerhoff, Miriam (eds) *The Handbook of Language and Gender*. Blackwell, Oxford.

Goodwin, Marjorie Harness and Goodwin, Charles (1987) Children's arguing, pp. 200–48 in Philips, Susan, Steele, Susan and Tanz, Christine (eds) *Language, Gender and Sex in Comparative Perspective*. Cambridge University Press, Cambridge.

Gough, Brendan and Edwards, Gareth (1998) The beer talking: four lads, a carry out and the reproduction of masculinities, *The Sociological Review*. August: 409–35.

Graddol, David and Swann, Joan (1995) Feminising classroom talk?, pp. 135–47 in Mills, Sara (ed.) *Language and Gender: Interdisciplinary Perspectives*. Longman, London.

Greif, Esther Blank (1980) Sex differences in parent–child conversations, pp. 253–8 in Kramarae, Cheris (ed.) *The Voices and Words of Women and Men*. Pergamon Press, Oxford.

Gunnarsson, Britt-Louise (1997) Women and men in the academic discourse community, pp. 219–48 in Kotthoff, Helga and Wodak, Ruth (eds) *Communicating Gender in Context*. John Benjamins, Amsterdam.

Haas, Adelaide (1978) Sex-associated features of spoken language by four-, eight-, and twelve-year-old boys and girls. Paper given at the 9th World Congress of Sociology, Uppsala, Sweden, 14–19 August.

Haas, Adelaide (1979) Male and female spoken language differences: stereotypes and evidence, *Psychological Bulletin* 86: 616–26.

Haas, Mary (1944) Men's and women's speech in Koasati, *Language* 20: 147–9.

Hall, Catherine (1985) Private persons versus public someones: class, gender and politics in England, 1780–1850, pp. 10–33 in Steedman, Carolyn, Urwin, Cathy and Walkerdine, Valerie (eds) *Language, Gender and Childhood*. Routledge, London.

Hall, Kira (1997) 'Go suck your husband's sugarcane!': Hijras and the use of sexual insult, pp. 430–60 in Livia, Anna and Hall, Kira (eds) *Queerly Phrased: Language, Gender and Sexuality*. Oxford University Press, New York.

Hall, Kira (2003) Exceptional speakers: contested and problematised gender identities, pp. 353–80 in Holmes, Janet and Meyerhoff, Miriam (eds) *The Handbook of Language and Gender*. Blackwell, Oxford.

Hall, Kira and Bucholtz, Mary (eds) (1997) *Gender Articulated: Language and the Socially Constructed Self*. Routledge, New York.

Harris, Sandra (1984) Questions as a mode of control in magistrates' courts, *International Journal of the Sociology of Language* **49**: 5–27.

Herbert, Robert K. (1998) Sex-based differences in compliment behaviour, pp. 53–75 in Cheshire, Jenny and Trudgill, Peter (eds) *The Sociolinguistics Reader.* Vol. 2: *Gender and Discourse.* Arnold, London.

Herring, Susan (1992) Gender and participation in computer-mediated linguistic discourse. Document No. 345552, ERIC Clearinghouse on Languages and Linguistics, Washington, DC.

Herring, Susan, Johnson, Deborah and **DiBenedetto, Tamra** (1995) 'This discussion is going too far!': male resistance to female participation on the Internet, pp. 67–96 in Hall, Kira and Bucholtz, Mary (eds) *Gender Articulated: Language and the Socially Constructed Self.* Routledge, New York.

Herring, Susan, Johnson, Deborah and **DiBenedetto, Tamra** (1998) Participation in electronic discourse in a 'feminist' field, pp. 197–210 in Coates, Jennifer (ed.) *Language and Gender: A Reader.* Blackwell, Oxford.

Hewitt, Roger (1997) 'Box-out' and 'taxing', pp. 27–46 in Johnson, Sally and Meinhof, Ulrike H. (eds) *Language and Masculinity.* Blackwell, Oxford.

Hirschmann, Lynette (1974) Analysis of supportive and assertive behaviour in conversations. Paper presented at Linguistic Society of America meeting, July 1974.

Hollway, Wendy (1983) Heterosexual sex: power and desire for the other, pp. 124–40 in Cartledge, Sue and Ryan, Joanna (eds) *Sex and Love: New Thoughts on Old Contradictions.* Women's Press, London.

Holmes, Janet (1984) Hedging your bets and sitting on the fence: some evidence for hedges as support structures, *Te Reo* **27**: 47–62.

Holmes, Janet (1987) Hedging, fencing and other conversational gambits: an analysis of gender differences in New Zealand speech, pp. 59–79 in Pauwels, Anne (ed.) *Women and Language in Australian and New Zealand Society.* Australian Professional Publications, Sydney.

Holmes, Janet (1988a) Paying compliments: a sex-preferential politeness strategy, *Journal of Pragmatics* **12**: 445–65.

Holmes, Janet (1988b) Sex differences in seminar contributions, *BAAL Newsletter* **31**: 33–41.

Holmes, Janet (1995) *Women, Men and Politeness.* Longman, London.

Holmes, Janet (1998) Women's talk: the question of sociolinguistic universals, pp. 461–83 in Coates, Jennifer (ed.) *Language and Gender: A Reader.* Blackwell, Oxford.

Holmes, Janet (2000) Women at Work: analysing women's talk in New Zealand, *Australian Review of Applied Linguistics* **22** (2): 1–17.

Holmes, Janet and **Meyerhoff, Miriam** (eds) (2003) *The Handbook of Language and Gender.* Blackwell, Oxford.

Holmes, Janet and **Stubbe, Maria** (2003) 'Feminine' workplaces: stereotypes and reality, pp. 573–99 in Holmes, Janet and Meyerhoff, Miriam (eds) *The Handbook of Language and Gender.* Blackwell, Oxford.

Holmes, Janet, Marra, Meredith and **Burns, Louise** (2001) Women's humour in the workplace: a quantitative analysis, *Australian Journal of Communication* **28** (1): 83–108.

Hudson, Emmet (1992) Swearing: a linguistic analysis. Unpublished MA dissertation, Birkbeck College, London.

Hughes, Susan (1992) Expletives of lower working-class women, *Language in Society* **21**: 291–303.

Humm, Maggie (1989) *The Dictionary of Feminist Theory*. Harvester Wheatsheaf, London.

Humphrey, Caroline (1978) Women, taboo and the suppression of attention, pp. 89–108 in Arderner, Shirley (ed.) *Defining Females: The Nature of Women in Society*. Croom Helm, London.

Hunt, Pauline (2003) Gender specifics, *Education Guardian* 11 February.

Hymes, Dell (1972) On communicative competence, pp. 269–93 in Pride, J.B. and Holmes, Janet (eds) *Sociolinguistics*. Penguin Books, Harmondsworth.

Ide, Sachiko (1991) How and why do women speak more politely in Japanese?, pp. 63–79 in Ide, Sachiko and McGloin, Naomi H. (eds) *Aspects of Japanese Women's Language*. Kurosio Publishers, Tokyo.

Ingram, David (1989) *First Language Acquisition*. Cambridge University Press, Cambridge.

Irigaray, Luce (1990) Women's exile, Interview with Luce Irigaray, translated by Couze Venn, pp. 80–96 in Cameron, Deborah (ed.) *The Feminist Critique of Language*. Routledge, London.

Irwin, Anthea (2002) The construction of identity in the spontaneous conversation of adolescents. Unpublished PhD thesis, University of Surrey, Roehampton.

Irwin, Anthea (in press) Policing peer group reproduction: adolescents' use of 'like', *Roehampton Working Papers in Linguistics*. Vol. 3.

Jenkins, Nancy and **Cheshire, Jenny** (1990) Gender issues in the GCSE oral English examination: Part 1, *Language and Education* **4**: 261–92.

Jespersen, Otto (1922) *Language: Its Nature, Development and Origin*. George Allen & Unwin, London.

Johnson, Sally (1997) Theorising language and masculinity: a feminist perspective, pp. 8–26 in Johnson, Sally and Meinhof, Ulrike H. (eds) *Language and Masculinity*. Blackwell, Oxford.

Johnson, Sally and **Finlay, Frank** (1997) Do men gossip? An analysis of football talk on television, pp. 130–43 in Johnson, Sally and Meinhof, Ulrike H. (eds) *Language and Masculinity*. Blackwell, Oxford.

Johnson, Sally and **Meinhof, Ulrike H.** (eds) (1997) *Language and Masculinity*. Blackwell, Oxford.

Jones, Deborah (1980) Gossip: notes on women's oral culture, pp. 193–8 in Kramarae, Cheris (ed.) *The Voices and Words of Women and Men*. Pergamon Press, Oxford.

Kamuf, Peggy (1980) Writing like a woman, pp. 284–99 in McConnell-Ginet, Sally, Borker, Ruth and Furman, Nelly (eds) *Women and Language in Literature and Society*. Praeger, New York.

Kelly, Alison (1987) The construction of masculine science, pp. 127–39 in Arnot, Madeleine and Weiner, Gaby (eds) *Gender and the Politics of Schooling*. Hutchinson, London.

Kelly, Alison, Whyte, Judith and **Smail, Barbara** (1984) *Girls Into Science and Technology: Final Report*. Equal Opportunities Commission, Manchester.

Kimmell, Michael S. (2000) *The Gendered Society*. Oxford University Press, Oxford.

Kirby, J. (1746) *A New English Grammar*. Scolar Press, Menston, Yorks, 1971.

Knowles, Gerald (1974) Scouse: the urban dialect of Liverpool. Unpublished PhD thesis, University of Leeds.

Kramarae, Cheris and **Treichler, Paula** (1992) *Amazons, Bluestockings and Crones: A Feminist Dictionary*. Pandora Press, London.

Kramer, Cheris (1974) Folklinguistics, *Psychology Today* **8**: 82–5.

Kramer, Cheris (1975) Stereotypes of women's speech: the word from cartoons, *Journal of Popular Culture* **8** (3): 624–38.

Kuiper, Koenraad (1998) Sporting formulae in New Zealand English: two models of male solidarity, pp. 285–94 in Coates, Jennifer (ed.) *Language and Gender: A Reader*. Blackwell, Oxford.

Kurath, Hans (1972) *Studies in Area Linguistics*. Indiana University Press, Bloomington.

Kyratzis, Sakis and **Sauntson, Helen** (eds) (2005) *Language, Sexualities and Desires: Cross-cultural perspectives*. Palgrave, London.

Labov, William (1972a) *Sociolinguistic Patterns*. Blackwell, Oxford.

Labov, William (1972b) *Language in the Inner City*. Blackwell, Oxford.

Lakoff, George and **Johnson, Mark** (1980) *Metaphors We Live By*. University of Chicago Press, Chicago.

Lakoff, Robin (1975) *Language and Woman's Place*. Harper & Row, New York.

Laqueur, Thomas (1990) *Making Sex: Body and Gender from the Greeks to Freud*. Harvard University Press, Cambridge, MA.

Leap, William (1999) Language, socialisation and silence in gay adolesence, pp. 259–72 in Bucholtz, Mary, Liang, A.C. and Sutton, Laurel (eds) *Reinventing Identities: The Gendered Self in Discourse*. Oxford University Press, Oxford.

Lee, Alison, Hewlett, Nigel and **Nairn, Moray** (1995) Voice and gender in children, pp. 194–204 in Mills, Sara (ed.) *Language and Gender: Interdisciplinary Perspectives*. Longman, London.

Leet-Pellegrini, Helena M. (1980) Conversational dominance as a function of gender and expertise, pp. 97–104 in Giles, Howard, Robinson, W.P. and Smith, Philip M. (eds) *Language: Social Psychological Perspectives*. Pergamon Press, Oxford.

Liebermann, Philip (1967) *Intonation, Perception and Language*. MIT Press, Cambridge, MA.

Livia, Anna and **Hall, Kira** (eds) (1997) *Queerly Phrased: Language, Gender and Sexuality*. Oxford University Press, New York.

Local, John (1982) Modelling intonational variability in children's speech, pp. 85–103 in Romaine, Suzanne (ed.) *Sociolinguistic Variation in Speech Communities*. Edward Arnold, London.

Lucas, Ian (1997) The colour of his eyes: Polari and the sisters of perpetual indulgence, pp. 85–94 in Livia, Anna and Hall, Kira (eds) *Queerly Phrased: Language, Gender and Sexuality*. Oxford University Press, New York.

Luhman, Reid (1990) Appalachian English stereotypes: language attitudes in Kentucky, *Language in Society* 19: 331–48.

Macaulay, R.K.S. (1977) *Language, Social Class and Education*. Edinburgh University Press, Edinburgh.

Macaulay, R.K.S. (1978) Variation and consistency in Glaswegian English, pp. 132–43 in Trudgill, Peter (ed.) *Sociolinguistic Patterns in British English*. Edward Arnold, London.

Maccoby, Eleanor E. and **Jacklin, Carol Nagy** (1974) *The Psychology of Sex Differences*. Stanford University Press, Stanford, CA.

MacLean, Ian (1980) *The Renaissance Notion of Woman*. Cambridge University Press, Cambridge.

Madhok, Jacqueline (1992) The effect of gender composition on group interaction, pp. 371–85 in Hall, Kira, Bucholtz, Mary and Moonwomon, Birch (eds) *Locating Power*. Berkeley Women and Language Group, University of California, Berkeley, CA.

Maltz, Daniel N. and **Borker, R.A.** (1982) A cultural approach to male–female miscommunication, pp. 195–216 in Gumperz, John (ed.) *Language and Social Identity*. Cambridge University Press, Cambridge.

Maynard, Douglas (1986) Offering and soliciting collaboration in multi-party disputes among children (and other humans), *Human Studies* 9: 261–85.

McElhinny, Bonnie (1998) 'I don't smile much anymore': affect, gender and the discourse of Pittsburgh police officers, pp. 309–27 in Coates, Jennifer (ed.) *Language and Gender: A Reader*. Blackwell, Oxford.

McIntosh, Angus (1952) *An Introduction to a Survey of Scottish Dialects*. Nelson, London.

McTear, Michael (1985) *Children's Conversation*. Basil Blackwell, Oxford.

Meditch, Andrea (1975) The development of sex-specific patterns in young children, *Anthropological Linguistics* 17 (9): 421–33.

Meyerhoff, Miriam (2003) Claiming a place: gender, knowledge, and authority as emergent properties, pp. 302–26 in Holmes, Janet and Meyerhoff, Miriam (eds) *The Handbook of Language and Gender*. Blackwell, Oxford.

Miller, Jean Baker (1978) *Towards a New Psychology of Women*. Penguin, Harmondsworth.

Miller, P., Danaher, D. and **Forbes, D.** (1986) Sex-related strategies for coping with interpersonal conflict in children aged five and seven, *Developmental Psychology* 22: 543–8.

Millman, Valerie (1983) *Sex Stereotyping in Schools: The Role and Responsibilities of the Teacher*. Equal Opportunities Commission, Manchester.

Mills, Jane (1989) *Womanwords: A Vocabulary of Culture and Patriarchal Society*, Longman, London.

Mills, Sara (ed.) (1995) *Language and Gender: Interdisciplinary Perspectives*. Longman, London.

Milroy, James and **Milroy, Lesley** (1978) Belfast: change and variation in an urban vernacular, pp. 19–36 in Trudgill, Peter (ed.) *Sociolinguistic Patterns in British English*. Edward Arnold, London.

Milroy, Lesley (1980) *Language and Social Networks*. Basil Blackwell, Oxford.

Milroy, Lesley (1982) Social network and linguistic focusing, pp. 141–52 in Romaine, Suzanne (ed.) *Sociolinguistic Variation in Speech Communities*. Edward Arnold, London.

Milroy, Lesley (1987) *Observing and Analysing Natural Language*. Basil Blackwell, Oxford.

Montaiglon, A. and **Raynaud, G.** (eds) (1872–90) *Recuil général et complet des fabliaux des XIIIᵉ et XIVᵉ siècles* (6 vols). Librairie des Bibliophiles, Paris.

Morgan, Marcyliena (1999) No woman, no cry: claiming African American women's place, pp. 27–45 in Bucholtz, Mary, Liang, A.C. and Sutton, Laurel (eds) *Reinventing Identities: The Gendered Self in Discourse*. Oxford University Press, Oxford.

Mulac, Anthony, Wiemann John, Widenmann Sally and **Gibson Toni** (1988) Male/female language differences and effects in same-sex and mixed-sex dyads: the gender-linked language effect, *Communication Monographs* 55 (4): 315–35.

Mullany, Louise (2003) Identity and role construction: a sociolinguistic study of gender and discourse in management. Unpublished PhD thesis, Nottingham Trent University.

Muscatine, Charles (1981) Courtly literature and vulgar language, in Burgess, G.S. (ed.) *Court and Poet: Selected Proceedings of the 3rd Congress of the ICLS (Liverpool 1980)*. Francis Cairns Arcas, Liverpool.

Nelson, Katherine (1973) Structure and strategy in learning to talk, *Monographs of the Society for Research in Child Development*, 149, 38 (1–2).

Nelson, Marie Wilson (1998) Women's ways: interactive patterns in predominantly female research teams, pp. 354–72 in Coates, Jennifer (ed.) *Language and Gender: A Reader*. Blackwell, Oxford.

Newbrook, Mark (1982) Sociolinguistic reflexes of dialect interference in West Wirral. Unpublished PhD thesis, Reading University.

Nichols, Patricia (1983) Linguistic options and choices for Black women in the rural South, pp. 54–68 in Thorne, Barrie, Kramarae, Cheris and Henley, Nancy (eds) *Language, Gender and Society*. Newbury House, Rowley, MA.

Nichols, Patricia (1998) Black women in the rural south: conservative and innovative, pp. 55–63 in Coates, Jennifer (ed.) *Language and Gender: A Reader*. Blackwell, Oxford.

O'Barr, William and Atkins, Bowman K. (1980) 'Women's language' or 'powerless language'?, pp. 93–110 in McConnell-Ginet, Sally, Borker, Ruth and Furman, Nelly (eds) *Women and Language in Literature and Society*. Praeger, New York.

Ochs, Elinor and Schieffelin, Bambi B. (eds) (1979) *Developmental Pragmatics*. Academic Press, New York.

Ochs, Elinor and Schieffelin, Bambi B. (1983) *Acquiring Conversational Competence*. Routledge & Kegan Paul, London.

Ochs, Elinor and Taylor, Carolyn (1995) The 'Father knows best' dynamic in dinnertime narratives, pp. 97–120 in Hall, Kira and Bucholtz, Mary (eds) *Gender Articulated: Language and the Socially Constructed Self*. Routledge, New York.

Ong, Walter J. (1967) *The Presence of the Word*. Yale University Press, New Haven, CT.

Orton, Harold (1962) *Introduction to the Survey of English Dialects*. E.J. Arnold, Leeds.

Patterson, D. (1860) *The Provincialisms of Belfast Pointed Out and Corrected*. Belfast.

Payne, Irene (1980) A working-class girl in a grammar school, pp. 12–19 in Spender, Dale and Sarah, Elizabeth (eds) *Learning to Lose*. Women's Press, London.

Pée, W. (1946) *Dialect-Atlas van West-Vlaanderen en Fransch-Vlaanderen*. De Sikkel, Antwerp.

Perkins, Michael (1983) *Modal Expressions in English*. Frances Pinter, London.

Pichler, Pia (2000) Bicultural femininities: the discursive accommodation of cultural diversity. *Roehampton Working Papers in Linguistics* 2: 93–138.

Pichler, Pia (2003) Young femininities: the discursive construction of class and culture-related gender identities in the talk of British adolescent girls. Unpublished PhD thesis, University of Surrey Roehampton.

Pichler, Pia (in press) Between gangsta rap and pet shop boys: the construction of cool girl identities in the talk of British adolescents.

Pilkington, Jane (1998) 'Don't try and make out that I'm nice': the different strategies women and men use when gossiping, pp. 254–69 in Coates, Jennifer (ed.) *Language and Gender: A Reader*. Blackwell, Oxford.

Pinter, Harold (1960) *The Birthday Party*. Methuen, London.

Pizzini, Franca (1991) Communication hierarchies in humour: gender differences in the obstetrical/gynaecological setting, *Discourse & Society* 2 (4): 477–88.

Pomerantz, Anita (1978) Compliment responses: notes on the co-operation of multiple constraints, pp. 79–112 in Schenkein, J. (ed.) *Studies in the Organization of Conversational Interaction*. Academic Press, New York.

Poole, J. (1646) *The English Accidence*. Scolar Press, Menston, Yorks, 1967.

Pop, Sever (1950) *La Dialectologie: Aperçu historique et méthodes d'enquêtes linguistiques*. Université de Louvain, Louvain.

Preisler, Bent (1986) *Linguistic Sex Roles in Conversation*. Mouton de Gruyter, Berlin.

Pujolar, Joan I Cos (1997) Masculinities in a multilingual setting, pp. 86–106 in Johnson, Sally and Meinhof, Ulrike H. (eds) *Language and Masculinity*. Blackwell, Oxford.

Reid, Euan (1976) Social and stylistic variation in the speech of some Edinburgh schoolchildren. Unpublished MLitt thesis, University of Edinburgh.

Reynolds, Katsue Akiba (1998) Female speakers of Japanese in transition, pp. 299–308 in Coates, Jennifer (ed.) *Language and Gender: A Reader*. Blackwell, Oxford.

Romaine, Suzanne (1978) Postvocalic /r/ in Scottish English: sound change in progress?, pp. 144–57 in Trudgill, Peter (ed.) *Sociolinguistic Patterns in British English.* Edward Arnold, London.

Romaine, Suzanne (1984) *The Language of Children and Adolescents: The Acquisition of Communicative Competence.* Basil Blackwell, Oxford.

Romaine, Suzanne (2003) Variation in language and gender, pp. 98–118 in Holmes, Janet and Meyerhoff, Miriam (eds) *The Handbook of Language and Gender.* Blackwell, Oxford.

Ryan, Colm (2003) Features of all-male talk. Unpublished undergraduate project, Open University, Buckingham.

Sachs, Jacqueline (1987) Preschool boys' and girls' language use in pretend play, pp. 178–88 in Phillips, Susan, Steele, Susan and Tanz, Christine (eds) *Language, Gender and Sex in Comparative Perspective.* Cambridge University Press, Cambridge.

Sachs, Jacqueline, Lieberman, Philip and **Erickson, Donna** (1973) Anatomical and cultural determinants of male and female speech, pp. 74–84 in Shuy, Roger and Fasold, Ralph (eds) *Language Attitudes: Current Trends and Prospects.* Georgetown University Press, Washington DC.

Sacks, Harvey (1995) *Lectures on Conversation* (Vols 1 and 2). Blackwell, Oxford.

Sacks, Harvey, Schegloff, Emanuel, A. and **Jefferson, Gail** (1974) A simplest systematics for the organisation of turn-taking for conversation, *Language* **50**: 696–735.

Sadker, Myra and **Sadker, David** (1985) Sexism in the schoolroom of the '80s, *Psychology Today* March: 54–7.

Sarah, Elizabeth (1980) Teachers and students in the classroom: an examination of classroom interaction, pp. 155–64 in Spender, Dale and Sarah, Elizabeth (eds) *Learning to Lose.* Women's Press, London.

Sattel, Jack (1983) Men, inexpressiveness and power, pp. 118–24 in Thorne, Barrie, Kramarae, Cheris and Henley, Nancy (eds) *Language, Gender and Society.* Newbury House, Rowley, MA.

Schick Case, Susan (1988) Cultural differences, not deficiencies: an analysis of managerial women's language, pp. 41–63 in Rose, Susanna and Lawood, Laurie (eds) *Women's Careers: Pathways and Pitfalls.* Praeger, New York.

Schieffelin, Bambi (1990) *The Give and Take of Everyday Life: Language Socialisation of Kaluli Children.* Cambridge University Press, Cambridge.

Sears, P. and **Feldman, D.** (1974) Teacher interactions with boys and with girls, in Stacey, J., Bereaud, S. and Daniels, J. (eds) *And Jill Came Tumbling After: Sexism in American Education.* Dell Publishing, New York.

Segal, Lynne (1990) *Slow Motion: Changing Masculinities, Changing Men.* Virago, London.

Seidler, Victor (1989) *Rediscovering Masculinity – Reason, Language and Sexuality.* Routledge, London.

Sheldon, Amy (1990) Pickle fights: gendered talk in preschool disputes, *Discourse Processes* **13** (1): 5–31.

Sheldon, Amy (1992) Conflict talk: sociolinguistic challenges to self-assertion and how young girls meet them, *Merrill-Palmer Quarterly* **38** (1): 95–117.

Sheldon, Amy (1996) 'You can be the baby brother, but you aren't born yet': preschool girls' negotiation for power and access in pretend play, *Research on Language and Social Interaction* **29** (1): 5–80.

Sheldon, Amy and **Johnson, Diane** (1998) Preschool negotiators: linguistic differences in how girls and boys regulate the expression of dissent in same-sex groups, pp. 76–98 in Cheshire, Jenny and Trudgill, Peter (eds) *The Sociolinguistics Reader.* Vol. 2: *Gender and Discourse.* Arnold, London.

Shipman, V.C. (1971) Disadvantaged children and their first school experiences, *Educational Testing Service Head Start Longitudinal Study*, USA.

Siegler, David and **Siegler, Robert** (1976) Stereotypes of males' and females' speech, *Psychological Reports* **39**: 167–70.

Smith, Peter and **Connolly, Kevin** (1972) Patterns of play and social interaction in preschool children, pp. 65–96 in Blurton Jones, N. (ed.) *Ethological Studies of Child Behaviour*. Cambridge University Press, Cambridge.

Smith, W.G. and **Heseltine, J.E.** (eds) (1935) *The Oxford Dictionary of English Proverbs*. Oxford University Press, Oxford.

Snow, Catherine, Perlmann, Rivka, Gleason, Jean Berko and **Hooshyar, Nahid** (1990) Developmental perspectives on politeness: sources of children's knowledge, *Journal of Pragmatics* **14**: 289–305.

Spender, Dale (1979) Language and sex differences, *Osnabrücker Beitrage zür Sprachtheorie: Sprache und Geschlect* **11**: 38–59.

Spender, Dale (1980a) *Man Made Language*. Routledge, London.

Spender, Dale (1980b) Talking in class, pp. 148–54 in Spender, Dale and Sarah, Elizabeth (eds) *Learning to Lose*. Women's Press, London.

Spender, Dale (1990) *Invisible Women: The Schooling Scandal*. Women's Press, London.

Spender, Dale and **Sarah, Elizabeth** (eds) (1980) *Learning to Lose*. Women's Press, London.

Stanford Research Institute (1972) Follow-through pupil tests, parent interviews, and teacher questionnaires, Appendix C. Stanford Research Institute, Stanford, CA.

Stanworth, Michelle (1983) *Gender and Schooling*. Hutchinson, London.

Stanworth, Michelle (1987) Girls on the margins: a study of gender divisions in the classroom, pp. 198–212 in Weiner, Gaby and Arnot, Madeleine (eds) *Gender under Scrutiny*. Hutchinson, London.

Stone, M. (1983) Learning to say it in cup of tea language, *The Guardian* (Women's Page), 19 April.

Streeck, Jürgen (1986) Towards reciprocity: politics, rank and gender in the interaction of a group of schoolchildren, pp. 295–326 in Cook-Gumperz, Jenny, Corsaro, William and Streeck, Jürgen (eds) *Children's Worlds and Children's Language*. Mouton de Gruyter, Berlin.

Strodtbeck, Fred and **Mann, Richard** (1956) Sex role differentiation in jury deliberations, *Sociometry* **19**: 3–11.

Stubbe, Maria, Holmes, Janet, Vine, Bernadette and **Marra, Meredith** (2000) Forget Mars and Venus: let's get back to earth! Challenging gender stereotypes in the workplace, pp. 231–58 in Holmes, Janet (ed.), *Gendered Speech in Social Context: Perspectives from Gown to Town*. Victoria University Press, Wellington, New Zealand.

Stubbs, Michael (1983) *Discourse Analysis*. Basil Blackwell, Oxford.

Sutton, Laurel (1994) Using USENET: gender, power and silence in electronic discourse, pp. 506–20 in Gahl, Susanne, Dolby, Andy and Johnson, Christopher (eds) *Proceedings of the Twentieth Annual Meeting of the Berkeley Linguistics Society*. Berkeley Linguistics Society, Berkeley, CA.

Swacker, Marjorie (1975) The sex of the speaker as a sociolinguistic variable, pp. 76–83 in Thorne, Barrie and Henley, Nancy (eds) *Language and Sex*. Newbury House, Rowley, MA.

Swacker, Marjorie (1979) Women's verbal behaviour at learned and professional conferences, pp. 155–60 in Dubois, Betty-Lou and Crouch, Isobel (eds) *The Sociology of the Languages of American Women*. Trinity University, San Antonio, TX.

Swann, Joan (1992) *Girls, Boys and Language*. Blackwell, Oxford.

Swann, Joan (1998) Talk control: an illustration from the classroom of problems in analysing male dominance in education, pp. 185–96 in Coates, Jennifer (ed.) *Language and Gender: A Reader*. Blackwell, Oxford.

Swann, Joan (2003) Schooled language: language and gender in educational settings, pp. 624–44 in Holmes, Janet and Meyerhoff, Miriam (eds) *The Handbook of Language and Gender*. Blackwell, Oxford.

Swift, Jonathan (1735) *Works*. Faulkner, Dublin.

Talbot, Mary (1992) 'I wish you'd stop interrupting me': interruptions and asymmetries in speaker-rights in equal encounters, *Journal of Pragmatics* 18: 451–66.

Talbot, Mary (1998) *Language and Gender: An Introduction*. Polity Press, Cambridge.

Talbot, Mary (2003) Gender stereotypes: reproduction and challenge, pp. 468–86 in Homes, Janet and Meyerhoff, Miriam (eds) *The Handbook of Language and Gender*. Blackwell, Oxford.

Tannen, Deborah (1984) *Conversational Style: Analysing Talk Among Friends*. Ablex, Norwood, NJ.

Tannen, Deborah (1990a) Gender differences in conversational coherence: physical alignment and topical cohesion, pp. 167–206 in Dorval, Bruce (ed.) *Conversational Organization and its Development*, Ablex, Norwood, NJ.

Tannen, Deborah (1990b) Gender differences in topical coherence: creating involvement in best friends' talk, *Discourse Processes* 13 (1): 73–90.

Tannen, Deborah (1991) *You Just Don't Understand: Women and Men in Conversation*. Virago, London.

Thomas, Beth (1989) Differences of sex and sects: linguistic variation and social networks in a Welsh mining village, pp. 51–60 in Coates, Jennifer and Cameron, Deborah (eds) *Women in their Speech Communities*. Longman, London.

Thornborrow, Joanna (2002) Questions, control and the organisation of talk in calls to a radio phone-in, *Discourse Studies* 3 (1): 119–42.

Thorne, Barry (1993) *Gender Play: Girls and Boys in School*. Buckingham, Open University Press.

Thorne, Barrie and Henley, Nancy (eds) (1975) *Language and Sex: Difference and Dominance*. Newbury House, Rowley, MA.

Todd, Alexandra Dundas and Fisher, Sue (1988) *Gender and Discourse: The Power of Talk*. Ablex, Norwood, NJ.

Tolson, Andrew (1977) *The Limits of Masculinity*. Tavistock, London.

Troemel-Ploetz, Senta (1991) Review essay: selling the apolitical, *Discourse and Society* 2 (4): 489–502.

Trudgill, Peter (1972) Sex, covert prestige and linguistic change in the urban British English of Norwich, *Language in Society* 1: 179–95.

Trudgill, Peter (1974a) *The Social Differentiation of English in Norwich*. Cambridge University Press, Cambridge.

Trudgill, Peter (1974b) *Sociolinguistics*. Penguin Books, Harmondsworth.

Tucker, Susie (1961) *English Examined*. Cambridge University Press, Cambridge.

Underhill, R. (1988) *Like* is, like, focus, *American Speech* 63: 234–46.

Walters, J. (1981) Variation in the requesting behaviour of bilingual children, *International Journal of the Sociology of Language* 27: 77–92.

Wareing, Shan (1993) Cooperative and Competitive Talk: The Assessment of Discussion at Standard Grade. Unpublished PhD thesis, University of Strathclyde.

Warnock, Mary (1987) Why women are their own worst enemies. *Daily Telegraph* 19 January: 10.

Weedon, Chris (1987) *Feminist Practice and Poststructuralist Theory.* Blackwell, Oxford.

Wells, Gordon (1979) Variation in child language, pp. 382–409 in Lee, V. (ed.) *Language Development.* Croom Helm, London.

Wenger, Etienne (1998) *Communities of Practice.* Cambridge University Press, Cambridge.

Wernersson, I. (1982) Sex differentiation and teacher–pupil interaction in Swedish compulsory schools, in Secretariat of the Council of Europe (ed.) *Sex Stereotyping in Schools.* Swets & Zeitlinger, Lisse, The Netherlands.

West, Candace (1984) *Routine Complications: Troubles with Talk between Doctors and Patients.* Indiana University Press, Bloomington.

West, Candace (1998a) Not just 'doctors' orders': directive–response sequences in patients' visits to women and men physicians, pp. 328–53 in Coates, Jennifer (ed.) *Language and Gender: A Reader.* Blackwell, Oxford.

West, Candace (1998b) When the doctor is a 'lady': power, status and gender in physician–patient encounters, pp. 396–412 in Coates, Jennifer (ed.) *Language and Gender: A Reader.* Blackwell, Oxford.

West, Candace and **Zimmerman, Don** (1983) Small insults: a study of interruptions in cross-sex conversations between unacquainted persons, in Thorne, Barrie, Kramarae, Cheris and Henley, Nancy (eds) *Language, Gender and Society.* Newbury House, Rowley, MA.

West, Candace and **Zimmerman, Don** (1987) Doing gender, *Gender & Society* 1: 125–51.

West, Candace and **Zimmerman, Don** (1998) Women's place in everyday talk: reflections on parent–child interaction, pp. 165–75 in Coates, Jennifer (ed.) *Language and Gender: A Reader.* Blackwell, Oxford.

Whyte, Judith (1986) *Getting the GIST,* Routledge & Kegan Paul, London.

Wilson, T. (1560) *The Arte of Rhetorique.* Clarendon Press, London, 1909.

Wilson, T. (1724) *The Many Advantages of a Good Language to Any Nation.* Scolar Press, Menston, Yorks, 1969.

Winter, Joanne (1993) Gender and the political interview in an Australian context, *Journal of Pragmatics* 20: 117–39.

Wodak, Ruth (1981) Women relate, men report: sex differences in language behaviour in a therapeutic group, *Journal of Pragmatics* 5: 261–85.

Wodak, Ruth (1997) 'I know, we won't revolutionise the world with it, but . . .': Styles of female leadership in institutions, pp. 335–70 in Kotthoff, Helga and Wodak, Ruth (eds) *Communicating Gender in Context.* John Benjamins, Amsterdam.

Wolfson, Nessa (1983) An empirically-based analysis of complimenting in American English, pp. 82–95 in Wolfson, Nessa and Judd, E. (eds) *Sociolinguistics and Language Acquisition.* Newbury House, Rowley, MA.

Wolfson, Nessa (1988) The bulge: a theory of speech behaviour and social distance, pp. 21–38 in Fine, J. (ed.) *Second Language Discourse: A Textbook of Current Research.* Ablex, Norwood, NJ.

Wood, Kathleen (1999) Coherent identities amid heterosexist ideologies: deaf and hearing lesbian coming-out stories, pp. 46–63 in Bucholtz, Mary, Liang, A.C. and Sutton, Laurel (eds) *Reinventing Identities: The Gendered Self in Discourse.* Oxford University Press, Oxford.

Woods, Nicola (1989) Talking shop: sex and status as determinants of floor apportionment in a work setting, pp. 141–57 in Coates, Jennifer and Cameron, Deborah (eds) *Women in their Speech Communities.* Longman, London.

Woolf, Virginia (1979) *Women and Writing.* Women's Press, London.

Yaguello, Marina (1978) *Les Mots et les Femmes*. Petite Bibliothèque Payot, Paris.

Zimmerman, Don and **West, Candace** (1975) Sex roles, interruptions and silences in conversation, pp. 105–29 in Thorne, Barrie and Henley, Nancy (eds) *Language and Sex: Difference and Dominance*. Newbury House, Rowley, MA.

Index

E18 RESOURCE BASE